The Heresy of Heresies

The Heresy of Heresies

A Defense of Christian Common-Sense Realism

TIMOTHY M. MOSTELLER

CASCADE *Books* · Eugene, Oregon

THE HERESY OF HERESIES
A Defense of Christian Common-Sense Realism

Cascade Books
An Imprint of Wipf and Stock Publishers
199 W. 8th Ave., Suite 3
Eugene, OR 97401

www.wipfandstock.com

PAPERBACK ISBN: 978-1-7252-5573-9
HARDCOVER ISBN: 978-1-7252-5574-6
EBOOK ISBN: 978-1-7252-5575-3

Cataloguing-in-Publication data:

Names: Mosteller, Timothy M., author

Title: The heresy of heresies : a defense of Christian common-sense realism / Timothy M. Mosteller

Description: Eugene, OR: Cascade Books, 2021 | Includes bibliographical references and index.

Identifiers: ISBN 978-1-7252-5573-9 (paperback) | ISBN 978-1-7252-5574-6 (hardcover) | ISBN 978-1-7252-5575-3 (ebook)

Subjects: LCSH: Realism | Metaphysics | Religion—Philosophy | Common sense | Critical realism | Knowledge, Theory of

Classification: BL51 M67 2021 (paperback) | BL51 (ebook)

Manufactured in the U.S.A.   10/08/21

To J. P. Moreland, for putting me on the path.
In Memory of James V. Schall (1928–2019)

Contents

Acknowledgments

THIS BOOK WAS MADE intellectually possible by the influence of several philosophers: Dallas Willard, J. P. Moreland, James V. Schall, and George Klubertanz. Through Willard's undergraduate course in metaphysics and several of Moreland's graduate courses in metaphysics, as well as many conversations in office hours and in personal meetings, my ideas on metaphysics have taken form through the influence of these philosophers. While Moreland introduced me to the idea that existence is essential exemplification, it is primarily through the thought of George Klubertanz that I was able to understand how we come to a common-sense understanding of the nature of existence through common-sense experience. James V. Schall's work is saturated with a love of "*what is*," and I have learned a great deal from him as a teacher whom I never met. I often tell my students that the true and interesting ideas in philosophy I owe to my teachers. That will be true of this book as well. All of the true and interesting ideas are derived from these thinkers, and the true but uninteresting, along with the false and interesting ideas, will be my own.

This book was made practically possible by several generous research grants from The Acton Institute that allowed me the time for research and study on the ideas of existence and how they connect to the areas of economics and human flourishing. I am also thankful to the leadership of California Baptist University, President Ronald Ellis, Provost Chuck Sands, the Board of Trustees, Dean Chris Morgan, and Associate Dean Tony Chute, for granting a sabbatical leave for the 2019–20 academic year to complete this book. I am also grateful to Professor Richard Colledge from Australian Catholic University for encouraging me to visit Australia to complete the book and for his expertise on Heidegger's thought. I am also grateful to Paul Tyson at the University of Queensland for his work on Plato and for his encouragement while in Australia. I am also indebted to Adiel Brasov and Eddie Colanter for reading early chapters on the book and for their ongoing friendship in all things philosophical. I owe a special thanks to William Vallicella for reading portions of the book as well as providing me with many things to think about regarding the nature of existence. I am also grateful to Josef Seifert, Mátyás Szalay, and the Instituo Filosofía Edith Stein in Granada, Spain, for their annual summer seminars where I was able to present some of the ideas in this book. Thank you as well to the Evangelical Philosophy Society, the European Society for Philosophy of Medicine and Healthcare, and the Pontifical University of Santa Croce in Rome for the conferences where I was able to present early versions of some of the main ideas in the chapters of this book. I also wish to thank the editors at *Acta Philosophica* for permission to reprint my article "The Incompatibility of a Thomistic View of Existence and Natural Existence Monism" (2017), in which portions of several chapters of this book first appeared.

I am extremely grateful to my family, who let me drag them half way around the world to find a quiet place to complete this book during my sabbatical leave, only to be cooped up with me during a global pandemic!

Ultimately, I wish to thank the Lord Jesus Christ: "All things have been created through him and for him" (Col 1:16b), including this book.

Introduction

THIS BOOK DEFENDS WHAT is often thought to be heretical: the validity of common-sense experience about the nature of reality and its implications for flourishing human life found within the Christian tradition. It is a response to what George Orwell anticipated in *1984*. "In the end the Party would announce that two and two made five, and you would have to believe it. It was inevitable that they should make that claim sooner or later: the logic of their position demanded it. Not merely the validity of experience, but the very existence of external reality, was tacitly denied by their philosophy. The heresy of heresies was common sense."[1]

In 1945, just a few years before Orwell wrote that common sense would become the heresy of heresies, C. S. Lewis wrote, "What we want is not more little books about Christianity, but more little books by Christians on other subjects—with their Christianity *latent*."[2] While Lewis wrote specifically about little books in the physical sciences, I've tried to take his advice on the topic of metaphysical common-sense realism. The connections to Christianity may not be as latent as Lewis wished for, but for a topic that is so closely related to the Christian faith, I simply couldn't help myself. To know the nature of reality which points to the Christian faith as I defend it in this book does not itself require a commitment to the Christian faith, or to any other faith whatsoever. It does require a commitment to being willing to look and see *what is*. Once one grasps *what is*, one has grasped something in which God and ultimately the Christian faith are indeed latent.

In the same essay, Lewis wrote, "Our business is to present that which is timeless (the same yesterday, today and tomorrow) in the particular language of our own age" and that our "teaching must be timeless at its heart and wear a modern dress."[3] I've attempted that in this book. Grasp-

---

1. Orwell, *1984*, 80.
2. Lewis, *God in the Dock*, 93.
3. Lewis, *God in the Dock*, 93–94.

ing the nature of existence through common-sense experience is a timeless endeavor. Humans have been doing this since there were humans. I defend common-sense realism from within the Christian tradition in the language of our own age by showing four things. (1) There are good reasons to maintain common-sense realism. (2) Common-sense realism about the nature of existence can be easily seen from common-sense experiences. (3) The alternatives to common-sense realism (relativism, materialism, idealism, pragmatism, and existentialism) do not fare well in comparison to common-sense realism. (4) Common-sense realism has important implications for human flourishing in religion, politics, economics, and ethics.

As you read this book, please keep in mind that it is written by a *generalist* philosopher. The majority of my twenty years as a professor of philosophy have been spent in the classroom, teaching across the philosophical curriculum, from upper division philosophy majors who've gone on to teach at top-tier universities, to night classes for working adults trying to finish their degrees. I am not a "scholar" of realism or metaphysics or much of anything else. I'm a professional "philosophy professor." I am also, or at least hope that I am, as Peter Kreeft said, an "*amateur philosopher*."[4] I am a philosopher who loves philosophy, wisdom, and reality, which we know through philosophy. This book is an *amateur* philosophers' defense of Christian common-sense realism.

G. K. Chesterton wrote that Robert Louis Stevenson had

> a splendid scorn for that most false and contemptible of maxims, the statement that if a thing is worth doing, it is worth doing well. Stevenson was one of the few modern philosophers who realized the essential truth that a thing is good in its quality and not only in its perfection. If music and wood engraving are really good things they must be good even to the disciple and the fool. If an invention is marvellous and beneficent, it must be worth beholding even partially and through a glass darkly. If a thing is worth doing it is worth doing badly.[5]

I believe that this little book on realism was worth writing, even if it was worth writing badly. It was worth writing because the challenges against common-sense realism in the academy, in philosophy, in politics, in culture, and in religion are legion. It is my prayer that this book will return common-sense realism from heresy to orthodoxy, to a reasonable view of reality available to all who seek *what is*.

---

4. Kreeft, *Philosophy 101 by Socrates*, 9.
5. Chesterton, "The Life of Stevenson," 6.

Part 1

Reality Revisited

As It Was in the Beginning, Is Now, and Ever Shall Be

CHAPTER 1

Common-Sense Realism

A Place to Begin

1.0 REFLECTING ON WHAT IS

I arrive at the beach. I feel the cool, wet sand on my feet. I taste the saltiness of the ocean water on my lips. I hear the sound of the crashing surf. I smell the freshness of the sea air. I see waves breaking offshore. These things are real. Every person knows what is real from ordinary common-sense experiences like these. They also tell us more. They tell us about the nature of reality itself, about existence, about *what is*.

The common experiences of my senses brings *reality* to me as a gift. The gift of *reality* brings joy. *Reality* is to be enjoyed for what it is. Yet, in addition to joy, there is knowledge. I gain knowledge from my reflection upon reality given in common-sense experience. Not only am I able to know *reality*, but I can also reflect upon *what* it is for *reality* to be *what* it is! I can think about what it is for sand to be sand, for waves to be waves, for gulls to be gulls, for salt to be salt, and for the ocean to be ocean. But, I can reflect further, and ask: What do the being of sand, waves, gulls, salt, and sea have in common with each other? What is it for these things to exist, and what is the nature of existence and reality itself that each of these things have in common? This book answers these questions.

This book argues that common-sense experience gives us direct knowledge of reality, of *what is*. From our common-sense experiences, we can know the nature of what it is for things to exist *and* the nature of existence itself. It argues that it is only by means of knowledge of *what is* that one can live well. This book defends common-sense metaphysical realism within the Christian tradition as the basis for being a good person and living a good life.

One of the main motivations for writing this book is to help my students. I am completing this book twenty-two years after teaching my first philosophy courses. Having taught at the university level for over twenty years, I have come to realize that the ideas of common-sense realism are in the minority today across the academy, but especially among my students. One of the reasons that real objective values (whether ethical or aesthetic) are largely rejected by students is due to a deep confusion regarding the nature of reality. Allan Bloom recognized this intellectual problem among his students in the latter half of the last century. He claimed in *The Closing of the American Mind* that "there is one thing a professor can be absolutely certain of: almost every student entering the university believes, or says he believes, that truth is relative."[1] The one thing that professors can count on is that almost all of their students are relativists about truth. More than a generation later, and twenty-plus years in the classroom, I can testify that things have gotten much worse.

The most tragic thing in the deepening intellectual fog of relativism, is that students are not just relativists about beauty, ethics, religion, or even truth as Bloom recognized. Students today are relativists about reality. Here is an example of this that occurred recently in an Introduction to Philosophy

---

1. Bloom, *Closing of the American Mind*, 25.

course. I was sketching for the students the main areas of the discipline of philosophy and introducing some terminology and questions that are pursued in those areas. When I got to the area of ontology (metaphysics), which asks questions like "What is the ultimate nature of reality?" a student raised a hand and with a straight face asked, "Is there just one reality, or does each person have their own?" As a philosophical question, this is a good one! This book will answer it.

One of the first things I do to answer my students' questions about reality is to help them to see the problems of philosophical relativism. I do this by showing that, first of all, relativism simply does not follow from epistemic or doxastic diversity. Second, I show how relativism is self-refuting. Third, I show them how it is unlivable. Having written books on this topic, and taught on it for two decades, I still believe that it is the job of every philosopher to help their students deal with the challenges of relativism. However, that is just the beginning. We cannot simply show our students what is unreasonable (e.g., relativism), we must also hold forth light. We must show them *what is*. My own strategy on this is to start with *truth*, and especially a defense of a robust metaphysical realist correspondence view of truth.[2] The book you are now reading will rest on my defense of truth as correspondence as a necessary component for an introduction to a common-sense realism about *what is*.

One might expect the sort of absurdity that we are faced with today regarding student's beliefs about the *irreality* of reality if one were living under a totalitarian system like George Orwell described when he wrote in *1984*, "In the end the Party would announce that two and two made five, and you would have to believe it. It was inevitable that they should make that claim sooner or later: the logic of their position demanded it. Not merely the validity of experience, but *the very existence of external reality*, was tacitly denied by their philosophy. The heresy of heresies was common sense."[3] But, my students are not yet living under a totalitarian *political* regime. They do, however, seem to be living under a totalitarian *spirit of the age*. The outcome of their philosophy by the time they enter college (and often worse when they leave) is the same as that of The Party in Orwell's dystopia: the existence of external reality is rejected. The denial of the objectivity of reality has been accomplished in the mind of my students not by force of some political party, but by poorly reasoned philosophy over many years. My students figure out very quickly that if reality itself is not real, then necessarily aesthetics, ethics, politics, and religion are not real either.

2. See Mosteller, *Theories of Truth*.
3. Orwell, *1984*, 80.

This book was written to ameliorate this condition. It defends the objectivity of reality through the resources of common-sense realism as understood within the Christian intellectual tradition. This is the "Heresy of Heresies." Common-sense realism is antithetical and heretical to the ontological relativism of our age. The fog must be lifted. Light must shine on *what is*, in a post-truth and post-real world: "For thou wilt light my candle: the Lord my God will enlighten my darkness" (Ps 18:28 KJV).

1.1 COMMON-SENSE ONTOLOGICAL REALISM

Since this book is a defense of common-sense ontological realism about existence and the nature of reality, as philosophers often do, let me begin by saying what I mean by "common-sense ontological realism."

1.1.1 Common

By *common*-sense ontological realism, I mean two things. First, I mean that the nature of reality can be known *in common* by multiple people simultaneously. This is the sense of *communis* understood as communal or public and is the opposite of *idiosyncratic*. We do not each have our own reality. Reality is something we have in common. The form of realism I defend in this book is one in which the very nature of reality can be grasped by any serious inquirer. It is the view that the understanding of reality is accessible and can be had in common with others. Of course, this notion of "common" requires that the very same reality can be present before the mind of all inquirers, and that each inquirer can equally perceive the same objects, and therefore have the same conception of the same reality. Now, of course this requires a longer story about the nature of perception, and a rejection of what Dallas Willard calls a "Midas Touch Epistemology."[4]

The second thing I mean by *common-sense realism* is that the nature of reality can be seen directly through everyday experiences. In chapters 2 and 3 I argue that common everyday experiences combined with careful and patient reflection can lead us to the nature of existence. This approach to metaphysics is one that takes the common ordinary experience of the world around us and our own mental life as the basis for our account of *what is*.

---

4. Willard, *Predication as Originary Violence*. Also see Willard, "Toward a Phenomenology," for a very good defense of the epistemology required for the realism I am promoting here. For a common-sense realist view of perception that is needed as a background account for common-sense realism, see Audi, *Epistemology*, ch. 1.

1.1.2 Sense

By common-*sense* realism, I mean that our understanding of *what is* comes to us primarily through our senses. I take the notion of "senses" to be sufficiently broad as to include an interior, mental sense or *awareness* of reality that is not sense perceptible. The notion of sense that I will be working with throughout this book is one that does not limit "sense" to the five senses. When we sense our pains, when we sense our emotions, and when we sense our thoughts as thinking and reflecting beings, neither what we sense (nor how we sense it) is physical; yet, we still sense these realities. So, by "sense" I mean *both* our five physical senses, *plus* "reflection." Reflection is our mind's ability to sense mental realities, which occur internal to ourselves.

1.1.3 Ontological Realism

By common-sense *ontological realism*, I mean realism pertaining to *being*; to what *is*! One can be a realist about many things in philosophy: physical objects, properties, universals, possibilia, ethical or aesthetic qualities, numbers, etc. Ontological realism is a realism about *existence itself*, and *anything which exists*. "Ontological realism" in the sense I am using the terms means that existing things exist, and *existence* itself exists. In addition, the existence of things and of existence itself is independent from whether there are human minds. Reality itself is *real* apart from how we feel about it.

1.2 WHY COMMON-SENSE REALISM? SOME ARGUMENTS

1.2.1 An Argument from Chesterton: Eggs Are Eggs!

It has been said that the big questions of philosophy often seem so profound as to merit answers so confusing that no one but a professional expert philosopher could even manage to understand. What is existence? What is truth? What is goodness? What is beauty? Thankfully, there have been thinkers through the ages who begin answering these big questions from simple, common-sense starting points. St. Thomas Aquinas was one such philosopher, and G. K. Chesterton was another. Chesterton's brilliant book on Aquinas shows us the stark contrast between those thinkers like Aquinas who start from common-sense experiences and those who do not. Chesterton wrote that modern philosophies start with a paradox, or something that "no normal man would believe" such as "everything is relative to a reality that is not there" or "that contradictories should exist together." Those thinkers who really get things right, who deserve our admiration, and whose ideas we should follow have philosophies that are grounded upon our common-sense experience. Chesterton tells us,

> The philosophy of St. Thomas stands founded on the universal common conviction that eggs are eggs. . . . The Thomist stands in the broad daylight of the brotherhood of men, in their common consciousness that eggs are not hens or dreams or mere practical assumptions; but things attested by the Authority of the Senses, which is from God. . . . To this question "Is there anything?" St. Thomas begins by answering "Yes"; if he began by answering "No," it would not be the beginning, but the end. That is what some of us call common sense. Either there is no philosophy, no philosophers, no thinkers, no thought, no anything; or else there is a real bridge between the mind and reality. But he is actually less exacting than many thinkers, much less so than most rationalist and materialist thinkers, as to what that first step involves; he is content, as we shall see, to say that it involves the recognition of Ens or Being as something definitely beyond ourselves. Ens is Ens: Eggs are eggs, and it is not tenable that all eggs were found in a mare's nest.[5]

Chesterton's delightful idea is an excellent starting point for our understanding of existence. We start with our ordinary experiences, and we develop our view of reality from there.[6] Doing so requires some careful reflection and elaboration. This is the task of philosophical thinking. Such thinking is always based on experiences that can be had by anyone capable of having experiences, whether they will reflect on those experiences or not. If one is willing to look and to see that "eggs are eggs," that things are real, and that there are certain kinds of things that are not others, then one is on the first step of a longer analysis of the nature of existence.[7]

Chesterton's argument is simple. If one needs an analysis of his argument, here it is. It takes the form of a simple disjunctive syllogism.

5. Chesterton, St. Thomas Aquinas, 94.

6. Stephen Boulter in his introductory defense of "Common Sense Philosophy" follows Aristotle on the authority of the senses in a similar was as it is expressed here by Chesterton. Boulter writes, "The authority of philosophy is of a decidedly inferior rank to that of common sense. . . . Common sense beliefs . . . do *not* have to establish a claim upon us; their claim is felt immediately and is in part responsible for the emergence of philosophical reflection in the first place" (Boulter *The Rediscovery of Common Sense Philosophy*, 22).

7. Logic Alert! If you want a little nerdy logical analysis of Chesterton's claims, keep reading. If not, skip to the next section.

P: There is nothing.

Q: There is something.

Premise 1: P or Q.

Premise 2: Not-P.

Conclusion: Therefore, Q.

The key premise in this argument is premise 2. There is not-nothing. Why? Because there is something! The evidence for this claim is fairly straightforward. If there were nothing, then there wouldn't be any argument for something. But there is an argument for something, therefore it is not the case that there is nothing. Similarly, even if one argued that there was nothing, the result would be the same. If there were nothing, then there wouldn't be any argument for nothing. But there is an argument for nothing, therefore it is not the case that there is nothing! Therefore, there is something.

This is the point where some readers simply say that the only thing that philosophers are good for is emergencies at pool parties, or gatherings around deep bodies of water. For they are able to go down deep, stay down long, and come up dry! Chesterton is simply stating that if we answer the question "Is there anything?" in the negative, then there is no philosophy either. But since we are philosophizing about reality, therefore there is something.

This is all fairly logically straightforward. But Chesterton has a slightly stronger conclusion in his next argument. He says, "Either there is . . . no anything; or else there is a real bridge between the mind and reality." What are we to make of this claim?

It looks as if Chesterton has the makings of another disjunctive syllogism. Where the first disjunct is:

R: There is nothing.

And the second disjunct is:

S: There is a real bridge between mind and reality.

So, the argument looks like this:

Argument A:

1. R or S

2. Not-R

3. Therefore, S

This argument is perfectly valid in its logical structure. The main criticism that could be leveled, is that it is unsound in premise 1. One could claim that

R and S are both false. One could deny that there is nothing and deny that there is a real bridge between mind and reality. Thus, one could claim that this argument is valid, but unsound. It would be analogous to this argument:

R': $\quad$ 2 + 2 = 5

S': $\quad$ The moon is made of green cheese.

Argument B:

1. R' or S'

2. Not R'

3. Therefore, S'

Argument B is of course valid and unsound. So, one could argue that Chesterton's argument A is analogous to argument B; *both* are valid, but unsound. *But* is argument A analogous to argument B? I do not think that it is. Here is why.

The way in which the premises in argument A and argument B relate to one another are very different. In argument B, the premises are about two very different things. R' is about math, and S' is about the moon's material constitution. You might say that these two premises are externally related.

However, in argument A, the content of each of the premises *are* related to one another internally. Here is how. When we evaluate argument A for its soundness, we are making a judgment about the truth of the first premise. This judgment is about whether there is a real bridge between the mind and reality. If we say that S is false, we are saying that reality lacks a real bridge between mind and reality. Yet, *this just is a judgment* in which we claim that *our minds do connect with reality*, but they do not find any such bridge. In other words, we claim that our minds are bridging to reality, but not finding any bridges. This is like saying that one is looking through a pair of binoculars in search of binoculars, and not finding any in the search, concluding definitely that there are no binoculars. It is a bit absurd. To claim that a proposition is false, is to claim something specific about a proposition, about the way the world is, and about *what is*. Further, to claim that an argument is *unsound* just is to claim that one's mind has bridged to reality, namely the reality that pertains to the falsity of at least one of the propositions in an argument. Therefore, to claim that premise S is false, just is to demonstrate that it is true. And, since S is true, argument A is sound.

This then seems to be Chesterton's point. Unless there is something that is real that our minds can directly connect to, then there can be no philosophizing at all. The very acts of experience and thought in philosophy already put us in touch with *what is*. This is the simplicity of the Chestertonian and Thomistic way of metaphysics. We can simply recognize the nature and essence of *what is* through our ordinary, common-sense experiences.

1.2.2 An Argument from Gilson: You Have Always Been a Realist!

Étienne Gilson has a brilliant treatment of common-sense realism in his "Handbook for Beginning Realists," which is the last chapter of his *Methodological Realism*. I encourage all of my metaphysics and epistemology students to read and reread it. Let us look at three arguments that Gilson offers for common-sense realism.

Gilson opens his "Handbook for Beginning Realists" at the end of his book *Methodological Realism* with the following steps on the realist path:

Step 1: "Recognize that one has always been a realist."[8]

Let us assume that step 1 is the conclusion of an argument. What would the evidence for this conclusion be? It could be the conclusion of an inductive generalization from past experiential reflection on one's own life. If we reflect back on our own grasp of *what is*, we will see that we have always been realists in our approach to reality. We have always lived our lives as realists. Gilson hints at this generalization of cognitive experience when he states, "The awakening of the intelligence coincides with the apprehension of things, which, as soon as they are perceived, are classified according to their most evident similarities. This fact, which has nothing to do with any theory, is something that theory has to take account of. Realism does precisely that and in this respect is following common sense. That is why every form of realism is a philosophy of common sense."[9]

Step 2: "Recognize that, however hard one tries to think differently, one will never manage to."[10]

This step is looks like a conditional claim, which could take the form of a simple hypothetical syllogism:

1. If you ought to be a non-realist, then you should be able reasonably to think of reality in non-realist ways.

2. However, you cannot reasonably think of reality in non-realist ways.

---

8. Gilson, *Methodological Realism*, 97.
9. Gilson, *Methodological Realism*, 97.
10. Gilson, *Methodological Realism*, 97.

3.   Therefore, you ought to be a realist.

Gilson does not spend a great deal of time defending this idea in the opening paragraph of the "Handbook," but it seems fairly easy to see why premise 2 is reasonable. Just try getting *what is* to be non-realist. Common-sense realism maintains that *what is* (i.e., all things that exist, and existence itself) are not dependent for what they are on human cognition, will, or feeling. It seems easy enough to try the anti-realist approach. Yet, when specific cases arises, the absurdity seems obvious enough. The existence of gas in the tank of my car does not depend on how I feel.[11] Now, of course, I may (or may not) have pumped the gas into the tank, but once the gas in the tank is there, its *existing* or *not-existing* is irrelevant to anything within my cognitive capacities, functions, realizations, emotional states, family history, or social status. As I drive hurriedly in my Prius to the beach to try to squeeze in a late afternoon surf session before it gets dark, I look at my gas gauge and realize that it's twelve miles to the beach, but I only have a quarter of a mile left on the on the gas gauge. No matter how hard I try to think that reality (the gas in the tank) is dependent upon my will, feelings, desires, beliefs, my politics, genes, self-identity, or whatever, the amount of gas in the tank simply doesn't change. In fact, the gas tank is running dry. I might think that this is unfair, oppressive, the result of societal bias against aging Prius-driving surfers, but *what is* (the gas my tank) doesn't change according to what I believe. Reality is real regardless of how I feel.

Step 3: "Realize that those who claim they think differently, think as realists as soon as they forget to act a part."[12]

Early in the semester when I teach Introduction to Philosophy, I have quite a few students who are vocal advocates of some form of non-realism about reality, usually aesthetic, moral, or religious reality. My students often default to anti-realism about *big* philosophical questions like: What is right or wrong? How should we live our lives? What is beauty? Yet, when it comes to *small* questions like: Should I complain about being short-changed? Or is it fair that I didn't get paid for the hours I worked? They claim that there are right answers to *these* philosophical questions, and they suddenly become very clear-cut common-sense realists.

I often present them with the following scenario. Imagine if you went to Starbucks and paid for a five-dollar drink with a twenty-dollar bill. Suppose

---

11. See Willard, "Truth: Can We Do Without It?"

12. Gilson, *Methodological Realism*, 93.

the barista only gave you five dollars back in change and said, "Thanks for coming to Starbucks! Have a nice day! Next please!"

You'd probably say, "Uh, excuse me. I paid you with a twenty for a five-dollar drink. Where's my other ten bucks?" Suppose the barista says, "Excuse me, but that's *your* reality? Next please!" Would you just say, "Oh . . . I'm sorry, I didn't realize that I was being so close minded and judgmental? You can just keep the change." No! You'd say something like, "Hey, you owe me ten dollars! Can I talk to your manager?!" Suppose the manager then comes up and says, "How can I help you?" You then explain how you paid for a five-dollar drink with a twenty-dollar bill and only got five dollars back, and that you want your other ten dollars. Suppose the manager then says, "That's what's real for you." Would you back down thinking, "Oh yeah! . . . It is just real for me because of how I feel, but not real for them"? No! You'd say, "What are you talking about?!" Suppose the manager then said, "Look, on our side of the counter, we have our own reality. And we'd appreciate it if you didn't try to push your reality onto us." Would you be happy with that? No! Because there's common-sense right answer to the question of whether correct change has really been given to us.

This is Gilson's point. Unless one is "playing a part" and not dealing with *what is*, then one must live as a realist. No one can live consistently as a relativistic anti-realist. The attempt to do so leads to absurdity.

To reiterate, the first three steps on the realist path are:

1) You've always been a realist.

2) You can't think reasonably as an anti-realist.

3) You can't live consistently as an anti-realist.

Immediately after this third step, Gilson concludes his opening paragraph with this claim: "If one then asks oneself why, one's conversion to realism is all but complete."[13] The idea here seems to be that once we start asking ourselves why have we always been realists, and why can't we think and live as an anti-realists, then we are well on our way to understanding both the reasonableness of and the need for a common-sense realist approach to philosophical thinking and to living our lives well.

In conclusion, Gilson is careful to distinguish mere common sense from philosophy. He states, "It does not follow from [realism being a philosophy of common sense] that common sense is a philosophy; but all sound philosophy presupposes common sense and trusts it, granted of course that, whenever necessary, appeal will be made from ill-informed to

---

13. Gilson, *Methodological Realism*, 93.

better-informed common sense."[14] Gilson is right to recognize that "common sense" alone is not a philosophy. Common sense is simply that ability, whether potential or actual, to know *what is*.

According to Gilson, all *good* philosophy will begin with common sense. Good philosophy beginning with common sense will apply to all areas of philosophy, whether it be ontology, epistemology, or axiology (both ethics and aesthetics). However, common-sense philosophy can be improved. Some common sense can be "ill informed," but it can become "better-informed." This, I think is analogous to C. S. Lewis's idea in his *Abolition of Man* (more on this work in chapter 11). Lewis contrasts two different approaches to the very common-sense realist doctrine of objective value (the idea that values are real) that he defends throughout his lectures. He says, "It is the difference between a man who says to us: 'You like your vegetables moderately fresh; why not grow your own and have them perfectly fresh?' and a man who says, 'Throw away that loaf and try eating bricks and centipedes instead.'"[15]

It is easy to imagine a debate about something like "healthy eating." There are several ways the debate about a healthy diet can be had. It can be had between two realists, between a realist and a non-realist, or perhaps between two non-realists. The intramural realist debate would accept the common-sense idea that there is a right way to eat healthily, and that healthy eating isn't dependent on how we feel about it. Further, both common-sense realists might agree that to eat healthily in one's diet, one should consume a significant proportion of vegetables. However, the realists now differ as how to best do that. One realist might say that you should eat fresh vegetables, and the other might say that you should eat canned or frozen vegetables. A further realist might say that it is better to eat fresh organic vegetables grown in your own garden without pesticides. Now this debate moves from ill-informed to better informed healthy eating habits. It is common sense to recognize that healthy eating is a good thing, albeit ill-informed if that is as far as one gets. It is better informed common-sense philosophy of eating to recognize that one should consume a healthy proportion of vegetables in one's diet. It is even better informed common-sense philosophy of eating that one should eat really nutritious vegetables, whether fresh, frozen, or from one's own garden.

The debate about healthy eating would be very different it were between a realist and a non-realist, or between two non-realists. For in either case, the non-realists would claim that "healthy eating" is not *real*, or at

14. Gilson, *Methodological Realism*, 93.
15. Lewis, *Abolition*, 30.

least not real independent from how the eater feels. So, it would seem to follow that a steady diet consisting only of Twinkies and Mountain Dew is as healthy as a diet of a proper proportion of carbs and protein. But this is absurd. Healthy eating can no more be determined by the contingent features of your desires, will, or feelings any more than your feelings alone can determine the amount of gas in the tanks of your car.

Gilson explains that the scientific inquiry that is so useful in the modern world is part and parcel of the kind of common-sense realism that will be defended in this book. He states,

> This is how science goes about things; science is not a critique of common sense but of the successive approximations to reality made by common sense. The history of science and philosophy witness to the fact that common sense, thanks to the methodical use it makes of its resources, is quite capable of invention. We should, therefore, ask it to keep criticizing its conclusions, which means asking it to remain itself, not to renounce itself.[16]

A common-sense realism about the nature of what exists and of existence itself is not a static, passive, stultified, "one-and-done" approach to reality. It is capable of invention. It is capable of a never-ending grasping of the limitless nature of *what is*. It is a philosophy of hope and optimism, a philosophy in which boredom is *anathema*. It is the philosophy that goes further up and further in! We were made for *all that is*, and given the immortality of our souls, we can never exhaust the gift of *what is*.

1.2.3 An Argument from Schall via Belloc: A Gift Most Obvious!

I distribute a cheat sheet for the final for all of my Introduction to Philosophy courses. The final is how my students live their lives, and the cheat sheet for the final is a list of books that will help my students stay sane, and several of the books on that list are by James V. Schall. Schall has a way of making things simple. He is a master of *metaphysical docility*: the ability to take someone willing to learn to the truth of *what is*.

In an essay on Hilaire Belloc. Schall wrote,

> If you want to get Belloc's point, try to command something before it exists, to exist. We do not have the power of existence as such in our arsenal. This is the great Thomist truth, the truth of existence. Existence is the Gift we do not give ourselves, but

---

16. Gilson, *Methodological Realism*, 93.

only receive it. This is why, from our side, to recall Belloc's friend Chesterton, gratitude is the first response to being.[17]

Schall's main point here is that when we study metaphysics (ontology, the study of being qua being) we begin with a recognition that *what is*, existence, is not of *our* own making. It is something *given* to us. Thus, the metaphysician should be the most grateful of students. For the metaphysician is thinking carefully in wonder and awe about a gift that need not have been given.

Further in the same essay, Schall writes, "This is the most marvelous of [Belloc's] sentences. *To delight in existence itself*, this is the highest mark of sanity and reality. If we can delight in existence itself, we can, even more, delight in the tiny particular being that exists—the 'strong sense of individual existence.'"[18] There is a delight to metaphysics, to the study of being, of existence. If Schall (and Belloc) are right about this, then we have a good reason to study existence. Existence should be studied because it is delightful! Surfers often use the term "stoke" to describe the delight of wave riding. Metaphysicians are stoked! Ontology is the second-most stoked of the sciences! Theology is likely the most stoked, for ontology gives us an account of *what is*, and theology reveals *Who is*! The joy of metaphysics is the delight that we find in the gift of what is, given to us by our direct awareness of what is.

In another essay, Schall elaborates further on the importance of why we should study existence. He writes,

> These reflections were caused by an e-mail, which I received the other day. A young man, evidently a teacher, wrote to me something he admitted sounded "strange" and almost "funny." He observed that "for the majority of my students the existence of things is almost irrelevant; for them everything is how you choose to think about it. But then I suppose that the job of the philosopher, especially the Christian philosopher, is to insist on the obvious because that's what's most likely to be taken for granted."[19]

What Schall refers to as "strange" and "funny" would be so, if it weren't so tragic. The existence of things and the existence of existence itself is irrelevant. To insist otherwise is heretical today!

---

17. Schall, "On Disliking Champagne but Delighting in Existence."
18. Schall, "On Disliking Champagne but Delighting in Existence."
19. Schall, "Why Do Things Exist?"

Gratefully, Schall and the wise down through the ages recognize that "the existence of things is the most relevant fact about the things we daily encounter."[20] Schall and other true ontologists down through the ages continue to insist on the obvious, because that is indeed what is most taken for granted today.

The obviousness of existence is truly amazing, according to Schall. He states, "What is amazing about something is not how we feel about it, or even what we will do with it. Before we can have any of these reactions, we must know, acknowledge, and even celebrate the very existence of things."[21] The joy of metaphysics, of delight, stoke, and celebration of *what is*, can only come to us when we recognize that *what is* is a gift to us.

This leaves us with a question, according to Schall. He states,

> The question is this: What understanding of the existence of things can support this gift status of things? Only that understanding, I think, that finds in existence itself as we know it no reason why it must be, no reason, in itself, why it might not be. The existence of things bears all the marks of choice, abundance, and truth. And if this is so, what is the primary human reaction to the existence of things, one that must be there before all others? It can only be, I think, that of gratitude.[22]

The gratitude for existence should motivate us to be very clear on what existence is. A gift given is surely motivation to know not only the gift itself, but also the Giver? Is it reasonable to be given the greatest of gifts and ignore both the gift and the Giver? One can of course choose to ignore both, and Schall has pointed out that institutions of "higher" learning are filled with people for whom the things that exist, *what is*, are irrelevant.

1.3 CONCLUSION: CAN WE IGNORE SUNSETS?

I seem to recall Peter Kreeft pointing out that when people go to the beach they do not sit facing the parking lot or the snack bar. Every summer day, especially on holidays, the beaches of San Diego, where I live, and beaches around the world are literally packed wall to wall with people. Nearly all of them are looking at the sea, even more so at sunset. Nobody ignores a beautiful sunset when it is right in front of them, or at least very few do. Yet something greater than the sea is in front of us at every moment. Something

20. Schall, "Why Do Things Exist?"
21. Schall, "On Disliking Champagne but Delighting in Existence."
22. Schall, "Why Do Things Exist?"

greater than a sunset is always before us. Reality is a gift that is right in front of us, always with us. *What is*, is a gift that has been given. One of the main reasons to continue reading this book is to explore the gift of *what is* and to begin to have some knowledge of the Giver.

PART 2

Reality Regained

From Common Sense to God and Back

CHAPTER 2

The Exterior Path to Existence
Sense Experience

2.0 FROM COMMON-SENSE EXPERIENCE TO EXISTENCE

I arrive at the beach. I feel the cool, wet sand at my feet. I taste the saltiness of the ocean water on my lips. I hear the sound of the crashing surf. I smell the freshness of the sea air. I see waves breaking offshore. These things are real. Every person knows what is real from ordinary common-sense experiences like these. They also tell us more. These physical sensory experiences tell us about the nature of reality itself, about existence itself.

These external experiences are the first place we begin to understand the nature of reality. Dallas Willard once wrote, "Such basic ontological questions as those about the distinction between existence and non-existence . . . are thoroughly worked out in the course of the basic descriptive work of phenomenology as the descriptive theory of the essences of experiences."[1] In this chapter, we will do some basic descriptive work about the nature of existence from the essence of common-sense experience.

Common-sense realism about the nature of reality takes sense experience seriously as the starting point to begin to grasp the nature of reality. Jacques Maritain took this approach when he said, "It is in things themselves that metaphysics finds its object. It is the being of sensible and material things, the being of the world of experience, which is its immediately accessible field of investigation."[2] One of the strengths of the broadly Thomistic route to knowledge of existence advocated by Maritain, Gilson, Klubertanz, and Wippel (among others) is that it begins with ordinary sense experience and draws out existence directly from what is present before the intellect by means of those experiences. Let's call this a "common-sense" advantage to our knowledge of existence. It requires very little in the way of either conceptual analysis or complex logical apparatus and makes no assumptions or commitments to our beliefs about what must be the case, according to our preconceptions. It does, however, require some patient reflection upon what one has experienced in the ordinary course of human life.

1. Willard, "Phenomenology and Metaphysics."
2. Maritain, *Existence and the Existent*, 31–32.

Common-sense realism is committed to the fact that through sense experience we are all aware of what existence is, even if we are not aware of the fact that we are aware of what existence is. The philosopher's specific task is to make this clear and show how we can come to be aware that we are aware of what existence is. I believe that this is what Willard had in mind when he discusses the "basic descriptive work of phenomenology as the descriptive theory of the essences of experiences"

This approach also requires an ordinary commitment to common-sense epistemology, the kind of which G. K. Chesterton spoke so highly. It is a philosophy that "stands founded on the universal common conviction that eggs are eggs," and we simply stand "in the broad daylight of the brotherhood of men, in their common consciousness that eggs are not hens or dreams or mere practical assumptions; but things attested by the Authority of the Senses, which is from God."[3]

Chesterton was following one of the greatest common-sense realists in the history of philosophy. Thomas Aquinas maintained that the nature of reality is one of the first things that human beings grasp in their intellectual activities. Aquinas claimed in his work on truth (*De Veritate*) that "what is first apprehended by the intellect is being. Hence the intellect must attribute this (being) to whatever is apprehended by it. And so, when it apprehends the essence of any being, it says that that essence is a being."[4] It is from our acts of simple apprehension that we ground a theory of existence. We take those acts of simple apprehension, and we reflect on them. We consider what those simple acts tell us about the nature of existence. This chapter will elaborate and clarify how we come to know the nature of existence as it was developed by the twentieth-century philosopher George Klubertanz.

2.1 THE EXTERIOR ROUTE TO EXISTENCE: GEORGE KLUBERTANZ AND SOME THOMISTS

George Klubertanz claims that "according to St. Thomas, the human intellect must begin with sensible things, and hence all principles must somehow

3. Chesterton, *Thomas Aquinas*, 94.

4. Aquinas, *Truth*, 21. Aquinas also says, "Now, as Avicenna says, that which the intellect first conceives, as in a way, the most evident, and to which it reduces all its concepts, is being" (Aquinas, *Truth*, 5). In *Quaestiones Disputatae De Potentia Dei* (*On the Power of God*), Aquinas writes, "The first object of the intellect is being" (145). On the importance of good starts in metaphysics, Aquinas, following Aristotle, reminds us that "a small error in the beginning of something is a great one at the end, . . . moreover, being and essence are what the intellect first conceives. . . . Hence we ought to state what the terms 'essence' and 'being' signify" (Aquinas, *On Being and Essence*, 33).

be found in sense experience."[5] Not only does this mean that "sensible things can be understood as being" but also that we must find in the being of our direct experience all the intrinsic principles of being.[6] This means that when we have ordinary experiences, we know that the things we experience are real, and we can come to know the nature of reality itself. When we have a sense experience, seeing a crow on a fence for example, we know that the crow and the fence exist, but we also know what existence itself is. Klubertanz puts it this way: "The things that we directly and immediately assert to exist are the sensible things of our experience . . . and the judgments that we make about immediately experienced things are called perceptual judgments. The act of existing thus attained is the esse [essence in act] of a material, singular thing."[7]

In what follows, I present a brief summary from Klubertanz of how the process works. It shows how our minds move from common-sense ordinary experiences to an understanding of the nature of existence. There are four steps in the process.[8]

Step 1

We have ordinary sense experiences and we apprehend (or simply see) objects as they are presented to us in our experiences. For example, I look out

5. Klubertanz, *Introduction*, v.

6. Klubertanz, *Introduction*, vi.

7. Klubertanz, *Introduction*, 47. By *esse*, Klubertanz means essence in act, or essential actualization.

8. The key passage from Aquinas's work on this is from his commentary on Boethius's *De Trinitate*.

> We conclude that there are three kinds of distinction in the operation of the intellect. There is one through the operation of the intellect joining and dividing which is properly called separation and this belongs to divine science or metaphysics. There is another through the operation by which the quiddities of things are conceived which is the abstraction of form from sensible matter, and this belongs to mathematics. And there is a third through the same operation which is the abstraction of a universal from a particular, and this belongs to physics and to all the sciences in general, because science disregards accidental features and treats of necessary matters. And because certain men (for example, the Pythagoreans and the Platonists) did not understand the difference between the last two kinds of distinction and the first, they fell into error, asserting that the objects of mathematics and universals exist separate from sensible things. (Aquinas, *The Divisions and Methods*, 33)

See also Wippel, *The Metaphysical Thought*, 46, for an additional discussion of this, which relies in part on Klubertanz's work.

my window and see a black crow perched on the backyard fence. There they
are: crow and fence.

Step 2

I can see or reflect upon the fact that each of these objects exist. I am aware
that the crow is real, and the fence is real. I see that each of them exists or
has existence. There *is* the crow. There *is* the fence.

Step 3

We can see that there are both differences and similarities among the objects
of our experiences. We see that the crow has being, and we can see the fence
has being. We see that there is a difference between the crow existing and
the fence existing. One exists as a *crow*, and the other exists as a *fence*. We
see pretty clearly that *being a crow* and *being a fence* are two *very* different
things. Crows exemplify "crowness" and fences exemplify "fenceness." But,
we also see something in common between them. We see that the both have
being. They both *exist*. Existence is shared by the crow and by the fence. We
see that being or existence is something that both have in common. So now
we have two very different things, crows and fences, but the main thing that
they have in common is that they both exist. So, now we make a generalized
judgment about these two things. We judge that existence is something over
and above the two particular things that we have apprehended.

Klubertanz puts it this way: being cannot be reached by abstraction,
but it can be reached by judgment. Klubertanz claims that "the knowledge
of being is not a simple concept (apprehension) of an essence."[9] He maintains that we can have *knowledge* of being *qua* being, but not by apprehension. He claims that there are other forms of intellectual knowledge other
than apprehension. One such form is judgment, which he calls "that act of
the mind by which we assert (or deny) that something *is*."[10] He claims that
an act of judgment "directly reaches the esse [being in act, what I am calling
essential exemplification] of a thing."[11] Although the judgment is distinct
from an act of apprehension, it does "virtually" contain an apprehension of
an essence. He states that the judgment "does not contain an apprehension

---

9. Klubertanz, *Introduction*, 46.
10. Klubertanz, *Introduction*, 46.
11. Klubertanz, *Introduction*, 46.

as a distinct act but has *a function equivalent to that of an apprehension.*"[12] This is an eminently realist approach to existence. Judgment is a faculty of our minds by means of which our minds directly reach and connect with existence itself. Judgment has the same kind of direct connection to the nature of existence as apprehension does through simple seeing and the mind's grasp on the objects of our experience.

To help with this step, think of the way we come to make judgments about universals. For example, suppose I've never experienced a spherical object before. Suppose someone hands me a bag of ten round marbles, each one a different size and color. I dump out the bag of marbles, and I immediately see spheres.[13] I examine each marble and see and feel the roundness of each one. I go through the whole bag this way, and I see that each marble is *different* (different size, different color), but they are also similar.[14] There are different marbles, but each share in being spherical. Because I see that this is so, I can make the judgment that "sphereness" is something that all the marbles have in common. The marbles are each different individuals, but they have something in common, namely "sphereness" or the property of being spherical. I see now that "being a sphere" is something over and above the particular things that are spheres. So too in the account of existence we are working through here, when I see a crow and see a fence, I see that they are different, but what they have in common is existence. So, in the example of the marbles, existence is like the "sphereness" which is had in common by particular things.

Step 4

At this step, we take the evidence (from the simple apprehension) that we have so far and make one final judgment. We judge that *what* each thing is, the crow and the fence, is not the same as each of these things' *existence*. We simply see that "crowness" (being a *crow*, or existing *crowly*) and "fenceness" (being a fence, or existing *fencely*) is different than existence itself. Or to put it the other way around, we can see now that existence itself is not the same thing as any essence had by a particular thing. We judge that there is a difference between existence itself and the essences of things that do exist. We judge that there are essences to crows (that which makes *the thing perched on the fence* a crow and not a cat or a cabbage), and we judge that there are

---

12. Klubertanz, *Introduction*, 46n19, emphasis mine.

13. Even if I didn't have a word to describe the property of being a sphere, I could still see the sphere, even if I didn't see it *as* a "sphere."

14. This is a way to understand the negative aspects of the judgment of separation.

essences to fences (that which makes *the thing the crow is perched on* a fence and not a cat or a cabbage). We now have arrived at the end of our foundation for ontology, a study of existence. *We now judge that what makes crows and fences exist is the unity of the thing's essence with its act of existing. For a crow or a fence to exist is for each of them to actualize their essences.*

In this last judgment, being able actually to see the exemplification of an essence allows us to judge that existence is essential exemplification. J. P. Moreland, following Husserl, explains how this is possible:

> While focusing one's attention on a moment (a Husserlian property-instance), one can *directly perceive the universal in the moment.* The direct perception of a Universal is, on this view, a different mental act from an ordinary perception of a moment, but it in no way involves attending to something outside the moment itself. Indeed, it is while the eyes are on the moment that the universal is originally *given as a constituent of the moment in eidetic intuition.*[15]

This allows us to see universals and essences in the things that have them in order to judge that their existence is the exemplification of their essence.

Thus, we can conclude that existence is essential actualization. Crows exist because they exemplify the essence of crows, and fences exist because they exemplify the essence of fences. *Essences are different from existence, and things exist because they exemplify essences.* This will be the starting point of our reflection on what follows from the fact that existence is the actualization of an essence.

Let us turn at this point to a brief recapitulation of the four steps that we have just been through. These steps are written in a more formal way with direct quotations and reference from Klubertanz's work.[16]

1. S apprehends (i.e., has direct sensory experiences, i.e., simply sees) objects $O_1 \ldots O_n$.

2. S sees "O_1 is," "O_2 is" ... "O_n is."[17]

3. S apprehends that there is a difference between $O_1, O_2, \ldots O_n$ and the "is" or "being" of $O_1, O_2, \ldots O_n$, since $O_1, O_2, \ldots O_n$ are many/particular but "is" or "being" is one/general (i.e., "truly applied" equally to $O_1, O_2, \ldots O_n$).[18]

15. Moreland, "Grossman on Property Instances," 183, emphasis mine.

16. For a similar treatment of these four steps, see Maritain, *Existence and the Existent*, 26–28n13.

17. Could anyone really deny this?

18. Klubertanz, *Introduction*, 47.

3.1 Klubertanz calls this a "disengagement" of "a common intelligibility from its original presentation in the completely singular sensible thing."[19]

3.2 Klubertanz claims that this is *not* an abstraction, as nothing is left out when we judge that being is not identical to any particular $O_1 \ldots O_n$.

3.3 Judging that "is" or "being" is distinct from particular things "expresses indefinitely a completely determined, singular thing . . . it has an indefinite reference to the singular as such."[20] He calls this "the negative judgment of generalization."

4. Moving from sensible being to being of metaphysics involves the "discovery that 'is' asserts the *actuality* of, not the *nature* of" particular kinds of things.[21]

4.1 The "discovery of the act of existing—esse—is the moment of discovery of metaphysics."[22]

4.2 From direct perceptual judgment "This is," we make a negative judgment, "and its actuality is not identical" to a particular thing. This is a "judgment of separation."[23] This judgment separates "the intelligibility of what it means *to be* from the intelligibility of what a sensible, material quiddity or essence is."[24]

5. Summary

5.1 S simply apprehends $O_1 \ldots O_n$.

5.2 S judges that being is general from particulars $O_1 \ldots O_n$ (judgment of generalization).

5.3 S judges that being is separate from properties of $O_1 \ldots O_n$ (judgment of separation).

5.4 S knows that "to be" is in general "to be in act," or to actualize an essence; being is essential actualization.[25]

---

19. Klubertanz, *Introduction*, 47.

20. Klubertanz, *Introduction*, 47.

21. Klubertanz, *Introduction*, 50.

22. Klubertanz, *Introduction*, 50.

23. Klubertanz, *Introduction*, 51.

24. Klubertanz, *Introduction*, 51. Also see Wippel, *The Metaphysical Thought of Thomas Aquinas*, 46.

25. Here is what Aquinas claims about the meaning of the word "being." "*Being* properly signifies: something-existing-in-act" (Aquinas, *Introduction to the Metaphysics*, 22.) This quotation comes from the *Summa Theologica* (*ST* 1, 5, 1 ad 1).

2.2 ESSENTIAL EXEMPLIFICATION: HOW TO BE JUDGMENTAL

The key aspect to our knowledge of existence is the act of "judgment," through which we see that existence is essential exemplification. Jacques Maritain in his *Existence and the Existent* writes this about the insight gained through judgment:

> In forming this judgment, the intellect, on the one hand, knows the subject as singular (indirectly by "reflection upon phantasms"),[26] and, on the other hand, affirms that this singular subject exercises the act of existing. In other words, the intellect itself exercises upon the notion of this subject an act (the act of affirming) by which it [the intellect] lives intentionally the existence of the thing.[27]

According to Maritain, it is "by the judgment itself" through the "intuition of sense" that the intellect "grasps by immaterializing" the experience and "reaches the *actus essendi*."[28] The *actus essendi* is what I am here calling the act of essential exemplification in a singular particular which we know by experiencing it through common-sense experience. Maritain says that in judgment, the intellect receives intentionally the act of existence which is really in the thing that has it. Since things exist, and since our minds are able to receive the existence of things, our minds can know through judgment that existence is essential exemplification.

This is only slightly different from the way the intellect receives the forms of an object through perception. The soul can become all things; it can receive any essences that are exemplified. If this is right, that "the intellect lives intentionally the existence of the thing" then the soul can receive the act of existing of any existing thing through any sense (or other) experience, and it can become aware of the existence of the thing in an act of judgment. It seems to me that in any experience (sense or otherwise) of any reality, the intellect, given its ability to receive the forms, has already intentionally received the essential exemplification of the thing it experiences. If you have had any sense experience at all, then you have experienced the nature of existence, even if you haven't thought about the nature of existence. Judgment is that act of our minds which brings to light an awareness

---

26. These are qualities of objects received by the mind in an intentional (directed toward the object) state.

27. Maritain, *Existence and the Existent*, 26–27.

28. Maritain, *Existence and the Existent*, 27.

to the intellect of that which is already present to it, namely that existence is essential exemplification.

Klubertanz puts it this way: "Judgment, therefore, directly reaches the esse [essential actualization] of a thing, for in the judgment we know *that* a thing is. . . . A direct perceptual judgment is a knowledge that some existent is. . . . The act of existing thus attained is the esse of a material, singular thing."[29] So, we attain knowledge of essential exemplification (*esse* in Klubertanz's words) by means of judgment of what is already present to the intellect through common-sense experience.

So, if the intellect has intentionally before it the essential exemplification (esse) of the thing of experience, cannot the intellect hold before itself this very intentional state and wonder about it? Yes, it can! This is the starting point of metaphysics. If this is correct, then any metaphysics that does not begin here will be quickly off course.

However, if we *compare* multiple experiences of essential exemplification, what then are we to conclude? For example, suppose experience E1 of object O1 has essential exemplification (esse) EE1, and E2 of O2 has EE2, and E3 of O3 has EE3, etc. Are we then to conclude that EE is something over and above EE1, EE2, EE3, etc? We might. But then what? An idea from Frederick Wilhelmsen might be helpful here.

When we consider the universe, the totality of possible objects of experience, by means of which the intellect might be able to "live intentionally the existence of the thing," we are in fact struck by an obvious fact. It is the fact that what "the universe has in common is existence."[30] Then we are faced with a dilemma: (A) there is something that is not existence, or (B) there is existence itself. The first horn of this dilemma, *there is* something that *is not existence* is a contradiction and is really saying that "something exists that doesn't exist." If the logical relation of contradiction really does have bearing on reality, then option (A) is a non-starter.

So, we are left with option (B): existence itself exists. Wilhelmsen claims that existence found in the universe, or any possible object of common-sense experience "points to Pure Existence." Wilhelmsen claims that this is a Christian discovery and moves us beyond all metaphysical systems from the ancient world. He writes, "If a Christian metaphysician had to designate the contingent being he encounters from without and experiences from within, he might do well to call it 'Providential.' In its radical contingency, being points to its Author and thus proclaims itself a gift."[31] The universe of the

29. Klubertanz, *Introduction*, 46–47.

30. Wilhelmsen, *The Paradoxical Structure*, 120.

31. Wilhelmsen, *The Paradoxical Structure*, 121.

Christian common-sense metaphysical realist is a world of joy of receiving existence from him whose essence is His existence!

2.3 THE BRADLEYEN REGRESS OBJECTION TO ESSENTIAL EXEMPLIFICATION[32]

So far, I have argued that existence is essential exemplification, and that our knowledge of it is derived from common-sense experiences in the sections above. Yet, the very idea that existence is essential exemplification is not without its challenges. I would like to consider one such challenge here, namely the challenge of the Bradleyen regress regarding relations. If existence is essential exemplification, then there is a distinction between essence and existence and a relation involved.

In addition to my arguments here, the idea that existence exists has also been argued by several recent philosophers. Two of them, William Vallicella and J. P. Moreland, are realists about existence. They think that existence exists, and we can know it. Moreland's view is similar (although derived differently) from my view that existence is essential exemplification. Vallicella, although he agrees with Moreland's realism about existence, disagrees with Moreland (and me) that existence involves any sort of relation. Let me first sketch both Vallicella and Moreland's approaches to existence, and then show how Vallicella tries to argue against the idea that existence is essential exemplification by raising an argument against relations from William Bradley. Then I will provide some rejoinders to the challenge of Bradley's regress objection.

2.3.1 Moreland's Desideratic Approach

This book is dedicated to J. P. Moreland. I've learned a great deal about existence (and many other areas of metaphysics) from Moreland. His view of existence is essentially the same as the one I advocate in this book. However, Moreland does not derive his view of existence from common-sense experience in the way that Klubertanz does. Moreland's approach starts from theoretical desiderata and builds the theory from there. Moreland's approach to understanding existence is derived from the following theoretical desiderata. A theory of existence must:

---

32. Logic Alert! These next sections are difficult. If you are content with the understanding of existence as essential exemplification, then proceed to chapter 3. If you love really detailed, nitty-gritty metaphysical arguments, then enjoy!

1) Be consistent with and explain what actually does and does not exist.

2) Be consistent with and explain what could have existed but either does not exist or is not believed to exist.

3) Allow for the fact that existence itself exists (not be self-refuting).

4) Not violate the fundamental laws of logic.

5) Allow for the existence of acts of knowing.[33]

Moreland elaborates on these desiderata for a theory of existence in a response to the question of whether existence is a property. Following Kant's argument that existence is not a property, Moreland claims that to assert "x is real" "does add something to x because there is, in fact, a real difference between existence and nonexistence."[34] Moreland then proceeds by considering an existential *statement*, "Tigers exist." And from this derives a distinction between the property of being a tiger and the belonging of that property to an individual, e.g., Tony. From this, he concludes, "The claim that tigers exist is the claim that the essence of being a tiger (the what of being a tiger) is actually exemplified by or belongs to something (the that or fact of an individual tiger existing)" and then generalizes to the claim that existence is "the entering into the nexus of exemplification."[35] Moreland then shows that this view fits the five desiderata of a theory of existence.

2.3.2 Vallicella's Paradigmatic Approach

Another view of existence put forward by William Vallicella is similar to Moreland's, and one with which I am somewhat sympathetic. Vallicella develops his theory in two parts. First, he claims that a theory of existence "be anchored in an actual existent so that the theory of existence is at the same time both a theory of existence and a theory of an actual existent."[36] Second, he proceeds to show the failure of several attempts at a theory of existence (e.g., first-level property theories, "no difference" theories, property of property theories, and mondial attribute theories). Upon offering arguments against each of these views—Vallicella calls this a *via negativa*—he begins by asking the reader to "think of ordinary individuals as concrete states of affairs of facts" that are contingent unities of their constituents.[37]

---

33. Moreland and Craig, *Philosophical Foundations*, 188–89.

34. Moreland and Craig, *Philosophical Foundations*, 190.

35. Moreland and Craig, *Philosophical Foundations*, 190.

36. Vallicella, *A Paradigm Theory of Existence*, 8.

37. Vallicella, *A Paradigm Theory of Existence*, 160.

For example, he states "the fact of *a's being F* is plausibly taken to have three constituents, *a*, *F-ness* and the asymmetrical tie of instantiation."[38] He then proceeds to present arguments to the conclusion of a paradigm theory of existence which is understood as:

> (PT) Necessarily, for any contingent individual x, x exists if and only if (i) there is a necessary y such that y is the paradigm existent, and (ii) y, as the external unifier of x's ontological constituents, directly produces the unity/existence of x.[39]

2.3.3. A Brief Evaluation of Moreland and Vallicella's Approaches

Moreland's approach to a theory of existence has the following strengths. (1) It gives us clear desiderata for any theory of existence. (2) It draws from a consideration of ordinary language statements by means of which we refer to things in ordinary experience. (3) It connects directly to an overall realism about properties/universals. Similarly, Vallicella's approach to existence is logically rigorous, carefully argued, and extremely thorough. It also points to something, "the paradigm" of existence, which might be consistent with Christian theism.

However, neither Vallicella's nor Moreland's approach begins with the ordinary data of sense experience. This need not count against the conclusions in their arguments, which should stand or fall on their own merits. However, it might count against a robust theory of existence if that theory does not consider the data of ordinary sense experience as a contributing feature to what we know about the nature of existence. In other words, it is theoretically possible to have a coherent and logically rigorous account of existence but fail to connect that theory with the data that is derived from our experience of existence. While neither Vallicella nor Moreland explicitly reject the "exterior route" from Klubertanz, discussed above, the omission of such an approach in an account of existence from two thinkers whose views of existence is nearly identical to this approach seems puzzling to me.

Although Moreland and Vallicella are both realists about existence, Vallicella maintains that the idea of existence as essential exemplification (Moreland's view and the one that I defend here) falls prey to a "Bradleyen regress" argument against relations. Let us look at that argument and offer some rejoinders to it.

---

38. Vallicella, *A Paradigm Theory of Existence*, 160.
39. Vallicella, *A Paradigm Theory of Existence*, 2.

2.4 EXISTENCE'S REGRESS?

2.4.1. Vallicella's Agreement with Moreland

Although Vallicella offers a strong criticism of Moreland's and my view of existence, there is a great deal of agreement about existence. First, Vallicella agrees with Moreland that existence is not a property of individuals. This was a view held by Frege and Russel claiming that "existence is a second-order property . . . based on the idea that seemingly singular existential and negative existential sentence like 'Bill Gates exists' and 'Ronald McDonald does not exist' are, in their deeper logical form, general existential and negative existential claims."[40] Vallicella calls this view "Fressell's" view. He claims that Fressell "holds that existence cannot be a property of individuals any more than numerousness can be."[41]

Second, Vallicella also agrees with Moreland that existence cannot be an ordinary property of individuals, *pace* Kant. Kant made a distinction between two sorts of predicates:

i.   real or descriptive predicates, which describe what a thing is, e.g., hard, sweet, round, heavy, etc., and

ii. modal predicates or non-descriptive predicates, which describe the "mode" or manner of a thing's being, e.g., existence, possible, necessary, etc.

Kant held that for any concept (C) of object (O) one does not enlarge one's understanding of O through C by saying that O exists. Both Moreland and Vallicella agree with Kant here.

Third, Vallicella and Moreland agree that existence is not a classificatory property. Vallicella states, "Existence cannot be a property that classifies or sorts objects into the existent and the nonexistent."[42]

Fourth, they both agree that existence makes a real, indeed an "abysmal," difference to a thing that exists.[43] Vallicella claims that "existence does not contribute to the whatness of a thing" but adds "the thatnesss without which the whatness would be nothing at all," and "a veritable abyss separates being and nonbeing."[44] Vallicella quotes Moreland, "It follows that '[t]here is a fundamental difference between essence (whatness) and

40. Nelson, "Existence."
41. Vallicella, "The Moreland-Willard-Lotze Theory," 28.
42. Vallicella, "The Moreland-Willard-Lotze Theory," 29.
43. Vallicella, "The Moreland-Willard-Lotze Theory," 29.
44. Vallicella, "The Moreland-Willard-Lotze Theory," 29.

existence (thatness)' (Moreland, [*Universals*,] 137). This implies that a (contingent) individual cannot be identified with its existence."[45]

Fifth, they both agree that existence itself exists. Quoting Moreland again, Vallicella writes, "'If existence itself does not exist, then nothing else could exist in virtue of having existence' (Moreland, 135). Reinhardt Grossman takes the same line: 'If existence did not exist, then nothing would exist.'"[46]

2.4.2 Vallicella's Disagreement with Moreland

To recap, in his book *Universals*, Moreland states, (i) existence is the "having of a property" or (ii) "being had by a property."[47] Here in this book I have offered a view similar to Moreland's but based on common-sense experiences to the conclusion that existence is essential exemplification. Vallicella criticizes this understanding of existence as essential exemplification by focusing on Moreland's disjunction that existence is the: (i) "having of a property" or (ii) "being had by a property." Vallicella claims that (i) is clear, and (ii) is unclear. He claims that (ii) should read "being had of a property" to make explicit the relational nature of existence on Moreland's view.[48]

In another place Moreland says, "Existence is either the belonging of some property or the being belonged to by a property or, more simply, the entering into the nexus of exemplification."[49] This seems to make more explicit Vallicella's interpretation of Moreland's view of existence and the relation of exemplification. Vallicella states that according to Moreland, existence is "the relation of exemplification" and "existence itself exists because existence itself is the universal exemplification relation which is itself exemplified."[50] Having established that according to Moreland existence is a relation of exemplification (what I have been calling "essential exemplification"), Vallicella proceeds to offer of a criticism of this relation.

45. Vallicella, "The Moreland-Willard-Lotze Theory," 29.
46. Vallicella, "The Moreland-Willard-Lotze Theory," 30.
47. Moreland, *Universals*, 157.
48. Vallicella, "The Moreland-Willard-Lotze Theory," 30.
49. Moreland and Craig, *Philosophical Foundations*, 191.
50. Vallicella, "The Moreland-Willard-Lotze Theory," 30–31.

2.4.3. The Bradleyan Objection Applied

Vallicella's "Bradleyan Objection" is this: if existence is the universal/essential exemplification relation (EX), then for any particular existing thing, for example: Tony-the-tiger (T-t-t) will equal the following:

i. bare particular (individuator), plus

ii. EX (exemplification relation), plus

iii. property of being a tiger.[51]

The problem Vallicella sees is that i + ii + iii "do not add up to Tony-the-tiger." This conclusion follows because of these reasons:

1. T-t-t is not a sum but a unity.

2. EX unifies i and iii together.

3. EX unifies itself with i and iii.

4. If EX unifies i and ii, then EX unifies itself with i and ii.

5. Given 4, the view "succumbs to Bradley's famous regress argument against external relations," and an infinite regress of relations will follow.[52]

6. Thus, "EX is a relation external to its terms."[53]

7. Thus, "Each of the three ontological constituents [i, ii, and iii] can exist without the other two even if none of them can exist apart from all the others."[54]

2.5 REJOINDERS TO THE BRADLEYEN OBJECTION

2.5.1 Is EX an Internal or an External Relation?

Vallicella's understanding of Moreland's concept of existence as a relation need not be one that is external to its terms, given the distinction between external and internal relations. The exemplification relation (EX) need not be an *external* relation. It is possible that it could be understood as an *internal* relation.

---

51. Vallicella, "The Moreland-Willard-Lotze Theory," 31.
52. Vallicella, "The Moreland-Willard-Lotze Theory," 31.
53. Vallicella, "The Moreland-Willard-Lotze Theory," 31.
54. Vallicella, "The Moreland-Willard-Lotze Theory," 31.

A relation is an *internal* relation (IR) just in case: if x is IR to y, then x cannot exist without y. Or to put it another way, if x does not stand in IR to y, then x no longer exists as x (or is not at all). For example, Aristotle pointed out that a hand separated from a man is no longer a hand.[55] Being a hand is internally related to the whole man. The relata in an internal relation depend for their existence on their relation to the whole, or on the existence of the relation itself.

On the contrary, a relation is an external relation (ER) just in case: if x is ER to y, then x can exist without y. Or to put it another way, if x does not stand in ER to y, then x can still exist as x. For example, consider an eraser removed from a pencil, it can still be what it is without its relation to the whole. The parts can of the pencil can exist without their dependence on the whole.

Moreland's view of existence could be interpreted as seeing the exemplification relation, EX, as an internal relation to the whole. EX would not exist without being in the relation to the other two. If EX is exemplified, then EX exists. A proponent of existence as "essential exemplification" could simply say that if anything exists, then EX is exemplified.

2.5.2 Is EX Necessarily an External Relation?

Vallicella seems to be claiming that the relationship of i, ii, and iii can be contingent and thus EX must be related externally. But why must this follow? T-t-t can be a contingent being even if it is necessary that existence involves i, ii, and iii. So, even though it is true that EX doesn't necessitate that T-t-t exist, this does not mean that necessarily EX is external to the other terms.

Some internal relations are necessarily had by contingent beings. It might be necessary that if a hand is to be a hand, it must stand in an internal relation to a man, but it is not necessary that the man (or the hand) exist. The man (or hand) can be contingent, even if it is necessary that if the man is exemplified, his parts stand in an internal relation to him as a whole. So, it might be necessary that if EX is to be EX, it must stand in an internal relation to the other two relata (an indivuduator / bare particular and some property/universal/essence), but that does not mean that the whole

---

55. "For they cannot even exist if severed from the whole; for it is not a finger in any and every state that is the finger of a living thing, but a dead finger is a finger only in name. . . . For it is not a hand in any and every state that is a part of man, but only when it can fulfil its work, and therefore only when it is alive; if it is not alive it is not a part" (Aristotle, *Metaphysics*, 799, 1035b25).

complex is necessary, at least not for contingent beings. So, while it is true that "there is no necessity that a exemplify F-*ness*," this simply implies that a exemplifying F-*ness* is contingent, but it *doesn't* imply that the relation of exemplification between a and F-*ness* is external or necessary.

2.5.3 How Should We Understand Bare Particulars and the EX Relation?

There is a second way that Vallicella offers a summary and critique of the essential exemplification view of existence and the regress problem which misunderstands bare particulars. If Moreland's view is correct, this may militate against the regress problem. Here is Vallicella's argument.

Again, Vallicella claims that on the essential exemplification view, for a particular being, say Tony-the-tiger (T-t-t), to exist then three things are present:

i. bare particular,

ii. EX (the exemplification relation), and

iii. the property of being a tiger (which Vallicella calls F-ness).

Vallicella adds that i, ii, and iii are externally related, and this will generate the Bradleyan regress problem. Here is why.

We can imagine a possible world (W1) where only one particular exists: Tony-the-tiger. This will entail: i. a (bare particular) ii. EX (exemplification relation) and iii. F-ness (property of being a tiger). But, we can also imagine a second possible world, W2: with two particulars:

p1. Bugs Bunny: Bare particular a exemplifies G (being a bunny).

p2. Joanie the tigress: F-*ness* (being a tiger) exemplified by b (with a "different" bare particular than the one had by a).

According to Vallicella, the following can be considered. If W1 has a, *EX*, and F-*ness*, and W2 has a, *EX*, and F-*ness* (but separated), it follows that a, *EX*, and F-*ness* are related externally (or at least EX is related externally to a and F-*ness*). This external relation will therefore fall prey to the Bradleyan regress raised above.

Does this follow? Consider the following objection to this version of Vallicella's Bradleyen regress argument based on how we should understand bare particulars.[56] One can understand bare particulars as simples which are

___

56. For his discussion of the natures of bare particulars and their relations to universals, see Moreland, *Universals*, 14, 93–94, 102, and 155.

numerically but not intrinsically distinct. Therefore, in W_2, F-$ness$ exemplified by b is not intrinsically distinct from F-$ness$ exemplified by a in W_1. If there is merely numerical difference but not intrinsic difference between bare particulars a and b then the exemplification of F-$ness$ in b in W_2 is not intrinsically different than the exemplification of F-$ness$ in W_1. Thus, EX need not be understood as an external relation. Thus, to say that in W_2, a, EX, and F-$ness$ exist but separately seems to beg some questions about bare particulars. Here is one such question.

Does Vallicella understand bare particulars in the same way that Moreland does? Moreland's view of existence seems to be operating from the notion of bare particulars found in Gustav Bergmann, as Moreland quotes Bergmann, "Bare particulars neither are nor have natures. Any two of them are not intrinsically but only numerically different. That is their bareness. It is impossible for a bare particular to be 'in' more than one ordinary thing . . . a bare particular is a mere individuator . . . it does nothing else."[57]

Vallicella seems to be treating bare particulars "as wholes, namely states of affairs with properties as constituents within them" as Moreland points out in a rejoinder to critics of his notion of bare particulars.[58] If bare particulars are, as Moreland argues, "simples with properties tied to them" and are "not intrinsically but only numerically different" as Bergmann claims, then to assert that F-$ness$ is tied to bare particular a in W_1 and F-$ness$ is tied to bare particular b in W_2 is to assert that a and b are merely numerically distinct but not intrinsically different.[59] This would seem to imply that a and b could be swapped out with no resulting difference to Tony-the-tiger being Tony-the-tiger in W_1 and Joanie-the-tigress being Joanie-the-tigress in W_2. Simply put, Moreland's understanding of bare particulars does not entail the kind of externality between i, ii, and iii that Vallicella claims. Thus, the regress is avoided.

2.5.4 Is the EX Relation Primitive/Basic?

Moreland's view needs not maintain that the nexus of exemplification relation EX is simply "added" as a third sort of thing. EX is a basic/primitive relation that exists when any universal, including EX itself, is actualized. The universal-particular relation just is a case of the exemplification relation. So, in any particular "Timmy being fat," there are three things:

57. Moreland, *Universals*, 148.
58. Moreland, *Universals*, 155.
59. Moreland, *Universals*, 155.

1) an individuator (a bare particular for Moreland),

2) an instance of a universal (fatness in this case) present in the particular by means of EX,

3) an instance of EX.

There is an "internality" to these three things. Numbers 1 and 2 stand in an internal relation to one another because of the particular instance of EX. If either 1 or 2 were separated from this instance of EX, they would quit existing as these particular instances (although the universal fatness could still exist and other particular instances of fatness would exist if exemplified by another particular, say Tammy). Further, 3 is related (by its own nature as an instance of EX) to 1 and 2 internally as well. If this particular instance of EX were removed from 1 and 2, it would cease existing (although the universal EX could still exist, and other particular instances of EX could exist if exemplified by other contingent particulars). Thus, understanding instances of EX as an internal (as opposed to external) relation prevents the Bradleyen regress.[60]

2.6. THEORIES OF EXISTENCE: PROGRESS BEYOND INTRAMURAL DEBATES

One way that philosophers (among others) can come to have knowledge of something is to pay attention to particular cases of that thing. One such strategy in epistemology is found in understanding truth. Dallas Willard suggests that one way that we can understand truth is to pay attention to particular cases of the phenomenal experiences of truth.[61] I think that the same can be said for a theory of existence. It is by paying attention to these cases that we can begin our understanding of existence. I would like to suggest that the kinds of intramural debates like the one discussed above can be largely avoided if our account of existence qua existence is rooted in a careful analysis of actual cases of things that exist and our experience of them. This sort of task may be the best road for the Christian metaphysician. We should follow Willard's advice toward a common-sense phenomenology. Willard states, "Such ways of exploration do not rest upon *inferences* or efforts to *explain* why things are as they are, and are ways which confirm

60. If my interpretation of Vallicella's ideas are inaccurate, then these objections will need to be revisited.

61. See Willard "Toward a Phenomenology" and my defense of this view in Mosteller, *Theories of Truth*.

themselves to anyone not already committed to how things *must be* in the cases at hand."[62]

After seeing crows perched on fences (or any other sense perception) we come to know quite a bit about the nature of existence. We know that things exist, and they exist because they actualize their essences. If existence is essential actualization, then it will follow that everything that exists actualizes an essence. Maritain says, "The act of existing is the act *par excellence*, whether we consider it in this humble blade of grass or in the feeble beating of our heart, it is everywhere the act and the perfection of all form and all perfection."[63] It may also cause us to ask further questions like: Why do things actualize their essences at all? What is the cause of things actualizing their essence? Is there something or someone whose essence and existence are the same? Once you start down this path of ontological reflection, there are many more questions to pursue for a fruitful area of inquiry.

62. Willard, "Toward a Phenomenology of the Correspondence Theory of Truth."

63 Maritain, *Existence and the Existent*, 36.

CHAPTER 3

The Interior Path to Existence

Self Experience

3.0 FROM THE INSIDE AND OUT?

I arrive at the beach. I feel the cool, wet sand at my feet. I taste the saltiness of the ocean water on my lips. I hear the sound of the crashing surf. I smell the freshness of the sea air. I see waves breaking offshore. These things are real. Every person knows what is real from ordinary common-sense experiences like these. They also tell us more. They tell us about the nature of reality itself, about existence itself. These experiences occur in *me*, a subject of experience. When I begin to reflect on myself and my experience of myself, I can add to my knowledge of the nature of reality which begins from common-sense experience.

Common-sense realism need not preclude knowledge of "what is" that comes to us from an immediate grasp of what we experience internal to our own minds. Some philosophers might take this as a bad idea. After all, when Descartes set out to find a solid foundation for all knowledge, he looked within himself. He attempted to get to all of external reality from knowledge of himself through the famous "Cogito" or "I think, therefore I am." Although not a skeptic, Descartes's use of methodological skepticism opens a disastrous decline of philosophy through to Kant's permanent division of the internal from the external, the uncrossable *noumenal/phenomenal* divide.

For the common-sense realist, looking to what occurs within experience of the self, apart from sense experience, is still commonsensical. Common-sense realism is not limited to the five senses. The realist need not limit common sense to physical experience but can have a broader notion of experience that is still common to all human beings. We have direct awareness of ourselves, and we all know what it is like to experience ourselves as ourselves. What would it mean to deny this? Could someone really deny that they have never had a self experience? Philosophers can deny anything they want, but would doing so be reasonable, given our wealth of common, internal, self-experience. The common-sense realist would suggest that denying common experience of one's self would be as silly as denying that "eggs are eggs."

In this chapter, we will examine our knowledge of existence derived from interior common-sense experiences. When Aquinas indicates that "what is first apprehended by the intellect is being" he does not limit the intellect's apprehension to sense experiences. In fact, one of the first (if not temporally first, at least often experientially first) things we are aware of is ourselves. One of the first things that our intellect apprehends is itself.

We know that we exist.[1] This is the interior route to our understanding of the nature of existence. We might call the exterior route Thomistic, and the interior route Augustinian. The significance of this idea was put forward by St. Augustine in *On the Trinity*, whom Edith Stein quotes: "Of all the things we know, how much do we know the same certitude as we know that we exist?"[2] In this section, we will examine a more recent description of this route given by Edith Stein.

3.1 EDITH STEIN'S INTERIOR PATH TO EXISTENCE

According to Edith Stein, "Whenever the human mind in its quest for truth has sought an indubitably certain point of departure, it always encountered the inescapable *fact of its own being or existence*."[3] She goes on to quote Augustine, Descartes, and Husserl as each in their own way pointing to the undoubtable existence of the self, found in "the reality of my perception" of myself.[4] Each of us can have the certitude of our own existence. We know that we exist.

A question now arises. This question is part of the philosophical journey which moves us beyond a simple seeing of ourselves as existing to an elaboration of existence itself. Once our intellect sees its own existence, it raises from this fact the question "What is that being of which I am conscious?" This question is about the being of the self. It is about the nature of the existence that I have. Stein says that when we ask this sort of question, two things are revealed to us. First, we are aware of being, but we are also aware of not-being.[5] Second, it is from this certitude that one can come to have knowledge of the idea of pure and eternal being.

Here is how these two things are revealed to us. We come to know the difference between being and not-being by starting with self-knowledge, where the self can "contemplate the simple fact of its own being."[6] But, we

1. This sort of self-knowledge need not be part and parcel of a Cartesian search for epistemic certitude. It is simply an awareness of one's self which occurs in the ordinary course of human experience.

2. Stein, *Finite and Eternal Being*, 35.

3. Stein, *Finite and Eternal Being*, 35.

4. Stein, *Finite and Eternal Being*, 36.

5. Stein seems to indicate that we can be aware of "not-being." I think this is impossible, unless she means something like a "change of being." From common-sense realistic experiences, we have seen that existence is essential exemplification. If this is right, then unless something exemplifies an essence, it does not exist, but if something doesn't exist, then you can't be aware of it. Therefore, we can't be aware of "not-being."

6. Stein, *Finite and Eternal Being*, 37.

are also aware that the self, the "I," can change. Thus, we are aware of being and not-being. Stein then claims that it is from our awareness of the difference between being and not-being that the "idea of pure being is revealed to us as unchanging, and eternal."[7] This brings us to the starting point of our understanding of the nature of existence. Here is an elaboration of Stein's interior route:

Step 1: I am aware of my own being.

Step 2: I am aware that the being that is my being is subject to change.

Step 3: I can infer that since being and the intellectual movement (i.e., my awareness of my own being) are not separated, the being which is my own is likewise subject to change.[8]

Step 4: I experience a movement from former past states of being to present states of being.

Step 5: This means that "the being of which I am conscious as mine is inseparable from temporality."[9] So, I know that my own being (the being which I am, which I have) is temporal.

Step 6: From our awareness of ourselves as temporal beings, we are aware of being that is always "now." When we are aware of ourselves it is always "now." The being that we are aware of when we are aware of ourselves is always "now" and this is always between a "no longer" and "not yet." This is what Stein calls eternal being.

You might try a little experiment to get to step number 6. Get a timer and set it for 5 seconds. Right when you push "start" begin thinking of yourself and your own existence. Do this for the entire 5 seconds. (Use less time if you are easily distracted!) When the buzzer on the timer sounds, reflect on what just occurred. For five seconds you were "seeing" your own being. At each second, you were aware of your own being, and you were aware of time passing. So, there is here a distinction between being, and the movement of being which reveals change in being. When the buzzer sounded, the event was over, it no longer existed. At 5 seconds, the first 4 seconds no longer existed, but the being that you have still existed. So, your being that endures through time is distinct from temporal being, which passes away after a given time.

7. Stein, *Finite and Eternal Being*, 37.

8. In a footnote to this quotation, Stein indicates that Husserl uses the notion of *act* here to refer to that which she calls "intellectual movement" (Stein, *Finite and Eternal Being*, 37n9.)

9. Stein, *Finite and Eternal Being*, 37.

Another way to think of this is the similar way in which we engage in "separation" of being from our experience of particulars. Think of it this way. At the first second, s1, we were aware of our being at s1. At s2, we were aware of our being at s2. At s3 we were aware of being at s3, etc. When we reflect on this, we see that there is a distinction between being at s1 and s2 and s3. S1, s2, and s3 are each very different points in time, and each has its own being. In addition, there is the change of being between the moments of time. At s4, the being of s1 and s2 is over and done with. Those moments of being are past and no longer exist,[10] after the intellectual movement that we were aware of during our five-second experiment.

Here's where the separation/abstraction comes in. We can reflect back on s1, s2, s3, s4, and s5 and see that there is something in *common* that is had in the being of each of those moments of reflection. There is being that is had at each moment (analogous to the way in which circularity is common to many circles), and being that is the same at each different temporal point.[11] When we see this difference, the difference between being at different points in time (which fluctuates, comes and goes), and being over time, Stein says that "the *idea of pure being* is revealed to us."[12] We see now that "pure being is not temporal but *eternal*."[13]

3.2 ONCE WE GO IN, CAN WE GET OUT?

The great strength of Stein's interior route is comparable to the exterior route discussed in chapter 2, due to the fact that any individual can think this through for themselves. Our knowledge of being is found from within our experience of ourselves, which is an experience the type of which is undeniable. Yet, this view is not without its weaknesses.

3.2.1. What Happened to Essential Exemplification?

One of the weaknesses of Stein's approach is that it seems to point to the eternality of being without illustrating how existence involves essential ex-emplification. When I am aware of being, even though it is through my

10. This discussion here presupposes of an "A" theory view of time, which maintains that the past and future do not exist.

11. This is analogous to the way in which we can see that there is being which is common between the crow and the fence. Although each of these has its own being, there is being independent of these two things which makes them both exist.

12. Stein, *Finite and Eternal Being*, 37.

13. Stein, *Finite and Eternal Being*, 37.

own internal experiences, I do not, *via* a judgment immediately grasp that being is the exemplification of an essence (whether an essence of the self, an essence of a moment of time, or an essence of a change over time). So, if existence is essential exemplification, then does Stein's account of being as eternal conflict with the notion of existence derived from sense experience?

I think that the answer must be "No." The two ideas ([1] existence is essential exemplification and [2] existence is eternal) are compatible. The exterior route simply shows us what existence is, and the interior route adds additional information to the concept of existence derived from the exterior route. So, conceptually speaking, the two views of existence do not militate against one another.

3.2.2 From Finite to Eternal: Fallacy of Weak Induction?

A more serious objection to Stein's view is a logical one. The objection is that her argument is a fallacy of weak induction, a hasty generalization. Her argument seems to go like this: temporal phenomenal experiences (tpe) have being as the most salient of features in our awareness. We can be aware of tpe-1 through tpe-*n* in a series of time. Tpe-1 through tpe-*n* have being. Therefore, there is being "over and above" tpe-1 through tpe-*n* which is eternal.

Is this a hasty generalization? If we have awareness of some small set of change in being, does that necessarily or only probably imply eternal being? A hasty generalization is a type of weak induction in which a sample of a class is too small to make a general claim about the whole class. So, if I meet three New Yorkers and they are all rude, and I generalize that all New Yorkers are rude (or even worse that New Yorkers are essentially rude); then I've committed a weak induction fallacy of hasty generalization. Is Stein's argument like this?

I think that the answer is "No." Stein's argument does move from the being of individual particular experiences of discreet moments of time, and then infers the existence of being that is eternal, over and above these discreet moments. However, this is not a move from an ascription of a feature (i.e., being) of a few moments of time to *all* moments of time. It is rather a move from the reality of the feature of the being of moments of time to being which is nontemporal and eternal. So, since Stein's inference is not a generalization at all, it cannot be a hasty one.

Stein's argument seems to involve an induction, and as with all inductions, the conclusion only follows probably from the premises. So, the better question here is this: How strong is Stein's induction? How likely is it that there is eternal being, given that there is finite being? Stein's conclusion seems to have good explanatory power. Her claim is that eternal being can explain certain features of temporal being, e.g., the commonality of being across distinct and different moments of eternal being. Eternal being can be seen as that which informs each moment of finite being and unifies them as the same kind of reality, in a similar way in which the universal "redness" can explain the unity across all red things. So, Stein's argument from particular to universal, although inductive, appears to be strong.

3.3 HOW CAN KNOW WHAT IS NOT THERE TO KNOW? STEIN'S INTERIOR PATH AND NON-BEING

A much more serious problem for Stein's view is a metaphysical problem, and it has to do with the idea of "non-being." Stein is very clear that when we grasp being from within our experience of ourselves, we also grasp "non-being." She says, "When I turn toward being, it shows me, as it is in itself, two faces: the face of being and the face of nonbeing [*Nichtsein*]."[14] This seems like a flat out contradiction. If being can be shown as "it is in itself" as both "being" and "non-being," then being itself is "non-being." How is this not contradictory?

3.3.1 Heidegger and *Seinfeld*: Shows about Nothing

One might be tempted to follow Stein on the concept of "non-being" as some sort of positive reality that does things, or that can be used to do things. This temptation might come from reading Heidegger, who has a lot to say about nothing in his essay "What Is Metaphysics?" Stein admits to the influence of Heidegger on her views in her preface to *Eternal and Finite Being*. She indicates that she was deeply impressed with Heidegger's *Being and Time* and that "certain reminiscences may have found their way into" her own views in *Eternal and Finite Being*.[15] Whether Heidegger's discussion of "nothing" from "What Is Metaphysics?" also found its way into Stein's chapter is difficult to say, other than Stein does have a place for "non-being" in her discussion of how we come to see that existence is eternal.

Stein seems cautious and judicious in her view of non-being. As I have indicated above, it appears that what Stein may mean in her discussion of our knowledge of eternal being relying on knowledge of "not-being" may

---

14. Stein, *Finite and Eternal Being*, translated by Walter Redmond.

15. Stein, *Finite and Eternal Being*, xxxi.

simply mean "change of being" rather than "nothing." Heidegger's "What Is Metaphysics?" is an entirely different matter. Heidegger plows right into a discussion of "nothing" throwing caution and logic to the wind. He states, "If, however, we refuse to be led astray by the formal impossibility of an enquiry into Nothing and still continue to enquire in the face of it, we must at least satisfy what remains the fundamental pre-requisite for the full pursuit of any enquiry. If nothing as such is still to be enquired into, it follows that it must be 'given' in advance. We must be able to encounter it."[16]

Once you let logic go (formal impossibilities), you can pretty much get away with anything, so why not go ahead and talk about how you can *encounter* "nothing."[17] I find it really odd that since Heidegger seems to follow Kant's metaphysical disaster of separating the noumenal from the phenomenal, then if we are going to encounter "nothing" it's still behind and constructed by the categories of the understanding, or the schema of space and time. If Dasein is all there is, and you can encounter "nothing" in Dasein, then Dasein and "nothing" go together. Something and nothing together at last!

Alas, Heidegger has given us a love story! The logical relation of contradiction (that dreaded formal reality) had been keeping the contradictories "Some S are P" and "No S are P" apart. They have been staring at each other from opposite corners of the square of opposition from time immemorial, longing for the day when they might embrace! Heidegger, unconstrained by the formal impossibility of something and nothing uniting, has brought two estranged lovers finally embracing as one!

3.3.2 Finding Nemo[18]

The discussion of nothing or non-being always brings to my mind the story of Odysseus, Polyphemus the cyclops, and Polyphemus's cyclopes neighbors. Here is the relevant conversation:

> Odysseus: "Nobody—that's my name. Nobody—so my mother and father call me, all my friends."
>
> [Odysseus gouges Polyphemus's eye and plots his escape. Polyphemus's cyclopes neighbors hear his cries for help and respond.]

16. Heidegger, "What Is Metaphysics?," 362.

17. I am tempted to say, "Once you let logic go, then you can get away with *nothing*." This seems to me among the most diabolically disastrous beliefs in philosophy.

18. "Nemo" is Latin for "nobody."

Cyclopes: "Surely no one's rustling your flocks against your will—surely no one's trying to kill you now by fraud or force!"

Polyphemus: "*Nobody*, friends"—Polyphemus bellowed back from his cave—"Nobody's killing me now by fraud and not by force!"

Cyclopes: "If you're alone . . . and nobody's trying to overpower you now—look, it must be a plague sent here by mighty Zeus and there's no escape from *that*. You'd better pray to your father, Lord Poseidon . . ."

Polyphemus: "That, that Nobody . . . who's not escaped his death, I swear, not yet."[19]

In one way, Polyphemus is right. Nobody does not escape death, because Nobody doesn't exist, and neither does Nothing. Let me say that again, "Nobody doesn't exist, and neither does Nothing." Nobody and Nothing don't exemplify any essences; so Nobody or Nothing can't do anything. Odysseus uses the word "Nobody" as a proper name to confuse Polyphemus, but that's just a funny use of language. Polyphemus's cyclopes friends think that Polyphemus is using the word correctly, when Polyphemus shouts out that "Nobody" is killing him. Even the cyclopes understand that when the term "nobody" is used correctly, it can't possibly mean that something is being done to Polyphemus by something that doesn't exist. Confusion about "nobody" and "nothing" is a plague and requires prayer together with a lot of careful thinking to overcome.

3.4. GOD AND NOTHING

Since Heidegger does not let logic get in the way of his discussion of Nothing, then why not get theology on board too? Heidegger even tries to get Christian theology to agree with him about "nothing." He says, "Christian dogma . . . gives a twist to the meaning of Nothing, so that it now comes to mean the absolute absence of all 'being' outside God: *ex nihilit fit—ens creatum*: the created being is made out of what truly and authentically (*eigentlich*) 'is'; it becomes the *summum ens*, God as *ens in-creatum*."[20] Is this a reasonable view?

19. Homer, *The Odyssey*, 224.
20. Heidegger, "What Is Metaphysics?," 376.

3.4.1 The God of the *Ex*-es

One might be tempted to agree with Heidegger's view from what Aquinas says in his discussion of *creatio ex nihilo* (creation from nothing). In the *Summa*, first part, question 45, article 1, "Whether to create is to make something from nothing?" Aquinas answers the question by affirming the following: "For nothing is the same as no being. Therefore as the generation of a man is from the 'not-being' which is 'not-man,' so creation, which is the emanation of all being, is from the 'not-being' which is 'nothing.'"[21] This seems to imply that "nothing" (non-being) is used to create both human beings and all of creation.

Interpreting Aquinas to give positive existence (essential exemplification) to nothing (non-being) based on this passage in support of Heidegger would be too hasty. Thankfully, Aquinas makes very clear what he means by the notion of being coming from (*ex*) nothing (non-being). Before he gives his answer above, he presents a possible objection. He states, "Objection 3. Further, the preposition 'from' [*ex*] imports relation of some cause, and especially of the material cause; as when we say that a statue is made from brass. But 'nothing' cannot be the matter of being, nor in any way its cause. Therefore, to create is not to make something from nothing."[22]

Aquinas affirms *creation ex nihilo* (from nothing) but responds by distinguishing two senses of the preposition "from" (*ex*). The two senses are ordinal and causal. "From" (*ex*) could mean order, and Aquinas provides a temporal example: "from morning comes midday." "From" (*ex*) could also mean a material cause (e.g., "The spoon is made from wood"). When Aquinas advocates creation from (*ex*) nothing, he is careful to affirm that he does not mean a *causal* "from" but rather an *ordinal* "from." So, "creation from nothing" in no way, according to Aquinas, implies that "nothing" plays a causal or material role in creation. "Nothing" or "non-being" is not a positive thing lurking around "out there" or "outside of the Godhead" from which God causally creates. Thus, Aquinas, apparently distinct from Stein and Heidegger, does not give room to "non-being" (nothing) functioning in any way as a part of the created order.

3.4.2 God and That Which Is Not

There is a relevant passage from the Bible that should be considered here in this brief detour about non-being. In his Letter to the Romans, the Apostle

21. Aquinas, *Summa Theologica*, 241 (I, Q45 A1, a1).
22. Aquinas, *Summa Theologica*, 242 (I, Q45 A1, o3).

Paul says the following in his discussion of faith and grace in the life of Abraham: "As it is written: 'I have made you [Abraham] a father of many nations.' He is our father in the sight of God, in whom he believed—the God who gives life to the dead and calls into being things that were not" (Rom 4:17). The context here regards the faith of Abraham that he had in God regarding the promise of his son Isaac, and that God would use that promise to fulfill the greater promise of faith of making Abraham a father of many nations. But the kind of God who could do that is what I want to focus on here.

The kind of God in whom Abraham had faith is a God who can "give life to the dead." The context here speaks of Abraham and Sarah's old age and barrenness, but also looks ahead to the resurrection of Jesus and ultimately all those who have faith. But, in addition to being a god who can give life to the dead, he can do this, because he is a god who "calls into being things that were not." The context here is the calling into being of an heir for Abraham, namely Isaac, whom God had promised to Abraham. God promises Abraham an heir; God carries out his plan; Abraham has faith, which is a "step of trust to rely on what we have good reason to believe is so."[23] The most relevant part of this verse for our purposes is the phrase "calls into being things that were not." Let us look at this in the light of the discussion of nothing we have covered so far.

Following Stein, it seems that one could view "things that were not" as things that have "non-being."[24] That is the "non-being" of these things is something from which God causes things to be. However, if Aquinas is right, then the notion here is one of order, not cause. So, when God calls Isaac into being, he does not *use* "something that was not" (i.e., non-being) as a means to bring Isaac into being. Rather, God calls Isaac into being in a specific temporal order. Once, Isaac was not, but now Isaac is. It is important to remember that even the notion that "Isaac was not" does not mean that Isaac, the promised son of Abraham and Sarah, was floating around somewhere waiting to be exemplified.

23. Koukl, *The Story of Reality*, 137.

24. For a very thorough discussion of Stein's view of "nothing," see Walter Redmond's "A Nothing That Is: Edith Stein on Being without Essence." My main objection to Stein's view of "a nothing that is" is that she maintains that there can be being without essence, or essence-less being. Following the common-sense realism defended in this book, if existence (being) is essential exemplification, then without an essence exemplified, there can be no existence, no being whatsoever. Essence-less being is like a relation without relata. (Even the simplest relation of identity has one relatum).

Aquinas comments on this passage twice in the *Summa*.[25] The first is in a discussion of God's foreknowledge (I, Q14, a9) under the question: "Whether God Has Knowledge of Things That Are Not?" Aquinas cites this passage in his "On the contrary" just prior to his "I answer that." Aquinas claims that although Isaac is not actual (before God causes him to exist), God foreknows Isaac, and is able to make his promise about Isaac. It is through his "act of understanding, which is His being, [and] is measured by eternity . . . the present glance of God extends over all time, and to all things which exist in any time, as to objects present to Him."[26] When God makes his promise to Abraham, Isaac does not yet exist in time. God foreknows that Isaac will be and calls Isaac into being at the right time in order to fulfill his promise to Abraham who exercises his faith, his *active* trust in God for the promise of an heir.

The second time Aquinas refers to this passage is in a discussion of eternal law (II–I, Q91, a1) when he answers the question "Is There Divine Law?" The first objection considered to eternal law is the idea that there is no eternal law because there hasn't been someone from eternity to impose it on. Aquinas responds to this objection by stating the following: "Those things that are not in themselves, exist with God, inasmuch as they are fore-known and preordained by Him, according to Romans 4:17."[27] Since God foreknows what the eternal law will govern in the future, outside of himself, there is eternal law even prior to creation.

The metaphysical import of Aquinas's use of this passage should not be ignored. "Those things that are not in themselves exist with God" due to God's eternality, and eternal vision of all time at once. This is not to say that Isaac exists prior to his existing! What would that even mean? It is to say, that from God's perspective from eternity, God sees the times when Isaac was not, and sees the time when Isaac's essence is instantiated. God is the cause of the coming into being of Isaac from the order of the time when he was not to the time that he is. But, there is no hint of some sort of non-being of Isaac that exists (exemplifies properties) prior to God's creative act to fulfill his promises to Abraham.

Heidegger on the other hand seems to view "nothing" in the same way that the devil in Milton's *Paradise Lost* views evil. The devil's "Evil, be thou my good"[28] becomes Heidegger's "Nothing is also an original part of

---

25. For a clear discussion of some of the differences between Aquinas and Stein, see Sharkey, "Edith Stein and Thomas Aquinas on Being and Essence."

26. Aquinas, *Summa Theologica*, 1:83.

27. Aquinas, *Summa Theologica*, 1:208.

28. Milton, *Paradise Lost*, 82 (bk. IV, line 110).

essence,"[29] which is to say, "Nothing, be thou my being." Just as the devil takes evil, the opposite of good, and makes it his good, Heidegger takes nothing, the opposite of existence, of essential exemplification, and makes it his essence exemplified. I'm not sure that a philosophy such as Heidegger's can get much further afield from Chesterton's broad daylight of the brotherhood of men. When you've got nothing and something united; when you've got "nothing" being an original part of essence, and of God whose essence is his existence, then you know that something has gone deeply wrong.

3.5 A HORSE AND HIS NOTHING

This discussion about "nothing" would not be complete without a few comments from James V. Schall. Professor Schall is a philosopher closest to the ideal of a common-sense realist. One of the things that Schall says about Heidegger is related to us in a story from Hilaire Belloc's essay "The Roman Road." In that essay, Belloc writes, "I saw my horse Monster standing by himself, regarding nothingness."[30] Schall says of this passage, "A horse that 'regards nothingness' is, no doubt, a very metaphysical animal, obviously anticipating the arrival of Heidegger on the intellectual scene."[31]

I do not think that Belloc thought that Monster was examining Dasein and the thrownness of despair, rather, Monster just wasn't thinking about anything, just taking life in the most equine way possible. Belloc does however ask his horse a metaphysical question at another time at the stable of the The Sign of the Lion inn. Belloc writes, "As he [Monster] ate his oats, I said to him: 'Monster, my horse, is there any place on earth where a man, even for a little time, can be as happy as the brutes? If there is, it is here at the Sign of the Lion.' And Monster answered: 'There is a tradition among us that, of all creatures that creep upon the earth, man is the fullest of sorrow.'"[32] Monster was a philosophical horse indeed! The essay "At the Sign of the Lion" ends with a dialog between Belloc and a man of about fifty years of age.

They discuss what Heidegger hints at but confuses terribly. Heidegger is concerned with anxiety and the dread of nothing. Monster the horse recognizes that the beast that is fullest of sorrow is man, but neither Belloc nor Monster follow Heidegger. It is not from dread that we take charge of our lives and act to have meaning in the light of nothingness. Rather, it is faith

---

29. Heidegger, "What Is Metaphysics?," 370.

30. Belloc, "The Roman Road," 216.

31. Schall, "To Go and Look at the Roman Road," 46–48.

32. Belloc, "The Sign of the Lion," 289.

and hope in the common-sense experiences that God gives us in this life, which display, like a window, the permanent things that lie beyond them.

Belloc visits the Sign of the Lion to experience the real drink, fire, companionship, and food that give him hope of permanent things. Belloc writes, "'You think, then,' said I, 'that some immortal part in us is concerned not only with our knowledge, but with our every feeling, and that our final satisfaction will include a sensual pleasure: fragrance, and landscape, and a visible home that shall be dearer even than are these dear hills?' 'Something of the sort,' he [the stranger] said, and slightly shrugged his shoulders."[33] Let Christians never forget that our Carpenter Savior has gone to prepare a home for us and will eat and drink with those who have loved his real life, death, and resurrection and who look for and love his appearing to make all things new!

3.6 CONCLUSION: MORE THAN NOTHING—FROM FINITE TO ETERNAL BEING

In summary, at the end of the interior route, we find a true beginning, according to Stein. We find that we know that being is both temporal/finite and eternal/infinite. From reflection of on our own existence, we derive an awareness of both temporal and pure eternal being. It is from our temporal awareness of being that we become aware of "that eternal being which is immutable and therefore plentitude of being at every moment."[34] Again, as with the exterior route to being, many more questions arise: Is there more to eternal being than being *qua* being? What is the relationship between temporal and finite being? What is the relationship between *my* being and eternal being? Each of these questions begins with simple reflection on one's ordinary experiences and draws us to the pursuit of metaphysical knowledge of nature, and with hard work, wisdom.

This gives us a sense of what being is. Yet, once we start thinking about infinite, unchanging, and eternal being, although we know *that* it is, we might wonder *what* it is and *why*. We move from considerations of what philosophers call "predication" or being exemplified (e.g., the way that the crow exemplifies the existence of "crowness") and wonder about "causality" that is *why* a thing is what it is. It is now at least possible we might find at the end of our inquiry that such being may be personal rather than impersonal. Stein's argument does not give us the God of Abraham, Isaac, and Jacob, but as Dallas Willard writes in a somewhat different context, "There is now a

33. Belloc, "The Sign of the Lion," 296.
34. Stein, *Finite and Eternal Being*, 37.

somewhat broader ontological 'space' for the God of religion which would not be there in a universe" without being of the kind Stein has led us to.[35] The end of metaphysical inquiry into the nature of being now has the space to bring us to a personal relationship with God, the one "whose essence it is to be." If this is right, it has profound implications for our ordinary common-sense lives.

35. Willard, "Language, Being, God," 212.

CHAPTER 4

The Personal Ground of Realism

"I Am"

4.0 INTRODUCTION: TAKING EVERYTHING PERSONALLY

I arrive at the beach. I feel the cool, wet sand at my feet. I taste the saltiness of the ocean water on my lips. I hear the sound of the crashing surf. I smell the freshness of the sea air. I see waves breaking offshore. These things are real. Every person knows what is real from ordinary common-sense experiences like these. They also tell us more. They tell us about the nature of reality itself, about existence itself. These experiences are the experiences of a person, namely me. But I am neither responsible for the existence of these experiences, nor of my own nature that has them, nor of the things that exist, which I experience, nor of their natures, nor of the nature of existence itself. Is there any relation between existence itself and something personal?

This chapter will defend the idea that the nature of reality is ultimately grounded in a person, namely, God. An argument to the conclusion that we can know God is a personal being as the one upon whom all of reality depends for its existence will be considered. This will be done in light of the ideas developed from both the interior and exterior paths to realism coupled with evidence from the Bible.

4.1 FROM PERSON TO PERSON

This book is about common-sense realism regarding the nature of reality. It is my view that we can know a great deal about the nature of reality from natural reason, as I argued in chapters 2 and 3. From sense experience, we can know that existence is essential exemplification. From self-experience we can know that existence is both finite and eternal. Having this knowledge of the nature of reality is not dependent on any particular religious revelation claim. Rather, knowledge of the nature of reality that comes from sense experience and self-experience can point us to the acceptance or rejection of particular religious claims.

If it is reasonable to believe that existence is essential exemplification that is both finite and eternal, then any particular religious claim that is consistent with it will be consistent with what we know to be reasonable, and any claim that is contrary to it will be contrary to what we know to be reasonable. What we know from common-sense experience serves as evidence in light of which we might consider particular religious revelation claims. Thus, religious claims (claims made by specific religions or claims that are part and parcel of specific religions) may be consistent or inconsistent with the evidence that we have about existence from sense and self-experience.

We can think of what we know about the nature of reality from sense experience as "general ontology." General ontology is a narrow set of data of what Christians call "general revelation" or revelation that comes to us from the natural world, through sense-experience and self-experience. So, if God reveals himself through the natural world (general revelation), and also through specific, direct revelation-events, what theologians call "special revelation," then one would expect that these two would not contradict each other but would be consistent. That is, if God reveals himself generally (through nature) and specially (through direct revelation in Scripture), these two modes of revelation should be consistent with one another.

To make this clear, consider this idea from the moral side of things, rather than the ontological. Would it make any sense (i.e., would it be reasonable) to believe that God would reveal to us through natural reason that intentionally murdering innocent people is always morally wrong, and then reveal directly to us (through a divine apparition, or through a prophet, or through the incarnation of God himself), that intentionally murdering innocent people is always good and morally permissible? Would it be reasonable to believe in such a god? Would such a god be reasonable? I think the answer is "no" to these questions.

So, if God reveals himself through the natural world so that we can know something (even if it is minimal) about him through natural reason, then it would be reasonable to believe that whatever God reveals about himself directly through special revelation will be consistent with what we know about him through general revelation. If this is right and we do know something about the ultimate nature of reality through general revelation, namely that the nature of existence is essential exemplification that is eternal, then this can help us to think carefully about revelation claims.[1]

Our knowledge from general revelation will rule out special revelation claims, or broad religious beliefs about the nature of reality. For example, any special religious revelatory claim that maintains that reality is monistic will be ruled out as inconsistent with what we know from natural reason. Any religious revelation which teaches that reality is determined by you and your beliefs will also be unreasonable. So, common-sense ontology rules out the reasonableness of some religious claims.

Now, of course the human will is such that it can believe contrary to reason, or suspend reason in order to believe something unreasonable, but why should this be applied to religion, when we don't apply it to other more mundane areas of human life without great disasters? If I suspend my reason and ignore the evidence from my senses that my car is running out of gas so that I can *believe* with all my heart that my car will make it to the gas station in fifty miles, when there's a good gas station right here at this spot in the road, is this a good way to live life? If you tell your boss at work that you *believe* with all your might that the project on your desk due tomorrow will be done at 5:00 p.m., when all the evidence points to it not even being close to completion, as you leave the office for the day at 2:30 p.m. to go to the beach to surf, how long do you think you will have that job? Common-sense reality and what we know from it can be a good guide for making decisions about the reasonableness of things, including religious belief. So, if we can use the evidence from our senses, and from self-experience to give us a basis of expectation of revelation from a God whose essence is essential exemplification, then we can examine the variety of religious claims that

1. It is still possible to maintain that reason is fallen, but still sufficiently functional to give us some knowledge about God (per Rom 1:20), even if that knowledge is what condemns us.

confront us in our pluralistic religious environment. Such a task might be especially helpful for Christian apologists. We can know antecedently what we are looking for from religious claims regarding the nature of reality, and the nature of God who is to be revealed. It would be a fascinating task to examine the major options within the religions of the world today and look to see how their religious revelation claims match up with what we know from general ontology. That is not my task here. My task here is to show that what is revealed about God from within Christian revelation is consistent with what we know about God from general ontology. I hope to clarify how Christian special ontology is consistent with common-sense general ontology. Christians throughout history have thought that we can know a great deal about God from general revelation. In fact, we may be able to know a great deal more about God than what I am suggesting here. But in this section, I only want to focus on this: we know from general ontology (general revelation) that existence is essential exemplification and eternal, and this is consistent with what we know from Christian special ontology (special revelation) in the Bible. Let us turn to that task now.

4.2 REALITY IN THE FIRST PERSON

From the beginning of creation within Christian Scripture, everything has been taken personally. "In the beginning God created the heavens and the earth" (Gen 1:1). The God of the Bible is a personal being (a trinity of persons). He created both nonhuman persons (angels), and human persons to inhabit the physical cosmos. All of what is, on the Christian view of things, is from persons and for persons. Everything is personal!

Throughout Hebrew Scripture, in the Old Testament, God was known by revelation of himself to his people from Adam and Eve to Noah to Abraham to Isaac to Jacob to Joseph and to Moses about three hundred years later. With Moses, God makes clear who he is. He fully reveals his name to Moses: "I Am that I Am."

The account of Moses at the burning bush, taken from a common-sense realist ontology, is fairly straightforward. God uses an anomalous sensory experience, a burning bush that does not burn up, to move Moses into an encounter with God. Moses really sees a great sight, a burning thing that doesn't burn up! Without this plain epistemic and ontological common-sense realism, Moses could not have encountered God. If we do not really see the objects in front of us, if objects do not really exist as we experience them, then when one has an anomalous sensory experience, why should we be puzzled? If the world is a construct of our own making, if we can never reach things as they are in themselves, then why be puzzled by a burning bush that is not burned up? A burning bush that did not burn up wasn't behaving like a run-of-the-mill burning bush that should normally burn up. This was something worth seeing, really seeing! And through this real event, God reveals himself to Moses.

God's revelation begins with Moses' experience with the senses. There is visual and auditory sensation, and the holiness of God permeates all of those things. But what Moses learns about God is not merely from an inference of a burning bush that does not burn up. God personally speaks to Moses and has a conversation with him. God reveals himself as a particular sort of person directly and immediately to Moses. God's revelation to Moses is clear, and God connects his revelation to Moses' own personal family history as a descendent of Abraham. When Moses hears God's plan to use him to deliver the children of Israel, Moses asks for God's name so that he can tell this to the Israelites in Egypt. God responds: "I Am That I Am" and "Say unto the children of Israel, I Am hath sent me unto you" (Exod 3:14).

In addition to the ontological implications about God that we learn from God revealing his name, there is something important about the nature of this account at the burning bush with respect to revelation beyond general ontology. When God reveals himself, he does not reveal himself in a way that is contradictory to either the ordinary use of our senses, nor is the content of his revelation about himself contradictory to what we know about God from common-sense experience. Let us look at each of these in turn.

First of all, Moses' experience of God was done through ordinary common-sense means of experience and communication. Of course, as mentioned above, a burning bush that doesn't burn up is not itself an ordinary occurrence, but the act of looking at a material object to try to understand what it is, is itself an ordinary occurrence. So, the manner in which God reveals himself is consistent with common sense.[2]

Second, the content of what God reveals about himself is consistent with general ontological revelation about the nature of existence. God reveals himself as the essence of existence: "I Am That I Am." If we can know from sense experience that existence is essential exemplification, and then

2. I am reading this narrative according to its plain, common-sense reading. I believe that the events really happened as Scripture says they happened. If someone wants to argue that this is not an actual event, or that it is a "spiritual tale" or allegory or parable or whatever, that is fine. Philosophers and theologians are free to argue about their views of scriptural stories however they wish. This defense of common-sense realism presupposes (although I think that one could make a case for reading this story as literal) that these events were real, ordinary common-sense experiences that Moses really had.

God reveals himself as a person who is the essence of existence (essential exemplification as such), then what we have is the fulfillment of our expectation from general ontology: a perfectly existing being whose essence is his existence, eternally so. Special revelation/ontology fills in the expectations given in general revelation/ontology. Thus, faith, actively trusting good evidence is possible because it is established by God's revelation to us from *both* common-sense experience *and* his own personal revelation to us in the Bible.

4.3 "I AM" AND ONTOLOGY

Since the ideas of existence as essential exemplification that were defended in chapter 2 are Thomistic, it is worth looking at what Aquinas has to say about God as "The I Am." Aquinas has a short exposition of Exodus 3:14 in his *Summa Theologica* (I, Q13, a11) under the question "Whether This Name, *He Who Is*, Is the Most Proper Name of God?" He claims that there are three things we can learn from God calling himself "I Am That I Am."

The first thing that we can learn is that God's name "I Am" signifies "existence itself," that God's existence is his essence.[3] This is consistent with what we can know from general ontology, that existence is essential exemplification. However, with God's revelation to Moses, we have additional information about the nature of existence than cannot be derived by natural reasoning through common-sense experience. Natural reasoning through common-sense experience is a faculty of being human due to our being created in the image of God, but it will not save us. Like the children of Israel in Egypt, all of us are in bondage to sin trapped in an evil and foreign spiritual kingdom. As with the children of Israel, we need liberation and redemption, including the redemption of our rational faculties. Reason itself needs to be redeemed.

What we know from fallen reason is that existence is essential exemplification. This is not a bad place to start, but it will get us out of "spiritual Egypt." Only a person who can pay the price of our bondage can do that. That person revealed himself to Moses as the person who would draw Israel out of slavery from Egypt as a prefiguring of the way in which Jesus, "I Am" incarnate, draws his chosen people to himself out of our slavery from sin. We are given clear indication through God's revelation of his name to Moses, that the being whose existence is his essence is also a personal being who wants us to be free from the slavery of sin.

---

3. Aquinas, *Summa Theologica*, 73–74.

This is a being very different from the "god of the philosophers." The God of the Bible is neither "The Good" of Plato, nor the "Prime Mover" of Aristotle. The God of the Bible entered personally into human history to show his love for his people.[4] The God whose name is "I Am" is existence itself, but he cares for and loves his people. He loves them enough to enter into a relationship with them. He is concerned about their suffering and wants to help them live their lives to the fullest. In his rescue of the Hebrews, God liberates through divine justice upon the Egyptians. In his rescue of humanity, God liberates us through divine justice taken upon himself, through Jesus on the cross. Only the I Am can satisfy the payment, the penalty due to God himself, to free us from our bondage to our own sin. God's special revelation of himself as the Person Who Is Existence Itself deepens our knowledge of existence as essential exemplification into an experience with a God who loves us, and makes new and eternal life possible.

Second, Aquinas points out that God's name has "universality." This means that, according to Aquinas, "we cannot know the essence of God itself in this life, as it is in itself."[5] Therefore, a universal "I Am" which is less determinate as a name is fitting for God. What Aquinas *does not* mean here is that we cannot know that God exists, nor does he mean that we cannot know that God is a being who is existence itself, nor does he mean that we cannot know that existence is essential exemplification.

What we cannot know in and of itself is "the essence of *being* a-being-whose-essence-is-to-exist." We cannot know this, because we are not God. We cannot experience *being* a-being-whose-essence-is-to-exist, because we aren't God. Only the being whose essence is *being* a-being-whose-essence-is-to-exist can know himself perfectly as he is in himself.

I think that it is interesting that Aquinas qualifies what we cannot know about God with "in this life." This is consistent with what St. John teaches in 1 John 3:2: "Dear friends, now we are children of God, and what we will be has not yet been made known. But we know that when Christ appears, we shall be like him, for we shall see him as he is." There will be a time for those who follow God that we will be able to see him as he is. What this means exactly for the next life is beyond my intellectual comprehension. So, there is a major constraint in this life. Yet, even in this life we can know a great deal *about* God whose essence is his existence.

Aquinas does say that God is existence itself (essential exemplification itself) and God's essential nature is to exist, but we cannot know what that it

4. Chris Morgan points out that God's declaration that he is "I AM" reveals to us three things: God's "covenant faithfulness," his "sovereign freedom" and "The Lord, who keeps covenant with his people" (Morgan, *Christian Theology*, 91).

5. Aquinas, *Summa Theologica*, 74.

like. As finite creatures we can know *that* a being exists whose essence is his existence, even if we cannot know through experience the *essence* of his existing. Only God can know that. But we can know the universality of God's existence as that on which all existent things depend for their existence, including ourselves.[6] Aquinas quotes John of Damascus: "Hence Damascene says (De Fide Orth. i) that, 'He Who Is, is the principal of all names applied to God; for comprehending all in itself, it contains existence itself as an infinite and indeterminate sea of substance.'"[7] God's existence determines all substances, but God as the great I Am is "indeterminate to all." We simply cannot determine, comprehend, know (or probably even imagine) what it is like to be the great I Am.

Third, Aquinas points out that God's name "signifies present existence." God is real now and always! God does not call himself, "I Was" or "I Will Be." God does call himself, "I Am." Aquinas says that God's "existence knows not past or future, as Augustine says (De Trin. v)."[8] We learned from Edith Stein's interior common-sense route that existence is eternal. In the Bible, both in the case of Moses as well as in the case of Jesus, God reveals himself to us as an eternal (*Am*) person (*I*). This is a consistent expansion of what we know from general ontology, but also brings with it a great deal of new information that can serve as the basis for rich ontological reflection and opens the possibility of entering into a relationship with God.

4.4 JESUS IS THE "I AM"

When God reveals himself as the "I Am" he does so as a divine person incarnating himself in the physical world. But Christian Scripture contains more special revelation regarding the God who is the great "I Am." The incarnation of Jesus Christ is the fullest revelation of the personal nature of God. In this section I would like to briefly point out three things that we learn about

6. In addition to our dependence on God for our existence, God's revelation to Moses as "I Am" demonstrates God's sovereignty. John Frame writes, "This emphasis on the Lord's sovereign rule can also be found in the mysterious terms of Exodus 3:14. However we choose to translate 'I AM WHO I AM,' the phrase certainly reflects God's sovereignty. Consider the possible renderings: I am what I am. I am who I am. I will be what I will be. I am because I am. I will be because I will be. I cause to be what I cause to be. I am present is what I am. I am the One who is. These sentences have different meanings, of course, and some of them can he interpreted in a variety of ways. But all of them certainly stress God's sovereignty. They indicate that Yahweh is very different from us, determining his own nature, or his choices, or even his own being, without any dependence on us" (Frame, *The Doctrine of God*, 44).

7. Aquinas, *Summa Theologica*, 74.

8. Aquinas, *Summa Theologica*, 74.

existence from Jesus' revelation of himself to the world. First, that Jesus is the cause of all that exists outside of the godhead. Second, that Jesus, as the second member of the Trinity, is the "I Am." Third, that these first two truths have radical implications for ontology as an area of human inquiry.

First, Christian Scripture bear witness that Jesus has something to do with existence, with the nature of reality as such and with the nature of things that are real. Jesus is the *cause* of all that has been made. Consider John 1:3, "Through him all things were made; without him nothing was made that has been made" (NIV). The English term "made" comes from the Greek word *ginomai* and can be translated as "come into being." So as a Christian philosopher who wants to take seriously the question of the nature of being, who wants to give robust answers to the nature of existence, we are presented here with John's claim that everything that came into being exists because of the person of Jesus. Jesus is the cause of all reality outside of the godhead.

Second, consider Jesus' claim in John 8:58. Regarding his own being, in response to antagonistic inquisitors, John writes, "'I tell you the truth,' Jesus answered, 'before Abraham was born, I am!'" On Jesus' identity and this passage, Groothuis in his book *On Jesus* states that this "is a claim that Jesus existed as God during Abraham's time. The phrase 'I am' harks back to God's self-revelation to Moses when he said, 'I am that I am' (Exodus 3:14)."[9] The significance of Jesus' identity with God the Father, should not be minimized, but for the ontologist, Jesus' claim to be the "I Am" qua the One who has absolute necessary existence is crucial.

Existence itself (existence himself) has taken on human nature. Thus, there is the possibility of human nature, including our own human nature, to participate in existence itself. In the last section (4.3) we looked at Aquinas's idea that we cannot know "in this life" God's essence as a being whose essence is to exist. However, after this life we will come to know more about the existence of our Lord, whose existence is his essence. Because of the incarnation, death, resurrection, and ascension of Jesus, our fallen human nature can be redeemed, perfected, and glorified. Because of Jesus' perfect human nature participating in the fellowship of the Trinity, our human nature and the *imago Dei* contained within it can now participate in that divine life as well. We can start on that journey now as his sufficient grace helps us to conform our selves to himself. When our journey is complete, then "we shall be like him, for we shall see him as he is." That's good news!

The third thing to consider regarding Jesus' relation to ontology comes from a consideration of Colossians 1:16–17. Paul writes, "For by him all

9. Groothuis, *On Jesus*, 89.

things were created: things in heaven and on earth, visible and invisible, whether thrones or powers or rulers or authorities; all things were created by him and for him. He is before all things, and in him all things hold together." There are four things the Christian ontologist must notice here.

First, note the force of the term "all." Paul seems to indicate that Jesus' relation to things that exist is exhaustive. It covers *everything*. All things which exist are deeply connected to Jesus in their being.

Second, note the ontological dualism involved: visible/physical things and invisible/spiritual things. This is important for Christian ontologists who want to continue ontological enquiry based upon both general and special ontology regarding the nature of existence. General ontology is relational, and existence is essential exemplification. General ontology, as revealed through special revelation of Jesus shows that reality is dualistic: there is physical being and spiritual being. Thus, certain types of general ontology may need to be ruled out by special revelation (e.g., monism).

Third, notice that this passage is infused with deep purpose. There is a telos, or final cause ascribed to Jesus. The "that-for-the-sake-of-which" things exist is Jesus himself. This gives us insight into the connection between ontology, axiology, and Jesus. Since all things tend toward him in their being, this implies that there is a way thing *ought* to be in their being. There is a Christo-teleological *normativity* to all things that have being. This has important implications for the ways in which general and special ontology serve as the basis for axiological (value—i.e., ethical and aesthetical) inquiry.

Fourth, notice that the very fabric of being involves Jesus. He is the cause of the unity of things that exist. Since he is "before" all things, he can be the cause of all things. He also holds all things together. This implies that the way in which thing are sustained in existence and the way in which all existent things relate to one another are caused to be so by Jesus himself.

The consideration of Jesus' relationship to being is a departure from the medieval understanding of the relationship of the transcendentals to the persons of the Trinity. St. Thomas Aquinas indicates (as do others) that the transcendentals "are appropriated as follows: being pertains to the essence, one to the Father, true to the Son, and good to the Holy Spirit."[10]

Jan Aertsen indicates that the term "appropriation" "refers to the distinction between what is common to the triune divinity and what is treated as proper to one of the Persons."[11] While the individual transcendentals are appropriated to each member of the Trinity, Aquinas maintains that each

---

10. Aquinas, *Truth*, 5.

11. Aertsen, *Medieval Philosophy*, 47.

transcendental appropriated to each member is not "really distinguished from being, which remains with the essence."[12] So, Jesus is connected with being, due to his essential nature as God. My motivation for connecting him comes primarily through those scriptural passages that connect him to being, although the relationship between the persons of the Trinity is crucial for a robust theology proper and our daily lives.

4.5 MAKING IT PERSONAL

Existence is personal. God, who is the great "I Am," has entered into all of reality to help us be set free from the slavery of sin that disorders our lives. The people of Israel were enslaved and miserable in Egypt. The I Am entered into human history, and through Moses led the people of Israel out of bondage. This is a message, a foreshadowing of further ontological revelation regarding the nature of reality. Through the incarnation of Jesus, the I Am, further reveals his triune nature. The I Am himself enters into human history in the person of Jesus. Jesus, who is the I Am, is just as concerned with your life and the slavery that it has to sin as he was with the slavery that bound the Israelites. God is concerned with the slavery to sin in our lives just as he was concerned with the slavery of the Israelites in Egypt. He Who Is has come to set us free. That is good news. How will you respond to it?

There are multiple ways that you can respond to the claims that Jesus is the I Am.

(1) The "intellectual" response. The proponent of this response recognizes that something interesting is being said by Jesus and the New Testament writers about his connection to ontology, but does not think that this implies anything for philosophers doing philosophy. These concepts are merely intellectually interesting, but they are idle wheels in the machinations of real philosophical work. The problem with this response, at least of the person who takes Jesus and Scripture seriously, is that it seems to ignore what is quite clear in the Bible. Jesus and his relationship to ontology should not be thought of as an intellectually idle concept.

(2) The "devotional" response. Christian philosophers who take the New Testament seriously, and who take their own work in philosophy seriously, might be moved to worship Jesus more devoutly given the recognition that Jesus has something to do with their academic discipline. I think this is a crucial response in a total use of these ideas in relation to one's philosophical work, but I think it is not enough. Without any direct application

---

12. Kretzmann, "Trinity and the Transcendentals," 93.

to philosophical puzzles and problems, especially the problem of how to become wise, it seems incomplete.

(3) The "philosophical" response. The advocates of this response would use the ideas presented here to develop their ontology (and epistemology and axiology). For example, the advocates of this response would use the concept of Jesus being the grounding of reality to develop a personalist account of a correspondence theory of truth or an account of free will or a robust ethical theory. I favor this response, although every individual discipline (including philosophy) needs to work out the specific application of these concepts to problems within that discipline.

In order to do so, there are at least two major questions that need to be addressed. First, there is the question of *relevance*. How relevant are concepts of philosophical Christology to philosophy as a discipline, especially for Christian philosophers engaged with a discipline that is primarily secular? Second, there is the question of *conceptual unity*. How do intellectuals get the concept of Jesus as the One in whom all things consist to do explanatory work in developing an account of, say, the nature of universals or puzzles in philosophy of mind?

Perhaps both of these questions can be answered if one begins with the intellectual response and then uses the devotional response as a springboard for the philosophical response. Philosophy as "friendship with wisdom" is first and foremost a friendship, an activity between persons: the philosopher and wisdom. Wisdom is personified in Scripture (e.g., Proverbs 8). So, as one seeks to answer puzzles in the philosophy of mind or epistemology, or respond to the skeptic about knowledge, or defeat relativism, one might first take the intellectual response by recognizing that Jesus has something to do with one's work in the discipline of philosophy. A scholar might then take the devotional response and ask the One in whom one's own life and discipline consists for help in applying the ideas of Jesus and his relationship to philosophy to specific projects and puzzles within the discipline. This might lead to the truly philosophical response of gleaning specific ways in which the truth that Jesus is the ground of realty affects real philosophical work and work in all disciplines in the academy.

(4) "The Personal Response." More important than these first three responses, which integrate Jesus into one's scholarship, is the integration of Jesus into one's life. If Jesus is the I Am, if he is the One in whom all things consist, and for whom all things exist (including you!), then how should you respond in your own life? If Christian special ontology is consistent with general ontology (and I've argued here that it is), and the other options in general ontology are found wanting (as I will argue in the next few

chapters), then this implies that Christian special ontology is reasonable. It is reasonable to believe that Jesus is our ontological foundation.

But, the New Testament claims that Jesus is still present to us, here and now. He is calling each of us into a personal relationship with himself. You can choose to enter into this relationship here and now simply by engaging in an act of prayer. There might not be a burning bush with a voice calling audibly out to you, but the reality of Jesus here and now is as real as it was with Moses. Jesus himself tells us that he will not turn away anyone who comes to him (John 6:38). This is a decision that each person, professional philosopher or otherwise, must make. What will you decide about Jesus who claimed to be the I Am?

PART 3

Reality Rejected

How Art Thou Fallen from Heaven

Chapter 5

A Short and Opinionated History of Realism

From Homer to Heresy

5.0 A SHORT HISTORY OF COMMON SENSE

I arrive at the beach. I feel the cool, wet sand at my feet. I taste the saltiness of the ocean water on my lips. I hear the sound of the crashing surf. I smell the freshness of the sea air. I see waves breaking offshore. These things are real. Every person knows what is real from ordinary common-sense experiences like these. They also tell us more. They tell us about the nature of reality itself, about existence itself. As I think about these experiences, I wonder, "Surely other people have said something about this?" And they have. Let us look at some of the things that have been said about common-sense realism. This chapter consists of a short, selective, and opinionated history of philosophical theories of existence. I argue that common-sense realism has suffered a long decline since the metaphysical realism of antiquity and the Middle Ages. There are at least two glaring omissions in my brief, opinionated history. The first is the lack of discussion of the eighteenth-century philosopher Thomas Reid (1710–96) and the Scottish Enlightenment thinkers influenced by him, as well as the influence his philosophy had on the United States. The second is the common-sense philosophy in the work of G. E. Moore (1873–1958). I am sympathetic with much that these two very influential philosophers have to offer, but their approaches to common-sense realism are slightly different from the more broadly Thomistic approach that I am taking in this book. I think that Reid was not realistic enough, especially about the distinction between primary and secondary qualities, and Moore seems to me to focus too much on the analysis of language, which I don't think has any bearing on our knowledge of existence. We do not know the nature of existence by analyzing language or how we use it. We do not get to know *what is* by analyzing the word "is" any more than we get to know a friend by analyzing the word "friend." Any such projects (e.g., C. J. F. Williams's *What Is Existence?*) might be fascinating inquiries into language use, but can tell us nothing about the nature of the things themselves. In addition, these two thinkers are exceptions to the "spirits of their ages" and those spirits are ones that motivate a decline from the common-sense realism of Christian philosophy in the Middle Ages.

5.1 A BRIEF HISTORY OF REALISM: FROM HOMER TO HERESY

If Chesterton is right, that all human beings stand in "the broad daylight of the brotherhood of men, in their common consciousness that eggs are not hens or dreams or mere practical assumptions" but that "eggs are eggs," then this "common consciousness" is inherently human.[1] But human beings existed before they wrote their history, developed theories, and engaged in philosophy. In this sense then, realism is pre-historical, pre-theoretical, and pre-philosophical.

Common-sense realism is possible, as Frederick Wilhelmsen writes, because human "certitudes, unsophisticated and without the burden of academic prejudice, arise from an immediate contact with things as they are. The common man turns spontaneously to reality for the sustenance of his spirit and he is right in so doing: his instincts are healthy. The common man is a realist simply because it is the nature of man to know reality."[2] The best evidence for Wilhelmsen's claim, is that we experience this all the time. We regularly turn *to what is* for the sustenance of our spirits. It would be odd if someone denied that they have never turned to reality to get by in life. What would it even mean to say such a thing?

In this chapter, I will briefly trace the ideas of reality as they appear in several themes throughout history. This historical survey is not exhaustive, nor does it cover every possible view of the nature of reality in the history of philosophy. It is meant to provide a general sense of how we arrived at our current situation of philosophical reflection on existence and the nature of reality. The story I wish to tell is a tragedy and a long defeat, which may not as of yet reached its nadir. The story begins, as I have alluded to above, with common-sense realism built into human nature. Common-sense realism shows up practically in pre-philosophical literature and stories. It is philosophically born and raised in ancient Greek philosophy. It enters into a happy marriage in Christian philosophy. The partners in that marriage are sundered by modern philosophy in the greatest divorce in intellectual history. The partners are estranged in postmodern, twentieth-, and early twenty-first-century philosophy. The bitterness of the divorce affects all of God's children to this day.

5.2 ANCIENT WISDOM LITERATURE AND SCRIPTURE: COMMON-SENSE STORIES AND SAYINGS

5.2.1 Homeric Epics

However our ancient human ancestors sustained themselves, they did so by recognizing reality. Now, one might argue that pre-historical, pre-theoretical, and pre-philosophical human life is not as good as human life with

1. Chesterton, *St. Thomas Aquinas*, 94.
2. Wilhelmsen, *Man's Knowledge of Reality*, 75.

history, science, philosophy, and religion. In many ways it certainly is not. However, to argue for that idea is not to give up realism about reality. In fact, it may be that realism is the only way to make sense of human progress in history, science, philosophy, and religion. Pre-theoretical realism need not preclude a realism that is responsible for human advances in both technology and wisdom.

Human legends and early histories are replete with the idea that existence is knowable and not of our own making. From this, it does not follow that literature and legends are accurate representations of what is real, but it does show that common-sense realism is built into our natural ability to deal effectively with reality. Let us examine a few examples.

While Homer's *Illiad* is no treatise on common-sense realism, it does tell us something about reality, as do all great works of literature. The way in which a great work of literature tells us something about reality must itself resonate with our common-sense grasp of what is. It is hard to imagine any story perennially capturing the imagination if it lacks common-sense metaphysical realism as a basis for the points it makes in the work of literature. Here is one such passage from the *Illiad*: "Glorious Hector stretched out his arms to his boy, but back into the bosom of his fair-girdled nurse shrank the child crying, affrighted at the aspect of his dear father, and seized with dread of the bronze and the crest of horse-hair, as he marked it waving dreadfully from the topmost helm."[3]

There is something about this passage, when I read it in middle age, having children of my own, that struck me in a way that I simply missed when I read it in my late teens. What struck me was the realistic frightened reaction of Hector's child to his war-torn father. The child is frightened by the reality that he experiences. It is a simple reaction. Hector's real battle-hardened visage in front of his child is markedly different from what the baby is used to when he sees his father. The reaction of the child is seemly. It is an apropos response. It would be odd if the child smiled and threw himself into his father's arms. Homer, throughout *The Illiad*, presents these simple cases of human responses to what is. This is not a philosophical argument for common-sense realism, but it does show that for a story to be believable, the ontological assumptions in it must match and be familiar to our ordinary direct awareness of reality.

Similarly, in the *Odyssey* Homer offers vivid realistic descriptions of ordinary things, like dogs . . . the most philosophical of animals.[4] Odysseus's

3. Homer, *The Illiad*, 297.

4. "Surely this is a refined quality in its [a dog's] nature and one that is truly philosophical. In what way philosophical? Because it judges anything it sees to be either a friend or an enemy, on no other basis than that it knows the one and doesn't know the

old hound Argos has fallen on hard time, not unlike his master, reduced to beggary. Homer speaks: "As they were thus talking, a dog that had been lying asleep raised his head and pricked up his ears. This was Argos . . . now that his master was gone he was lying neglected on the heaps of mule and cow dung that lay in front of the stable doors . . . and he was full of fleas. As soon as he saw Ulysses standing there, he dropped his ears and wagged his tail, but he could not get close up to his master. When Ulysses saw the dog on the other side of the yard, he dashed a tear from his eyes."[5] This sad passage is quite commonsensical in the sense that one perceives a real object in the world, receives it into one's soul, and responds accordingly. Everyone has had such experiences, which connect us directly with *what is*.

5.2.2 Hebrew Scriptures

Throughout Hebrew Scripture, realism is not argued for, it is assumed and presupposed. Realism is part of the human condition, according to the narratives of the creation. For example, in Genesis chapter 2, in the account of the naming of the animals, Adam sees what these beasts are and assigns names to them. Their existence, their reality is antecedent to their being named. Adam's naming neither makes the animals to be nor to be the kinds of things they are, nor gives them the accidental qualities they have. Adam responds to *what is* and names the animals by means of the concepts that are formed through his common-sense experiences.

The stories of the patriarchs are replete with common-sense realism. Consider the example of Lot and Abraham deciding to part ways as to avoid conflict among their clans in Genesis 13:10. "Lot looked around and saw that the whole plain of the Jordan toward Zoar was well watered, like the garden of the LORD, like the land of Egypt" (NIV). Again, Lot saw the water of the Jordan valley, he did not make it by his seeing. He saw what was real.

The wisdom literature of the Old Testament is also committed to common-sense metaphysical realism. For example, in Ecclesiastes Solomon writes, "Generations come and generations go, but the earth remains forever. The sun rises and the sun sets, and hurries back to where it rises. The wind blows to the south and turns to the north; round and round it goes, ever returning on its course. All streams flow into the sea, yet the sea is

---

other. And how could it be anything besides a lover of learning, if it defines what is its own and what is alien to it in terms of knowledge and ignorance? It couldn't." (Plato, *Republic*, 1015 [376b].)

5. Homer, *The Odyssey*, 216.

never full. To the place the streams come from, there they return again"
(Eccl 1:4–7 NIV).

While the genre of writing is neither scientific nor sociological, it is
not mere poetry. Solomon is reporting reality by observation of what exists.
"Generations come and generations go." We do not make this happen. It *is*.
The point of Ecclesiastes of course is not a defense of metaphysical common-
sense realism. But the point of the preacher in this moving book is about the
human condition *under the sun*. In the natural world, we can observe *what
is* and draw both moral and theological wisdom from our common-sense
observations. We are in deep need of the Author of all things and a right
relationship to him, in light of what we experience under the sun.

Not only in the Law and the Writings of the Hebrew Bible is common-
sense realism built into the text, but also in the Prophets, that third great
section of the *Tanach*. Consider this passage from Jeremiah 38:6, "So they
took Jeremiah and put him into the cistern of Malkijah, the king's son,
which was in the courtyard of the guard. They lowered Jeremiah by ropes
into the cistern; it had no water in it, only mud, and Jeremiah sank down
into the mud" (NIV).

It is highly unlikely that no one but Jeremiah has ever had their feet
stuck in mud. It is a ubiquitous experience. We know that the feeling of being in mud is real. It is not "something we know not what"; it is not created
by the categories of our understanding; it is not a quality of the mind but
not of an object. Mud is *muddy*! It oozes, squishes, and stinks. The realism of
Jeremiah's treatment is something that everyone can relate to. Direct, common-sense realism is part and parcel of our understanding of the human
condition, from the beginning, through the long narrative of the history of
Israel, and it builds to a crescendo in the expectation of Messiah.

5.2.3 Christian New Testament

The four Gospels could not have been written without presupposing common-sense realism. Consider the following passage from Mark 11:1–4 with
its similar passage in Luke 19:26–34.

> As they approached Jerusalem and came to Bethphage and
> Bethany at the Mount of Olives, Jesus sent two of his disciples,
> saying to them, "Go to the village ahead of you, and just as you
> enter it, you will find a colt tied there, which no one has ever
> ridden. Untie it and bring it here. If anyone asks you, 'Why are
> you doing this?' say, 'The Lord needs it and will send it back here
> shortly.'" They went and found a colt outside in the street, tied at

a doorway. As they untied it, some people standing there asked, "What are you doing, untying that colt?" They answered as Jesus had told them to, and the people let them go. (NIV)

According to a common-sense realist, when Jesus states, "You will find a colt tied there," he is making a statement to communicate propositional content to his hearers. The disciples listening received this content into their minds and have an idea/concept/belief, a mental state that is about (intentionally about) a possible object. They take this idea/concept/belief and use it to guide themselves to the place Jesus describes, and, lo and behold, they find the world to be as they thought it to be, as it was asserted by Jesus to be. They see the qualities of a colt exemplified in the world. They see the exemplified essence of a colt that is tied in a specific location. They see the match/correspondence between their minds and reality.

When Jesus says, "You will find a colt tied there," this proposition is true because it matched/corresponded to reality. Notice that it was not true because the disciples looked for the colt; it was true independently of their looking. The disciples went, looked, and saw that it was true. They went and found the colt tied just as Jesus said they would. It was because the qualities of "unridden-colt-tied-up-at-the-village-entrance" were exemplified in reality that Jesus' claim was true. Its truth was independent of verification and was not made true by the disciples' beliefs, feelings, or any cognitive processes.

So, when the disciples "went and found a colt outside in the street" they really saw and found a colt outside in the street. They were directly aware of the colt. They were not merely aware of their perceptions or their ideas or their language use. Luke's version of the story puts it this way: "Those who were sent ahead went and found it just as he had told them." They found the colt, not an idea, not a language construct, not a concept; reality was "just as he had told them" (Luke 19:32). The reality they experienced was exactly as the idea was presented to them. Nothing stood between them and their experience of the world as it really was.

This discussion of the case from Mark and Luke can be applied not only to the ordinary sense experience example given in these passages of the Bible, but to the text of the Bible as a whole. For example, consider the idea that the Bible has "truth, without any mixture of error, for its matter"; is "totally true"; and "is the true center of Christian union."[6] I believe that the metaphysics and epistemology (especially the notion of truth) that are necessary for this statement of faith must maintain: (1) ontological realism about the objects referred to in the biblical text (the objects exist

6. The Southern Baptist Convention, *Baptist Faith and Message 2000*.

independently of our beliefs/feelings/language use about them), (2) correspondence as the relation between the text and the world, (3) direct, immediate epistemic realism regarding the connection between our minds and the realities referred to by the text. Common-sense realism accepts all three.

If common-sense realism is rejected then one really never has direct access to any of the realities asserted to exist in the Bible. How can it be asserted that the Bible is true if one never really connects with the things that the Bible asserts to be real? If one rejects common-sense realism, this will pull against specific ideas about the nature of reality asserted in the New Testament.

Realism presupposed through holy history is fulfilled in the incarnation of the real God-man, Jesus. One of his closest followers put it this way, "That which was from the beginning, which we have heard, which we have seen with our eyes, which we have looked at and our hands have touched—this we proclaim concerning the Word of life" (1 John 1:1 NIV). The incarnation is real apart from what we think, believe, or feel about it. It is because of this reality that John was able to hear, see, look at, and touch Jesus, the Word of Life. John did not hear, see, look at, or touch his ideas of Jesus, or his concept of Jesus, or the linguistic practices of the early believers. He really touched heard, saw, looked at, and touched *Jesus himself*, the Word of Life.

This does not amount to an argument for common-sense realism. Nor does this amount to an argument for the truth of the New Testament. I am simply trying to show here that the New Testament authors presuppose common-sense realism in their historical accounts of Jesus' life, teaching, death, resurrection, and ascension. It will be extremely difficult to accept or make sense of the New Testament without the resources of common-sense realism. The two go together.

5.3 PRE-SOCRATIC PHILOSOPHY: A FIRST START

The next part of the story of common-sense realism unfolds with human philosophical reflection upon the real, upon existence. Here, we will consider a few passages from both pre-Socratic philosophers followed by some ideas from Plato and Aristotle. The ideas that seem most salient in this brief story are that existence can be known, and understood in a careful, rationally reflective way. I will argue that the use of reason in understanding the nature of existence provides a starting point for progress in metaphysical reflection generally.

To begin this quick overview of Greek philosophy, I would like to borrow an analogy from Peter Kreeft about how to think about the history of philosophy.[7] Kreeft writes, "Socrates was a simple virgin, Christians are like married women (married to God), and modernists are like divorcees."[8] The analogy for Kreeft is this: Socrates (and I would add Plato and Aristotle) did not have access to the information of Christian revelation. Their approach to ontology, the nature of reality, was simple, innocent, and did the best it could with natural reason. Christian philosophers, like devoted wives, are committed to their beloved, and unify *what is* into a seamless whole. The marriage of faith and reason with respect to careful reflection on the nature of existence is one that unites two sources of knowledge about reality. The philosophers whom Kreeft calls "modernists" might run the gamut from late medieval nominalism (the beginning of the breakup) up through twenty-first-century post-postmodernism (the long-term consequences of a broken marriage).

If Socratic philosophy is virginal, Christian philosophy matrimonial, and modern/postmodern philosophy is "divorceal," what then of pre-Socratic philosophy? I would add that pre-Socratic philosophy is childlike. I do not mean *childish*, immature and silly. I simply mean that it begins in *wonder*. What little pre-Socratic philosophy we have regarding rational reflection on the nature of *what is* is wonderful. It seems to look at the world as we experience it and wonder about it. This wonder, as Socrates says, "is an experience which is characteristic of a philosopher; . . . this is where philosophy begins and nowhere else (155d)."[9]

It is probable that at one time or another, each of us has wondered philosophically in a simple, childlike way about *what is*. We've wondered: Why does everything seem to change? And, why do things seem to stay the same? These two acts of wondering are ways of getting at *what is*. For the pre-Socratic philosophers, the philosophical answers to these questions of wonder took the form of two varieties of naturalistic monism: there is just one thing. However, two of the major pre-Socratic philosophers differed radically about what the one thing is. Thus, there were two major varieties of monism: the one thing is in constant flux (Heraclitus) and the one thing never changes (Parmenides).

For Heraclitus, the answer to the question of ontological wonder was: Vive le flux! Fragments of his writing that have come down to us claim:

7. If you are reading this book and have not read *Philosophy 101 by Socrates*, by Peter Kreeft, put this book down; go read Kreeft's book. Then, come back here and keep reading!

8. Kreeft, *Philosophy 101 by Socrates*, 33.

9. Plato, *Theatetus*, 173 [155d].

"Everything flows and nothing abides; everything gives way and nothing stays fixed. You cannot step twice into the same river, for other waters are continually flowing on."[10] To the question *what is*? Heraclitus answers: one thing that constantly changes.

For Parmenides the answer is, contrary to Heraclitus: Vive le stasis! Parmenides claimed: "There is left but this single path to tell thee of: namely, that being is. And on this path there are many proofs that being is without beginning and indestructible; it is universal, existing alone, immovable and without end; nor ever was it nor will it be, since it now is, all together, one, and continuous."[11] To the question *what is*? Parmenides answers: one thing that never changes.

Our common-sense awareness of reality seems to affirm both of these ideas. Change is real, and permanence is real. Must we choose one over the other? Plato did not think so.

5.4 CLASSICAL PHILOSOPHY: FIRST PHILOSOPHY AND FIRST PHILOSOPHERS

5.4.1 Socrates and Plato: Particulars, Forms, Being, and the Good

In *Republic* Book VI, Plato makes clear through the analogies of the sun, the divided line, and the allegory of the cave that reality has *both* change *and* permanence. Not only does he offer a solution to the pre-Socratic dichotomy between flux and stasis, but he also goes beyond both. Plato maintains that *both* the things in constant change and flux in the physical world *and* the things that are permanent, unchanging realities (e.g., mathematical truths, forms/universals like humanity, justice, or beauty) have their being because of something beyond these things. This Plato calls the Good.

In the analogy of the sun, of the Good Plato says, "You should also say that not only do the objects of knowledge owe their being known to the Good, but their being is also due to it, although the Good is not being, but superior to it in rank and power" (509b).[12] So, here Plato thinks that all things that are real, whether physical or nonphysical, owe their being to something that is above them in the order of what is real. Then, he adds that the Good "is not being, but superior to it in rank and power." And here is where some trouble begins.

10. Heraclitus, *Heraclitus*, 29.
11. Parmenides, "Fragments of Parmenides," 93.
12. Plato, *Republic*, 1130 (caps on "Good" added).

One major criticism of this Platonic view is presented by the common-sense realist philosopher Étienne Gilson in his *Being and Some Philosophers*. Of this passage from the *Republic* regarding the Platonic idea of the Good as "not being," Gilson asks, "How could we say what the Good is, since in virtue of its very supremacy, it is not?"[13] In other words, if the Good *is not*, then *we cannot say anything of it at all!* After tracing philosophical reflection on the Platonic notion of the Good and its relation to reality from the neo-Platonists through Christian philosophy and up to John Scotus Eriugena, he points out that the Christian identification of the Good with God has the same problem: "He Who Is, is the cause of all beings, only because He himself is not."[14]

Now, this is a flat-out contradiction regarding the Good or God: "The Good is" and "it is not the case that the Good is." There are at least three solutions to this problem. One option is to punt to mysticism, which Gilson suggests occurs in all forms of Platonism. This might be fine as far as it goes, but Gilson points out that mysticism is not much good "*in* philosophy," which is supposed to achieve "perfect intelligibility."[15]

A second option is to reject the idea that being is beyond existence, that is to deny the Platonic notion that ultimate reality is not being. That is, we should not, as Gilson suggests, remove existence (ultimate reality) from being: "Once removed from being, existence can never be pushed back into it, and, once deprived of its existence, being is unable to give an intelligible account of itself."[16]

A third option is to offer the idea that when Plato says that "the Good is not being, but superior to it in rank and power" he is not removing existence from being at all. It seems possible that one could interpret this passage to mean *not* that the Good doesn't exist, but that the Good's existence is not precisely *like* the being of all of the things, which it causes to exist and illuminates for the mind to know.[17] Another passage that might help with this interpretation of Plato's notion of the Good can be found in Plato's explanation of the allegory of the cave in *Republic* Book VII. Socrates states,

---

13. Gilson, *Being and Some Philosophers*, 20.

14. Gilson, *Being and Some Philosophers*, 34.

15. Gilson, *Being and Some Philosophers*, 40.

16. Gilson, *Being and Some Philosophers*, 40.

17. I am merely suggesting here a possible interpretation of this passage in the *Republic*. If the context of the *Republic* combined with Plato's ideas elsewhere in his works suggest that it is not reasonable to interpret the passage in the way I am suggesting, then it would be reasonable to interpret the passage in the way that Gilson does and work out a possible solution to the dilemma in ways that Gilson suggests.

> In the knowable realm, the form of the Good is the last thing to
> be seen, and it is reached only with difficulty. Once one has seen
> it, however, one must conclude that it is the cause of all that is
> correct and beautiful in anything, that it produces both light and
> its source in the visible realm, and that in the intelligible realm it
> controls and provides truth and understanding, so that anyone
> who is to act sensibly in private or public must see it[18]

Here are a few things which can be drawn from this passage about
the Good. First, it can be "seen." That is, we can have direct knowledge, i.e.,
rational awareness of it. Second, we can know specific qualities about it. The
Good is the ontological cause of the existence of goodness and beauty in
everything else that exists. Third, it is the epistemic cause of both the means
and content of truth and knowledge for both physical and nonphysical reality. Fourth, it this the basis of the goodness of justice for private and public
action.

So, the question here is this: if the Good is beyond being (i.e., is not),
then how can we know all of these things about it? Plato says that we can
know at least these things about the Good. Thus, it seems to me that for
Plato, the Good is not beyond being. It is not the case that the Good is
not. Thus, one of two things must be the case here. Either, Plato is deeply
confused in ascribing both "non-being" to the Good while simultaneously
asserting that we can know something, the Good, which is not. Or, the interpretation of the passage in Book VI that when Plato says that "the Good is
not being" he does not remove existence from the Good as Gilson suggests.
Rather, Plato is simply saying that the Good is being itself, the Good itself
is existence, and because it is what it is, it is "beyond," i.e., in a *sui generis*
way, unique from the things that it causes to exist and causes to be known.
If this is a reasonable interpretation of the Platonic notion of the Good, then
this seems reasonably consistent with what we can possibly know about existence from the process of deriving our knowledge of existence from our
ordinary sense experiences.

5.4.2 Aristotle: Substances and Essences

In his excellent introductory book of the history of philosophy, William
Lawhead writes that, for Aristotle, "fundamental reality is the collection of
substances which we find in our everyday experiences."[19] Everyday experiences, for Aristotle produce in us our desire to know. What we experience,

18. Plato, *Republic*, 1135 [517b–c] (caps on "Good" added).
19. Lawhead, *Voyage of Discovery*, 90.

according to Aristotle, are substances. Substances are combinations of both matter and form or matter and essences, and essences are what makes a thing exist and exist as the kind of thing that it is.

Aristotle's common-sense realism gives us a great foundation for exploring the nature of being. Reality is fully present in the combination of form and matter (or that which individuates form). In other words, we are at the foundational point of recognizing the idea that existence is the actualization of an essence (as I have argued in chapter 2). A full development of this idea was to be later developed in the thought of Thomas Aquinas and subsequent students right up through the twenty-first century.

What is key about Aristotle, for the purpose of this very brief survey, is this: we can know the nature of existence through our ordinary sense experiences. Our minds conform to it, not the other way around. Aristotle gives us good reasons to believe that reality is not dependent upon us for it to be what it is. However, given the nature of our own selves as substances with minds that can access reality, there is a deep unity possible between the human mind and reality. The recognition that existence deeply involves essences and has the potential to be known brings the possibility and actuality of unity of knower and reality. The tradition of Aristotelian realism is further developed with the advent of Jesus.

5.5 CHRISTIAN PHILOSOPHY: A FRUITFUL MARRIAGE

The third part of the story includes something very few people saw coming in the flow of the history of philosophy. This part of the story includes the special revelation of Jesus. Jesus himself provides the advanced information needed for philosophical reflection to progress beyond where Plato and Aristotle were able to take it. Without the incarnation, the pull of pre-Socratic monism, whether static (Parmenides) or dynamic (Heraclitus), is too strong to resist. The medieval synthesis between rational philosophical reflection, and revelation of the person of Jesus allows for the development of an understanding of existence that is more reasonable than ancient ideas, but that also opens the doors for the study of both existence and things that exist. This paves the way for scientific advancement.

Christian Philosophy begins with Jesus, and it never ends. On the Christian account of reality, the Christian life is an eternal one in relation to Jesus Christ.[20] Christian philosophy takes seriously both faith (active trust in what we know to be the case from God's revelations to us, including the

20. Peter Kreeft argues that "one advantage of being a philosopher . . . is that you have job security even after death" (Kreeft, *Philosophy 101*, 80).

incarnation of Jesus Christ) and reason. In chapter 4 on the personal ground to realism, we looked at the passages John 1:3, "Through him all things were made; without him nothing was made that has been made" (NIV); John 8:58, "'I tell you the truth,' Jesus answered, 'before Abraham was born, I am!'"; and Colossians 1:16–17, "For by him all things were created: things in heaven and on earth, visible and invisible, whether thrones or powers or rulers or authorities; all things were created by him and for him. He is before all things, and in him all things hold together." In the previous chapter, we showed how these passages ground reality in a *person*, namely Jesus Christ.

The history of Christian philosophy, from the time of the apostles up to the present day, of rational reflection on Christian revelation, is a working out of the relationship between the deep unity of the nature of God, the incarnation, and all of reality, including being human. The flow of history itself is portrayed in the Scripture as culminating in a wedding between the Author of all that is and human beings who love him. Christian philosophers, following Kreeft's analogy, are like married women. They are married to God in their devotion of careful, prayerful pursuit of understanding in the light of faith, active trust, in our true knowledge of *what is*, and the Author of *what is*.

The unification of faith and reason in the history of philosophy flourishes for over a thousand years, and arguably provides the foundation for human progress not only in theology, philosophy, literature, and the arts, but also in architecture, engineering, science, economics, and all other areas of human inquiry.[21] Yet, as with all things "under the sun," there is often a great decline. The fruitful marriage of Christian philosophy begins to have trouble. Perhaps this should not be a surprise to us.[22] Even Jesus himself asked: "When the Son of Man comes, will he find faith on the earth?" (Luke 18:8 NIV).

---

21. Two books by Rodney Stark, *The Victory of Reason* and *How the West Won*, are very persuasive regarding this idea.

22. Dallas Willard gives an excellent illustration of this: "When you go to Assisi, you will find many people who talk a great deal about St. Francis, many monuments to him, and many businesses thriving by selling memorabilia of him. But you will not find anyone who carries in himself the fire that Francis carried. No doubt many fine folks are there, but they do not have the character of Francis, nor do they do the deeds of Francis, nor have his effects.

"What is true in this case is not peculiar to it. Rather, this is simply one of the more obvious illustrations of a general tendency of human life—and of the spiritual life as well. It happens in the professional world, the world of business, of government, education, and the arts" (Willard, *The Great Omission*, 91).

5.6 MODERN PHILOSOPHY: THE GREATEST DIVORCE

The fourth part of this historical survey is a sad tale of a divorce. As with all tragic breakups, it is often hard to tell when they begin. It is possible to trace the relational dysfunction back at least to William of Ockham (1287–1347), who identifies a thing with its existence. Ockham considers whether "the existence of a thing and its essence are two entities extra-mentally distinct from each other."[23] He concludes that "existence is not a thing different from the essence of a thing."[24]

Ockham, according to Frederick Copleston, "did not deny that there are universal concepts in some sense."[25] He adds that "it would be an over-simplification of their [fourteenth-century philosophers'] anti-realism to say that it consisted in attributing universality to 'names or words alone.'"[26] Yet, what happens if existence is not distinct in creatures from their essence? What if essences themselves are mere names? What happens to existence then? This seems to me a slow detachment from reality. If existence is not distinct from an essence of a thing, and if essences themselves become mere names (i.e., nominalism), then existence itself becomes a mere name.

While this may not have been Ockham's view, it seems to be a consequence of it. Frederick Copleston writes, "There arose and spread in the fourteenth century a new movement, associated forever with the name of William of Ockham. The thinkers of this new movement, the *via moderna*, which naturally possessed all the charm of 'modernity,' opposed the realism of the earlier school and became known as the 'nominalists.'"[27] Nominalism, according to Copleston, "constituted the wedge which was driven between theology and philosophy, and which broke apart the synthesis achieved in the thirteenth century."[28]

By the time we get to Galileo (1564–1642), the differences seem irreconcilable. Galileo, in his *Assayer*, considers whether heat is in the objects we perceive it to be. He says that it is very far from the truth that heat is "a real attribute, property, and quality that truly inheres in the material by which we feel warmed."[29] Heat ends up being a "secondary" quality, and doesn't really exist in the things that feel hot, but only "primary" qualities, such

---

23. William of Ockham, *Philosophical Writings*, 103.
24. William of Ockham, *Philosophical Writings*, 105.
25. Copleston, *A History of Philosophy*, 3:11.
26. Copleston, *A History of Philosophy*, 3:11.
27. Copleston, *A History of Philosophy*, 3:11.
28. Copleston, *A History of Philosophy*, 3:11.
29. Galilei, "From The Assayer (1623)," 185.

as motion and extension really exist in things. So, a cup of steaming coffee is not *really* "hot," and following Galileo's example, a feather is not *really* ticklish. He maintains that all of creation, without minds, is odorless, taste-less, and silent. His nominalism is fairly clear: "Outside the living animal these are nothing but names," and such properties "which are considered to be qualities inherent in external objects, do not really have any other existence except in us, and that outside of us they are nothing but names"; more precisely he says, "I do not believe in the least that . . . there is in fire another quality [besides primary qualities], and that is heat."[30]

When one of the greatest scientific minds of history says something like, "Fire isn't hot!" we should probably pause and think very carefully about what he has to say. A great many things could be meant by this, but given our common-sense experience, fire seems pretty hot. We should, of course, distinguish between the quality of being hot and the sensation of feeling heat. The latter of course cannot exist without a mind to instantiate it, but "being heat" and "feeling heat" are two different things. If the second-ary qualities go the way of names, nearly everything else does too, including existence.

Within a century and a half, the divorces papers have been filed. They were filed by Continental rationalists like René Descartes (1596–1650). They were filed by British Empiricists like John Locke (1632–1704) and Da-vid Hume (1711–76). Each in their own way denied that secondary qualities are real. George Berkeley (1685–1753) went a step further and argued that neither secondary *nor primary* qualities are really in the things that have them. Even causation and substance (remember how important this was for Aristotle) are not real, according to Hume, and his skepticism concerning these things was part of his contribution to modern thought.

By the time of Kant (1724–1804), the modernist divorce papers have been signed, the household assets split and divided, and the intellectual children left to fend for themselves in postmodernity. Kant makes a dis-tinction between the "phenomenal" world and the "noumenal" world. The phenomenal world is the world that we experience through the categories of our understanding. The noumenal world is the world outside of our un-derstanding, outside our minds, outside of what is experienced. Our knowl-edge is only of the phenomenal world, but not of the noumenal world. For Kant, all of existence, including God himself, is mere noumena.[31] Kant adds we should still accept "reality." He writes, "We must therefore accept an

---

30. Galilei, "From The Assayer (1623)," 187–88.

31. Kant seems to make an exception for minds and the categories of the under-standing. Why these should escape is opaque.

immaterial being, a world of understanding, and a Supreme Being (all mere noumena), because in them only, as things in themselves reason finds that completion and satisfaction which it can never hope for in the derivation of appearances from their homogenous grounds. . . . *But as we can never cognise these beings of understanding as they are in themselves,* that is, as definitely, yet we must assume them."[32] Existence was once out in the world. Now it's all in our minds.

Chesterton, following Aquinas, thought that eggs are eggs. Yet when modern philosophers assert that the heat required to scramble eggs isn't real, then Kantian philosophy takes it one step further and denies that the eggs are real either; nor is anything else for that matter. Since there are no real eggs, we can just talk about our own personal scrambles.

5.7 POST-KANTIAN PHILOSOPHY: ONTOLOGICAL ESTRANGEMENT

The fifth part of the story is the history of postmodernism. The history of postmodernism begins with post-Kantian idealism in the nineteenth century. Idealism, as a historical movement was dominated by G. W. F. Hegel (1770–1831). Hegel viewed existence itself as Absolute Spirit, an Idea known only internal to one's thought. Thus reality is ideal. Perhaps post-Kantian idealism's slogan could be captured by "Reality, what a great Idea!" This view is a long, tragic history of a dysfunctional philosophical family born out of the great philosophical divorce of modernism. Multiple attempts to repair the divorce have been tried, and each ending in disaster: idealism, pragmatism, positivism, Marxism, and linguistic analysis. None of these philosophies can heal the damage done by the divorce of modernism. In the remainder of this book, we will look briefly at some attempts to do so within the last hundred years or so. These philosophical movements are still trying to cope with the dysfunction of the greatest divorce: reality separated from itself.

5.8 TWENTIETH AND TWENTY-FIRST CENTURY PHILOSOPHY: ONTIC BITTERNESS OR REMEMBERING OUR FIRST LOVE?

The saddest thing about the consequences of this divorce is that if some-one suggests a return to one's first love, a return to reality, to *what is*, one

---

32. Kant, *Prolegomena*, emphasis added.

risks ostracism. This usually shows up in particular discussions of certain aspects of reality, most frequently those connected with deep psychological and bodily desires that are connected to political ideologies. In the historical summary that I've presented here what started as a love of reality, fragmented into nominalism, primary/secondary quality distinctions, and phenomenal/noumenal divides. Yet the possibility of returning to reality by realistic common-sense philosophy is thought to be impossible and even heretical, especially in those systems that dominate the institutions of civic life. This is what Orwell recognized in the great political totalitarian movements of the twentieth century when he wrote, "In the end the Party would announce that two and two made five, and you would have to believe it. It was inevitable that they should make that claim sooner or later: the logic of their position demanded it. Not merely the validity of experience, but the very existence of external reality, was tacitly denied by their philosophy. The heresy of heresies was common sense."[33] The next section of this book is to show how these philosophical consequences of the greatest divorce fail to make sense of *what is*.

33. Orwell, *1984*, 80.

CHAPTER 6

Relativism
"Real for Me" and Other Absurdities

6.0 RELATIVISM: A PERENNIALLY BAD IDEA

I arrive at the beach. I feel the cool, wet sand at my feet. I taste the saltiness of the ocean water on my lips. I hear the sound of the crashing surf. I smell the freshness of the sea air. I see waves breaking offshore. These things are real. Every person knows what is real from ordinary common-sense experiences like these. They also tell us more. They tell us about the nature of reality itself, about existence itself. As I ponder my own experiences, I think: Is this just *my* reality? What about the other surfers out here? Don't they have their own experiences different from mine? Doesn't everyone just have their own reality? This chapter will examine a recent affirmation of relativism and offer some objections to it.

But, you might ask: hasn't relativism been refuted? This is a good question. Alasdair MacIntyre once wrote, "Relativism, like skepticism, is one of those doctrines that have by now been refuted a number of times too often. Nothing is perhaps a surer sign that a doctrine embodies some not-to-be-neglected truth than that in the course of history of philosophy it should have been refuted again and again. Genuinely refutable doctrines only need to be refuted once."[1]

It would be nice if MacIntyre were right about relativism. It would be nice if relativism only needed to be refuted once. Unfortunately, genuinely refutable (and refuted) doctrines like relativism often are taken up again and again. When they are, they must be refuted again and again. Contrary to MacIntyre, there is no truth to neglect in relativism, because there is no truth in it at all.

I was reminded of this quotation recently when I was attending a large academic conference. As most large academic conferences often have, there was a large ballroom full of publishers from a variety of academic and popular presses. As I was browsing through the books, I ran across a book with the title *Who's Afraid of Relativism?* I thought that was a nice title. No one should be afraid of relativism. For a philosophy so unreasonable, what is there to fear? So, I picked up the book expecting to find a lengthy critique of relativistic thinking. To my surprise, what I found was a defense of relativistic thinking from a Christian perspective. Some refuted doctrines are taken up again and again. The task of this chapter is to show, once again that relativism is unreasonable.

This chapter offers a critical response to James K. A. Smith's *Who's Afraid of Relativism?* First, I offer some clarification of how relativism should be understood. Second, relying on the philosophy of Dallas Willard, I offer criticism that will apply to some of the salient ideas with which Smith is sympathetic and which are taken from Ludwig Wittgenstein, Richard Rorty, and Robert Brandom. Third, I offer some ideas as to what type of work in epistemology should be of concern to Christian thinkers who wish to defend common-sense realism other than the ideas of contemporary relativism. The chapter concludes with a fictional dialog between Dallas Willard (whose epistemology and metaphysics I take to be a form of common-sense realism), James K. A. Smith (a defender of relativism), and C. S. Lewis's Screwtape (a devil) from the *Screwtape Letters*, taken from quotations from each of these thinkers' works.

---

1. MacIntyre, *Relativism, Power and Philosophy*, 22.

6.1 DEFINING RELATIVISM AND DEMONSTRATING ITS UNREASONABLENESS

6.1.1 Defining Relativism

When asking the question "Who's Afraid of Relativism?" one should be clear about what relativism is. James Smith's recent book, the title of which asks this very question, does little to specify what relativism is. Some notions of relativism are too broad. For example, "Any doctrine could be called relativism which holds that something exists, or has certain properties or features, or is true or in some sense obtains, not simply but only in relation to something else."[2] But this would entail that *any relation whatsoever* could be viewed as relativism. Other definitions are too narrow. For example: "Relativism [is] the denial that there are certain kinds of universal truths."[3] This definition could preclude ontological relativism. Smith claims that his own view is the former sort of relativism, while denying that his own view includes the latter broad notion of denying that there are certain kinds of universal truths. I will argue that Smith's own view amounts to a version of relativism that ought to be rejected. Let me turn now to a more precise definition of relativism and show how Smith's actual views meet that definition. A more precise definition of relativism is the following. Relativism = df:

> The nature and existence of items of knowledge, qualities, values or logical entities non-trivially obtain their natures and/or existence from certain aspects of human activity, including, but not limited to beliefs, cultures, languages, etc.[4]

This definition captures a variety of relativistic views, but Smith's book is primarily concerned with epistemic relativism (henceforth ER). ER is a view about knowledge of reality. ER maintains that knowledge itself and its constituent elements, such as truth and justification, are relative to something. In Smith's case, our knowledge of reality is relative to the use of language by a community. This view is not without difficulty.

6.1.2 Epistemic Relativism Is Self-Refuting

Philosophers have argued that ER has many problems, because maintaining ER will require the conjunction of two ideas.[5] First, it requires that one

2. Lacey, "Relativism," 206.
3. Pojman, "Relativism," 690.
4. Mosteller, *Relativism: A Guide*, 3.
5. See Siegel, *Relativism Refuted*.

believe that all knowledge claims are established by means of a standard or standards of epistemic evaluation (the standards conjunct). Second, it requires that there is no neutrality between competing standards of evaluation (the no-neutrality conjunct). The conjunction of these two notions entail that ER is self-refuting.

If one maintains ER, then ER itself will be established by means of some standard or standard of epistemic evaluation, and there is no neutrality between competing standards of evaluation. Thus, for anyone maintaining the contradictory of ER, the contradictory of ER will be established by means of some other standard of evaluation, and (according to ER itself) there will be no neutral way to adjudicate between ER and the contradictory of ER. ER and *not*-ER will both be items of knowledge, but this is absurd. For the sake of consistency, the definition of relativism will have to be applied to itself, but when it is applied to itself, it becomes false. So, if ER is true, then ER is false. Thus, ER is self-refuting.

Pointing out the self-refuting nature of epistemic relativism has been going at least since Plato's criticism of Protagoras. Unfortunately, in Smith's book there is no discussion of what exactly ER is or amounts to. No references are given to any academic discussion of ER or any other variety of relativism. To be fair, Smith does claim, "There are, no doubt, vast literatures that could have been consulted that don't appear in the footnotes."[6]

In an age of proliferation of knowledge in academic books and journal articles, this will of course be true of any book on any philosophical subject. Yet, if one is to answer the question of "Who's afraid of relativism?" one would hope for a brief statement of what ER is, or a brief account of its possible flaws followed by a sustained refutation of those flaws. None is given in Smith's book. Perhaps given the following quotation from Richard Rorty at the beginning of the book and quoted again in his chapter on Rorty, Smith believes that a sustained refutation of ER is impossible, and appears to agree with Rorty when he asserts, "We should not regret our inability to perform a feat which no one has any idea how to perform."[7]

Throughout Smith's book, he uses the terms relativism (without scare quotes), "relativism" (with scare quotes), and relative (in italics), but he never distinguishes between these three different expressions in the text. While there is no clear single definition given of either relativism,[8] "relativism,"[9]

6. Smith, *Who's Afraid of Relativism?*, 13.

7. Rorty, *Philosophy and the Mirror of Nature*, 340. Smith quotes this line from Rorty in *Who's Afraid of Relativism?*, 95 and 109.

8. Smith, *Who's Afraid of Relativism?*, 12.

9. Smith, *Who's Afraid of Relativism?*, 39.

or being *relative*,[10] there are different ways Smith uses language to describe relativism. It's probable that there are two broad ways of understanding relativism given what Smith does say, one of which Smith rejects and the other he accepts. Smith rejects relativism conceived as:

1. that which obliterates moral facts,[11]

2. that which threatens "absolute" truth,[12]

3. that which is rejected by "realism,"[13]

4. the "preclusion of norms,"[14]

5. "sophomoric,"[15]

6. "anything goes nihilism."[16]

Smith accepts relativism conceived as:

7. that which calls referentialism into question,[17]

8. being a necessary condition in the claim that: If we are "finite, contingent, historical, and social creatures," then our knowledge is relative to communities of practice,[18]

9. dependence,[19]

10. contingency.[20]

I agree with Smith that there are very good reasons to reject relativism understood in 1–6, so I won't touch on those ways of understanding relativism. Let me say something briefly about 7–8.

---

10. Smith, *Who's Afraid of Relativism?*, 87, 71, 105, 107, 141.

11. Smith, *Who's Afraid of Relativism?*, 26.

12 Smith, *Who's Afraid of Relativism?*, 29. Smith claims, "The frequent and sloppy use of the qualifier 'absolute' leads to a common confusion of 'relativism' with sheer arbitrariness" (29). I'm wondering if the same confusion is not the case for his own use of: relativism, *relativism*, and "relativism"; or realism (25), *realism* (102, 103) and "realism" (105).

13. Smith, *Who's Afraid of Relativism?*, 41.

14. Smith, *Who's Afraid of Relativism?*, 78.

15. Smith, *Who's Afraid of Relativism?*, 170.

16. Smith, *Who's Afraid of Relativism?*, 179.

17. Smith, *Who's Afraid of Relativism?*, 25.

18. Smith, *Who's Afraid of Relativism?*, 105.

19. Smith, *Who's Afraid of Relativism?*, 179–80.

20. Smith, *Who's Afraid of Relativism?*, 180.

Number 7 is true; relativism does call into question referentialism.[21] The problem is that calling referentialism into question requires that someone refer *to how things are* in a common-sense realistic way. Smith does this throughout the book. He tells us *the way language is*, but he denies that he is *referring* to anything. This is the gravest error of all forms of relativism, especially ER. It seems to take one aspect of reality (e.g., human language) and say that everything else in reality is relative to it. But somehow, language itself escapes this relativizing process. Relativists somehow forget that language itself is a bit of reality and maintain that it is somehow immune from relativism.

Number 8 is logically interesting insofar as it gives necessary and sufficient conditions. The problem is that it is obvious on a moment's reflection that the antecedent can be true, and the consequent false. We can be finite, contingent, historical, and social creatures and the epistemic relativism of Wittgenstein, Rorty, and Brandom be false. In fact, they are false! They are false because they are self-refuting. These relativistic attempts to reject our God-given common-sense understanding of the world fail every time they are tried. In fact, the overall tenor of the philosophies (broad worldviews) of these thinkers is generally antithetical, if not outright hostile to the Christian faith.

It is astonishing that in a book on a Christian approach to relativism, there is only one mention of this major problem of relativism (i.e., that it is self-defeating) and this only in a footnote in a discussion of Christian Smith's book *What Is a Person?*[22] This is astonishing in itself, as *What Is a Person?* is a book that is not dedicated as a sustained criticism of either relativism or pragmatism. Why not deal with a book on relativism to show how the self-defeating arguments fail? That is a much more formidable task indeed!

Smith's strategy is a bit different. He claims that we can have "standards without having to claim that they are 'objective.'"[23] His book tries to do that, but the problem with self-refutation lingers. For if there are standards for knowledge claims that are relative to language use, and there is no neutrality (i.e., no objectivity) between different standards, then there are two options. First, one can make this claim as objective based on some neutral standard, and thus gives up relativism. Second, one can maintain that the claim that

---

21. More on referentialism below. I will argue that Smith only rejects *one* way of understanding referentialism.

22. Smith, *Who's Afraid of Relativism?*, 21.

23. Again, one wonders if "objective" is different from objective (without the scare quotes) (Smith, *Who's Afraid of Relativism?*, 22, twice) or *objectivity* in italics (Smith, *Who's Afraid of Relativism?*, 147).

we can have standards without objectivity is only true within a language game, and that for any other language game which has different standards and claims that it is false, then it will be false within that language game.[24] Thus, the claim that we can have epistemic standards relative to language games will be true and false depending on the language game and given the absence of objective (neutral) standards between the two, there is no way to determine which it will be. This is absurd. Relativism really does need to be refuted again and again.

Numbers 9–10 are both true, but one doesn't need to follow Wittgenstein, Rorty, and Brandom to maintain a robust understanding of our dependence, or contingency. In fact, only a clear rejection of relativism and an acceptance of common-sense realism will allow us to truly come to know that we are dependent and contingent. For the claim that we are dependent and contingent is either true only within a language game, or true apart from language games (able to be seen to be true by anyone who is willing to engage their sensible faculties to see how God has made us).

If it is true apart from language games, then relativism must be given up. If it is true only from within a language game, and if there is another language game that denies that we are contingent and dependent, then the claim that we are not contingent and dependent will be true from within that language game. The self-refutation problem remains.

Smith is right to think that we should not avoid the fact that we are contingent creatures.[25] However, Smith can make the claim, "We are contingent creatures" only if the concept "We are contingent creatures" has intentional content that adequately corresponds to the real property of contingent creaturehood exemplified in us. But this is common-sense realism not relativism! Our concepts can, and do, correspond to the way things are, and we can know that they do.

So, for Smith (and anyone else), the only way to maintain that we are contingent creatures is to reject relativism, not to embrace it. Embracing it entails that the claim that we are contingent creatures has the same epistemic

24. By "language," Smith follows the philosopher Ludwig Wittgenstein (1889–1951) by claiming that there is a deep connection between language and "forms of life" (Smith, *Who's Afraid of Relativism?*, 46). According to Wittgenstein, a "form of life" "can be understood as changing and contingent, dependent on culture, context, history, etc.; this appeal to forms of life grounds a relativistic reading of Wittgenstein" (Biletzki and Matar "Ludwig Wittgenstein"). A "language game" according to Smith, again following Wittgenstein, "is the practical context in which our words and speech make sense—which is why understanding is bound up with, and relative to, the practical telos of the language-game, the end to which a community of practice is oriented" (Smith, *Who's Afraid of Relativism?*, 46).

25. Smith, *Who's Afraid of Relativism?*, 17.

status as the claim that we are not contingent creatures, depending on which language game you are playing. If you add that there is no neutral way to tell which language game to play, then the claim that we are contingent creatures can never be established. You can say it *louder* (like Americans speak English so as to be understood when they visit France); but that won't help make it so, and it's really annoying.

Smith claims that the sneering critic of relativism[26] doesn't appreciate our "finite creaturehood" as well as relativists.[27] However, a relativist who maintains a rejection of referentialism and claims that our knowledge of ourselves as finite creatures is relative to communities of practice would have to admit that being a finite creature is true only relative to some communities of language users, but not to others. Again, if one denies any objective or neutral way to determine which language community to join, then one can never reasonably claim that the claim that we are finite creatures is more reasonable than the claim that we are not finite creatures; nor can they more reasonably claim that it is more reasonable to believe that critics of relativism sneer than not sneer.

Only the common-sense realist has a way out of this relativist swamp. We all have ordinary sense experiences of ourselves as finite creatures. We know this bit of reality very clearly. In addition, there are two points to consider here, one epistemic and the other ontological. First, being a member of the category "finite human creatures" is irrelevant to language use. Human beings, whether unborn or in permanent vegetative states, are what they are apart from our language use or their language use. The use of a language does not make one a member of the category "finite human creatures." A relativist could claim that the unborn or those in permanent vegetative states are finite human creatures because of the way in which we speak. But can language really do that? On such a view, language would literally create reality. Just imagine if all of reality worked that way! I could power my car simply by talking to it! In addition, is it reasonable simply to define out of existence members of the human species simply based on what we say about them? The history of the twentieth-century genocides is replete with examples of this sort of thing happening. For these reasons, being "finite human creatures" is irrelevant to language use.

Second, we can know that we are finite human creatures apart from language use. Using language is neither necessary nor sufficient for thought and knowledge, especially self-knowledge. We can know what we are without saying anything, especially if we don't think in language.[28]

26. Why do defenders of relativism think that critics of relativism are sneering?

27. Smith, *Who's Afraid of Relativism?*, 16.

28. See Willard's "The Absurdity of Thinking in Language."

Language is a capacity of contingent finite human persons, and our knowledge of our own language use is of course dependent upon our actual use of language. But we know our own creaturely, dependent, and contingent finitude not because our linguistic communities say so, but because our minds grasp the real properties of creatureliness, dependency, contingency, and finitude that inhere in ourselves as we were created by a loving God who calls us into being what we are.

We know ourselves as we are in ourselves because our minds have the capacity to correspond to the way we are. Some language users can see the correspondence between our belief that we are finite creatures and the fact that we are finite creatures, others don't, but they don't, not because they don't use language in the right way, but because their minds are not conformed to the real way we are. It is not the realist advocate of a correspondence view of truth who "inflates our creaturehood to Creator-hood."[29] The exact opposite is the case. Relativists "do have something to teach us about being a creature" where a creature is something that creates. For the relativist, the linguistic community creates the truth that we are finite creatures, rather than the truth that we are finite creatures being true even if the linguistic community denies it.

Here is a slightly more formal way of putting this criticism. Consider the following four claims:

R1: All knowledge claims are made, justified, true, and reasonable only relative to linguistic communities.

R2: There is no neutral way to adjudicate between linguistic communities.

P1: Humans are finite creatures.

and

P2: It is not the case that humans are finite creatures.

According to a relativist view, P1 and P2 are both made, justified, true, and reasonable only relative to linguistic communities. Given R2, there's no neutral way to adjudicate between P1 and P2. Thus, P1 and P2 are on the same epistemic footing. But, Smith does not believe that P1 and P2 are on the same epistemic footing, but they must be, given R1 and R2. Thus, either relativism must be given up, or P1 and P2 are on the same epistemic footing. This should be a sufficiently good reason to reject relativism. Unfortunately, Smith does not consider this view in his treatment of Wittgenstein, Rorty, or Brandom, to which we now turn.

29. Smith, *Who's Afraid of Relativism?*, 78.

6.2 REFUTING RELATIVISM IN WITTGENSTEIN, RORTY, AND BRANDOM

In order to respond to Smith's account of Wittgenstein (and Rorty and Brandom with him), I begin with a quotation from the late Christian philosopher Dallas Willard. Willard claimed that epistemic relativism of the Wittgensteinian variety, which makes knowledge relative to language, will always be a theory of the real essential nature of language and consciousness, as well as the real connection between language and reality. The fact that this is the case leads to some serious problems with this view. Willard states,

> Relativisms in the theory of knowledge are sets of claims about how consciousness (language) and its objects really are related, without regard to how they (consciousness and its objects) are thought of or spoken of by the particular theorist or culture. They are quite general claims of essence about consciousness and its objects. The same is of course true for the claims of those theorists who oppose idealism or relativism, but that is consistent with their view.[30]

Thus, when Smith, following Wittgenstein, claims that human knowledge is contingent, finite, created, and social, one must immediately ask, is this because of the natural reality of human contingency, finitude, creaturehood, and social relations? In other words, if knowledge is contingent, finite, creaturely, and social, it will be because of the way these things *are*, and because our thoughts about them *correspond to those realities*. The problem for Smith is that Smith's own view prevents him from maintaining this. Let us consider a few propositions that Smith asserts and consider them both singly and conjointly.

In his opening chapter, Smith states:

P1: "Christians know their contingency is correlative to their status as creatures."[31]

Yet, as the book unfolds, Smith denies P1 corresponds to the way things are. For example, in his discussion of Wittgenstein, Smith follows Wittgenstein by claiming:

---

30. Willard, "Theories of Wholes," 164.
31. Smith, *Who's Afraid of Relativism?*, 36.

P2:   "Correspondence [of language and reality] . . . is itself game-dependent. What counts as correspondence is a connection that is game-
relative. Correspondence is conventional."[32]

If P2 is correct, then P1 is conventional. Our knowledge of our contingency is not knowledge of how human knowledge really is. P1 only corresponds in a conventional sense, and our knowledge of ourselves is a mere
matter of convention. Yet, P1 claims to be a claim about our nature, but then
given P2, it will not be a claim about our nature, or a claim that corresponds
to the reality of our nature as such. P1 itself cannot be a claim about our
nature, given P2. Even worse, P2 itself is only a matter of convention, and
the contradictory of P2 would also be a matter of convention. If there is no
neutral (game-independent, nonconventional) way of determining whether
P2 or the contradictory of P2 is the case, then a self-defeating form relativism will follow.

Smith claims (following Wittgenstein) that maintaining P1 and P2
does not result in "casting ourselves into the abyss of sheer arbitrariness."[33]
This is welcome news. He claims that we can be wrong about our use of
language, because the correspondence of language to the world depends
upon communal use of the language.

P3:   "There is no naming or reference that isn't rooted in such convention. Community precedes correspondence. And this is a feature of
finitude, a characteristic of creaturehood."[34]

The trouble now begins. There is a serious problem with P3, given P2.
According to Dallas Willard's criticism of Wittgensteinian relativism raised
above, P3 is a claim about how language (naming) "and its objects *really
are* related."[35] P3 is about how language and community (language games)
relate to their objects, but given P2, the correspondence of P3 which is supposed to be about how language and community relate to their objects will
itself be dependent on some game, say G1.

Suppose someone asserted, "Not-P3," which is the negation of P3.
Given P2, Not-P3 would be a correspondence of language to reality which
would also depend on another game, G2. But, P3 claims that there is no
reference that is nonconventional, and thus there is no neutral (nonconventional) way to adjudicate between P3 and Not-P3 (or P2 and Not-P2
for that matter). In other words, P1 meets the "standards conjunct" in the

32. Smith, *Who's Afraid of Relativism?*, 51–52.
33. Smith, *Who's Afraid of Relativism?*, 53.
34. Smith, *Who's Afraid of Relativism?*, 53.
35. Willard, "Theories of Wholes," 164.

definition of ER raised above, and P2 meets the "no neutrality conjunct," and therefore, this is a form of ER. It is self-refuting.

In addition, there an extremely serious logical problem here.[36] The negative generalization of P3 itself raises some serious logical difficulties, given the content of P6. On a traditional understanding of categorical logic, a statement of the form "No S are P," where S and P stand for any possible category of thing, is a denial of the overlap of two categories. It is possible to understand the possibility of the existence of members of the subject and predicate overlapping categories (OC) in three possible ways.

OC1: One category has no members (e.g., No leprechauns are humans), and since one category lacks members, they can't overlap.

OC2: Neither category has members, (e.g., No leprechauns are centaurs), and since neither category has members, the categories can't overlap.

OC3: Both categories have members, but it is a (contingent) fact that there is nothing which exemplifies both categories simultaneously (e.g., No humans are fish).

Let's simplify P1 to:

P3': No human acts of reference are nonconventional human acts.

Smith certainly doesn't believe that the categorical overlap in P3' should be understood in sense OC2, since he clearly maintains that there are human acts of reference, which he (and Wittgenstein) identify with the use of language in the slogan, "Meaning is use." Meaning just is the physical use of language on this view.

It is difficult to say whether Smith maintains the overlap in sense as OC1. He clearly maintains that there are human acts of reference (i.e., linguistic acts), but it is not so clear that he believes that there are nonconventional human acts. What might such nonconventional human acts amount to?

One clear case of a nonconventional human action is a mental state of which one is aware, whether a simple awareness of a pain state, or a complex mental state such as a belief or a desire. Let us say generally that if subject S engages in an act of being aware of mental state M, that this act is nonconventional. So, there are multiple acts which could exemplify a nonconventional state. S could engage in a mental act of being in pain, or engage in a mental act of thinking about pain, or believing that S is in pain.

---

36. Logic Alert! The next few pages involve some nerdy logical discussions. If you aren't into that, then skip to section 6.3.

There are two reasons why such mental acts are nonconventional. First, the properties of the act of awareness of the mental state's intentional states are intrinsically and essentially about something, but no conventional acts are intrinsically and essentially about something. Second, S's awareness that S is in pain, and the phenomenal felt quality of pain itself, does not depend upon language. Dallas Willard has argued persuasively that since language is always doing something with physical symbols, and if no thoughts involve physical symbols, then we don't think in language.[37] Considering the simple case of an act of being in pain, or an act of being aware that one is in pain, it is hard to see how these might be conventional.

Yet, Smith appears to advocate just such a view in his chapter on Robert Brandom.[38] There are three reasons to think this. First, Smith quotes Brandom as saying that we treat something as sapient when we explain its behavior "by attributing to it intentional states such as belief and desire."[39] Brandom seems to be saying that sapient beings don't have mental states that have a natural immaterial aboutness to them, rather we merely attribute such states to beings we believe to be sapient when they give reasons for their actions, but the giving of reasons is not the same as having a nonconventional mental state. Second, Smith claims that Brandom's pragmatism leads him to believe that we can understand how "linguistic expressions, or the functional role of intentional states, confers conceptual content."[40] This looks like an identification of linguistic expressions with intentional states, or at least their functional role in such expressions, which would entail that such states are going to be conventional (i.e., intentional meaning is use). Third, he quotes Brandom as saying "propositional content . . . is a feature we can make intelligible as a structure of the commitments and entitlements that articulate the *use* of sentences."[41] This would apparently lead us to think that there are no human acts, including mental acts, that are nonconventional.

Thus, it very well looks like Smith maintains OC1. There just are no nonconventional human actions, including mental acts (such as an act of being aware that one is in pain). This type of act on Smith's view (following Brandom) would be a conventional act. But, again, if there are mental acts

---

37. See Willard's "The Absurdity of Thinking in Language" and my defense of it in Mosteller's *Theories of Truth*, ch. 1. The quickest way to summarize the argument here is this: Since all language is physical, and no thoughts are physical, it follows that, no thought is linguistic. Thus, we do not think in language.

38. Smith, *Who's Afraid of Relativism?*, 118–23.

39. Smith, *Who's Afraid of Relativism?*, 118.

40. Smith, *Who's Afraid of Relativism?*, 122.

41. Smith, *Who's Afraid of Relativism?*, 148.

that are inherently nonconventional (and a very good candidate for such an act is any act that exemplifies a mental state that is itself possessing the property of intentionality), then Smith's (and Brandom's) view fails.

Intentionality is often thought to be the mark of the mental.[42] However, it is hard to see how the qualities of a mental state together with the intentional phenomenal realities that attend to them could in any way be conventional. The reason for this is straightforward. Simple phenomenal intentional states and their constituent qualia[43] are the ontological essences of mental acts, especially simple mental acts such as being aware of pain. Such essences are completely independent from anything conventional, including language. To clarify the argument, let us consider a few more propositions:

P4: No conventional states are acts of awareness of phenomenal qualia of pain.

P5: All acts of knowing that one is in pain are acts of awareness of phenomenal qualia of pain.

P6: Therefore, no acts of knowing that one is in pain are conventional states.

P7: Therefore, all acts of knowing that one is in pain are nonconventional states (from P6 by obversion).

P8: Therefore, some acts of knowing that one is in pain are nonconventional states (from P7 by sub-alteration).

If,

P3': No human acts of reference are nonconventional human acts

entails

P3": No human acts of knowledge are nonconventional,

and if P3" entails

42. The term "intentionality" refers the "aboutness" of a mental state. All mental states are *about* something, whether themselves or other things. For example, my thought of what I had for breakfast is *about* an omelet. My thought is about or directed toward an object in the past. Or for example, my belief that there is a bird on the fence is an "intentional" state. It is a state of my mind that is *about* the bird and its relationship of being on the fence. All mental states have intentionality. They are all *about* something.

43. The term "qualia" refers to the "what it is like to experience" a mental state. So, for example, when I look at a yellow banana, I experience the "quality" of yellow. Or when I taste chocolate chip cookies, I experience the "quality" of sweetness. The properties of red and sweetness are "qualia." They are present before my mind, and are things that I can describe in my experience. There is a specific "what it is like" to any experience of them that makes them what they are.

P3''':   No human acts of knowledge that one is in pain are nonconventional,

then P8 and P3''' are contradictory. Thus, necessarily, if one is false, then the other is true, but given P2, P8, and P3''' being contradictory is simply game-dependent. Thus, for Smith, P8 and P3''' can both be true depending on the game being played! The question that must be asked is whether Smith believes that contradiction is game-dependent or a natural feature of reality? His ideas so far seem to imply the former.

The logical relation of contradiction is not about language use, any more than the phenomenal qualia of pain states depend on my ability to say "Ouch!" It is about *what is* and *what is not*. It is an ontological reality. Something is, or it is not. Something exemplifies an essence, or it doesn't. If Wittgenstein's and Smith's view were correct, not only would the act of knowing be conventional and dependent upon human language use, so too would the act of *being*, including the being of logical realities, be dependent upon human language use. So, Smith must either: (A) give up relativism, or (B) follow it to the logical conclusion that *reality itself is dependent upon and relative to human language use*. The realist who stands in the daylight of our God-given senses and sees all that is as a great gift will not follow after the strange gods of the relativists.

In a very readable interview regarding truth, Dallas Willard was asked, "What can we do to help those who are advocating a relativist understanding of truth?" I believe that Smith's views do need a great deal of help with this. Willard responded by saying,

> Many of them are helped just by pointing out that they are making an absolute claim about the nature of truth itself. . . . They are telling you what it really is. And some people are helped by having this pointed out to them. Now a consistent person will at that point back off and tell you, "No, I'm just telling you what I think." But that's what you would call a Pyrrhic victory, because if he's only telling me what he thinks, that carries no weight with others. Obviously he is not. He wants to tell me what I should think. But why should I think what he thinks I should think? No reason, unless there is something called truth beyond opinion [i.e., use of language], the truth about truth.[44]

Smith does exactly what Willard indicates in his chapters on Rorty and Brandom, as he does in his chapter on Wittgenstein. He makes claims that supposedly tell us about how language really is, while denying that knowledge claims correspond to the way things are. In Smith's discussion

44. Willard, *Truth: Can We Do Without It?*

of Rorty and Brandom a similar denial of truth as correspondence of the mind with reality is quite pronounced. For example, in the chapter on Rorty, Smith says the following: "What *counts* as 'correspondence' is, at root a *social* production";[45] "Representation and correspondence . . . are games that we learn to play from a community of social practice, . . . our realisms (and attendant claims to correspondence) are *dependent upon* communities of practice."[46] In Smith's chapter on Brandom, he claims that Brandom does not "locate justification in correspondence," rather "reference is one kind of inferential game we can play, and what counts as a good inference is bound up with a community of know-*how*, a community of practice."[47]

The self-referential problem arises here for Rorty and Brandom just as it does for Wittgenstein. Do their claims correspond to the way things are or not? If they do, then their relativism is given up, if they do not, then the claim is false in just those language games that deny them. Willard points this out very clearly when he writes,

> The jury is still out, to say the least, on whether or not any philosophically significant degree of objectivity or realism can be salvaged within the relativization of identity and exis-tence to language in the manner of a Wittgenstein, Quine, or others. Of course I understand the general assumption today that nothing else could be possible. But to be consistent, this approach to identity and existence must also be applied to the elements of language themselves—the terms and expressions of various types that make it up, the rules, etc.—to which all identities and entities were supposed to be relativized. A regress obviously threatens, for the view is that what is (treated as) the same depends in general upon samenesses—of criteria, rules, expressions—in the domain of language. But these too must depend upon our ways of talking about them, unless identities and entities in language are to be arbitrarily exempted from re-quirements imposed on everything else. However, this problem is seldom even recognized, much less resolved.[48]

I would add that Smith's book does not resolve this problem, which is faced by Wittgenstein, Rorty, and Brandom. Advocating pragmatic relativism cannot maintain our knowledge of the real features of human

---

45. Smith, *Who's Afraid of Relativism?*, 85.
46. Smith, *Who's Afraid of Relativism?*, 107.
47. Smith, *Who's Afraid of Relativism?*, 130.
48. Willard, "Integrity of the Mental Act," 251.

community, finitude, contingency, and creaturehood. Here is an additional
claim by Willard that makes the same general point:

> And it must be pointed out that Wittgenstein (and his adher-
> ents) have never made clear exactly how the linguistic sign,
> being what it is, can function as identical in both the public do-
> main and within the individual linguistic or conscious act. . . . I
> think, one has to accept the fact that he is arguing in the manner
> of "transcendental arguments" generally, where one is told what
> must be the case, but no coherent account is given of how it is so.
> . . . He simply relies upon the magical powers of certain alleged
> components. I strongly doubt that much more can be done from
> within the prejudgments under which he, and most other Ana-
> lytical philosophers up to today, work. The vaguely empiricist/
> positivist/physicalist penumbra of assumptions about legitimate
> categories of analysis seem to me to make impossible any thor-
> ough analysis of the structure of linguistic acts, any complete
> understanding of their essential nature and possible relations,
> differences and similarities.[49]

6.3 REJECTING RELATIVISM AS OFTEN AS NECESSARY

I have argued that Smith's position, which embraces the pragmatic relativism of Wittgenstein, Rorty, and Brandom, not only falls prey to the general self-defeating nature of relativism but suffers from other flaws as well.
Rejecting relativism in the sense in which Smith asserts it does not entail
rejecting claims (which Smith rightly asserts) about human finitude, for
such claims correspond with the way things are. Human beings are contingent, finite, dependent, and creaturely. This claim, however, cannot be
maintained on the kind of relativism that Smith advocates. It can only be
maintained if these concepts in our minds really do correspond with the
way things are. It can only be known that we really are contingent, finite,
dependent, and creaturely if we accept what C. S. Lewis calls the "doctrine of
objective value": "the belief that certain attitudes are really true, and others
really false, to the kind of thing the universe is and the kind of things we
are."[50] This, however, is a radically different view of the nature of knowledge
than that presented by Smith in his book.

49. Willard, "Attaining Objectivity," 15–21.
50 Lewis, *Abolition of Man*, 12.

Of course, one might claim that this chapter criticizing Smith (and Wittgenstein and Rorty and Brandom) is just one more language game among others. As Willard believes, this would be to

> return to the authority of social practice as the basis for all critique, which means that social practice in general cannot be subject to critique. This is abundantly clear from, for example, Rorty's *Philosophy and the Mirror of Nature* as well as Lyotard's *The Postmodern Condition*. Such ancient precepts as "Thou shalt not follow a multitude to do evil" (Ex. 23:2) can be applied in specific cases, but postmodernism hardly leaves you a logical leg to stand on to oppose "professional practice," much less the spirit of the age.[51]

In the early twenty-first century, what we need to stand on is a clear account of knowledge that rejects the relativistic spirit of our age, which does so much harm to both academic and popular culture. We need a thorough account of a Christian view of knowledge and reality the type of which has been carefully defended in the work of Dallas Willard (among others), who defines knowledge non-relativistically. Willard states,

> I take knowledge in the dispositional sense to be identical with the capacity to represent a respective subject matter as it is, on an appropriate basis of thought and/or experience. In the occurrent sense it consists in actually representing, at a point in time, the respective subject matter as it is, on an appropriate basis of thought and/or experience.[52]

This is where epistemologists, especially Christian epistemologists, should spend their time, instead of failing to gain insights into the nature of knowledge from looking into epistemic relativism.

Smith begins his book from the famous quotation of St. Augustine where the great doctor of the church encourages Christians to plunder the treasures of philosophers like Plato who say things that are "true and agreeable to our faith." However, with the three philosophers discussed in Smith's book (Rorty, Wittgenstein, and Brandom) their cannons aren't thundering (as Jimmy Buffet reminds us). It isn't even clear that they have any treasure worth plundering, at least with respect to putative insights into epistemic relativism.

Let us look elsewhere for our epistemology following this advice from Dallas Willard:

51. Willard, "What Significance Has 'Postmodernism' for Christian Faith?"
52. Willard, *Knowledge and Naturalism*, 31.

One does have to make one's way, and that means coming to grip with how things are. How they *really* are. How they *truly* are. How one *knows* them to be. Rorty famously if not fatuously, says that "truth" is what your colleagues allow you to get away with. Is that so? Or is it just another thrust in the social flow of professionalized academic life? Clearly he thinks it is true, which must mean, then, that it is something that his colleagues allow him to get away with saying. It depends on who your colleagues are. But of course, he believes his statement is *true*, and not just permitted. He believes that his saying presents the situation in academic life *as it really is*, and on the basis of appropriate thought and experience. If it were "true" in the sense he states, it wouldn't be worth stating, and few people would care. But he really does care, and he thinks he has achieved valid insight into how things are. That, of course, is *knowledge* in the time-honored sense in which knowledge is necessary to human life.[53]

6.4. TAKING SCREWTAPE TO CHURCH: DONS AND DEVIL IN DIALOG

This section of this chapter consists of a fictional dialog between two dons, both Christian professors of philosophy. The dialog was motivated in part by C. S. Lewis's *The Screwtape Letters*. I tried to imagine what Screwtape would have to say about the different approaches between Smith and Willard on the topic of relativism, especially about the nature of reality, as it pertains to the Christian faith. I've taken some liberties with the textual quotations of each author but have tried to keep the central ideas intact in the flow of the conversation. Let's listen in . . .

> *Willard*: "Truth, along with goodness and beauty . . . are no longer generally thought of as realities independent of human attitudes. And that, of course, is simply what it means to say they are not 'objective.'"[54]

> *Smith*: "But, recognizing the social and communal conditions of knowledge—that our knowledge is *relative* to our social context—does not entail that everything is just made up."[55]

53. Willard, *The Bible and the University*, 30.

54. Willard, "Truth in the Fire." Notice the scope of Willard's claims.

55. Smith, *Who's Afraid of Relativism?*, 87. Smith appears to disagree with Willard here.

Willard: "That is certainly the message that comes to us from the polymorphous clouds of Postmodernism(s) that hang over all our intellectual, artistic and cultural life now."[56]

Screwtape: [I find this fascinating. I have always maintained that using rational argument,] "even if a particular train of thought can be twisted so as to end in our favor, you will find that you have been strengthening in your patient the fatal habit of attending to universal issues and withdrawing his attention from the stream of immediate sense experiences. [My] business is to fix his attention on the stream. Teach him to call it 'real life' and don't let him ask what he means by 'real.'"[57]

Smith: [But, with respect to rational argumentation and faith], "ultimately Christian faith is not something that can be proven or demonstrated."[58]

Screwtape: [Yes!] "The trouble about argument is that it moves the whole struggle on to the Enemy's own ground. He can argue too. . . . By the very act of arguing, you awake the patient's reason; and once it is awake, who can foresee the result?"[59]

Smith: [But, my view,] "appreciating that meaning is use, does not preclude a robust account of reason and logic, though it will require that we reconfigure our understanding of both."[60]

Willard: "The *main* task before us is . . . the redemption of reason, of the intellect itself. . . . It is reason itself, not just truth, that is now fighting for its life. And it, like truth, is lost as a resource of human existence unless it can be identified and used independently of the adoption or rejection of political and cultural outlooks deemed proper or improper."[61]

56. Willard, "Truth in the Fire." Postmodernism is hard to pin down.

57. Lewis, *The Screwtape Letters*, 2. The "patient" is the person with whom the devil is dealing and whom Screwtape wishes to join in hell.

58. Smith, *Who's Afraid of Relativism?*, 175. The notion of proof is ambiguous here. It could mean "prove with absolute certainty" or "have good reasons to believe."

59. Lewis, *The Screwtape Letters*, 2. The devils seem to abhor our *imago Dei* capacity of reason.

60. Smith, *Who's Afraid of Relativism?*, 116. What would it mean to reconfigure logic? Can the laws of non-contradiction or excluded middle be reconfigured?

61. Willard, "Truth in the Fire." Redeeming reason is much different than reconfiguring it.

Screwtape: [When dealing with one of my subjects on an important matter], "if I had lost my head and begun to attempt a defence by argument I should have been undone."[62]

Willard: "What we must be sure of now, and must act upon, is that only through the rescue of truth [can the Christian faith be defended]."[63]

Smith: [Well,] "ultimately, Christian faith is a know-*how* absorbed in a community of practice and can never be reduced to propositional content."[64]

Screwtape: [What I always advocate when dealing with people interested in Christianity is that] "above all, do not attempt to use science (I mean, the real sciences) as a defense against Christianity."[65]

Smith: "Evangelism [dealing with people interested in Christianity] is not just about convincing people to believe but rather inculcating them into a form of life, into a community of practice organized around a 'final story.'"[66]

Screwtape: [Indeed.] "It is no affair of yours whether those theories are true or false; the great thing is to make Christianity a mystery religion in which [the patient] feels himself one of the initiates."[67]

Smith: "Pragmatists [from whom I've learned a great deal regarding community initiation] reject *referentialist* or *representationlist* accounts of meaning and knowledge that posit a kind of magical hook between ideas 'inside' my mind and things

---

62. Lewis, *The Screwtape Letters*, 3. Even the devils recognize the power of redeemed reason.

63. Willard, "Truth in the Fire." Truth as correspondence is the crux of the matter.

64. Smith, *Who's Afraid of Relativism?*, 175. Jesus seems to make "know how" irrelevant to his kingdom: "Many will say to me on that day, 'Lord, Lord, did we not prophesy in your name and in your name drive out demons and in your name perform many miracles?' Then I will tell them plainly, 'I never knew you. Away from me, you evildoers!'" (Matt 7:21–23).

65. Lewis, *The Screwtape Letters*, 4.

66. Smith, *Who's Afraid of Relativism?*, 176. Should Christians try to convince the world that the Christian story is true?

67. Lewis, *The Screwtape Letters*, 133. The devil is all for "initiation" into a "community of practice" where truth is irrelevant.

'outside' my mind. Instead referential claims are understood as games we've learned to play *from* a community of practice."[68]

Willard: [But], "it has never been explained how, precisely, the mind (language, culture, [community]) being what it is could actually make or construct a world of things such as solar systems and blades of grass, being what they are. From the beginning of the effort centuries ago, we have many, many explanations of how and why we think of or perceive things in the world as we do. But that is, simply, quite another topic. Certainly, our thinking and perceivings themselves are, in a sense, made by us; but that is not so of what our thinkings and perceivings are about or of—our objects, our subjects."[69]

Smith: [I would say, following Rorty that] "our anxieties about correspondence [about truth] are symptoms of a contingent philosophical neurosis that needs to be *healed*, not satisfied."[70]

Screwtape: [Surely, one must] "keep [one's interlocutor's] mind off the plain antithesis between True and False."[71]

Smith: [Beyond that,] "representation and correspondence and even 'realism' are games that we learn to play from a community of social practice; . . . realisms (and attendant claims to correspondence) are *dependent upon* communities of practice. In short, our claims about 'reality' are *relative* to a community of social practice *and* the 'environment' we inhabit."[72]

Willard: [We must remember that] "thought and language, being what they are, have no ability to produce or to restructure the objects which they are about: that is, to 'construct' them.

---

68. Smith, *Who's Afraid of Relativism?*, 105. It looks like Smith and Screwtape have common ground on rejecting any notion that knowledge involves correspondence between the mind and the world.

69. Willard, "Truth in the Fire." "Communities of practice" for Smith are "language games." Willard points out here that language cannot make reality. What would it mean to say that the church's creeds or liturgies created the resurrection of Jesus?

70. Smith, *Who's Afraid of Relativism?*, 79. In 1 Cor 15:4, when St. Paul says Jesus was buried, and on the third day rose from the dead, St. Paul believed that this event was real, and that his claim to the Corinthian church accurately represented/corresponded to that reality. Smith apparently wants to heal St. Paul of his neurotic disorder.

71. Lewis, *The Screwtape Letters*, 47. Why do the devils want our mind off of the real distinction between truth and falsehood?

72. Smith, *Who's Afraid of Relativism?*, 107. Truth as correspondence is a linguistic game? Again, when St. Paul said that Jesus rose from the dead, is that true only for the Christian community or for the world too?

Of course thought and language (culture) are themselves facts or realities, and as such they have real *consequences* in the real world. But that is a very different matter from constructing objects by *merely* thinking or speaking of them."[73]

Screwtape: [Gentleman, what I always say, is that when "persuading" someone to believe something we should get them to] "believe [something], not because it is true, but for some other reason." That's the game."[74]

Smith: "So, far from being the prerequisite for Christian orthodoxy, claims to 'absolute' truth might almost be diabolical."[75]

Screwtape: "That might have been so if [one] had lived a few centuries earlier. At that time the humans still knew pretty well when a thing was proved and when it was not; and if it was proved they really believed it. They still connected thinking with doing and were prepared to alter their way of life as the result of a chain of reasoning. But what with the weekly press and other such weapons we have largely altered that. [People are now] accustomed . . . to have a dozen incompatible philosophies dancing about together inside [their] head[s]. [They don't] think of doctrines as primarily 'true' or 'false', but as 'academic' or 'practical', 'outworn' or 'contemporary', 'conventional' or 'ruthless'. Jargon, not argument, is your best ally."[76]

Willard: [I disagree. Only by defending] "'real truth' as correspondence with fact—can reason itself be salvaged, and thereby human life sustained in the power and dignity it cries out for by its nature and divine appointment. The excesses and mistakes of Modernity should not be allowed to obscure this fundamental point."[77]

---

73. Willard, "Truth in the Fire." It would be great if Willard were right about this. I'd have a lot more money in my bank account, if I only believed strongly enough.

74. Lewis, *The Screwtape Letters*, 126. The devil avoids truth-as-correspondence because it is his enemy.

75. Smith, *Who's Afraid of Relativism?*, 115. What is certainly diabolical is Srewtape's agreement with Smith to ditch the concept of "absolute truth."

76. Lewis, *The Screwtape Letters*, 1. Lewis wrote *The Screwtape Letters* in 1942. Smith is nearly eighty years too late in his claim. Over the last century of so, "absolute truth" is thought to be diabolical and the "heresy of heresies." That is why so many people reject it.

77. Willard, "Truth in the Fire." Neither modernism nor postmodernism will help, but only a philosophical realism grounded in the Christian tradition.

Chapter 7

Materialism

A Eulogy for a Metaphysical Myth

7.0 Eulogy for a Myth

7.1 Materialism and Existence: An Argument from Moreland

7.2 From the Existence of Anything Material to the Falsity of Materialism

7.3 Natural Existence Monism in Light of Existence as Essential Exemplification

7.4 Ontological Materialist Monism: Three Logical Problems

7.5 Conclusion: Materialism or Common Sense

7.0 EULOGY FOR A MYTH

I arrive at the beach. I feel the cool, wet sand at my feet. I taste the saltiness of the ocean water on my lips. I hear the sound of the crashing surf. I smell the freshness of the sea air. I see waves breaking offshore. These things are real. Every person knows what is real from ordinary common-sense experiences like these. They also tell us more. They tell us about the nature of reality itself, about existence itself. The sea, sand, surf are all material realities. I know I'm experiencing this stuff, but is this all there is? Is the material world the extent of reality?

In his essay "Funeral of a Great Myth," C. S. Lewis gives a eulogy for the mythical understanding of materialist evolution. The myth has a prelude, which as a philosopher is the place I want to focus. Lewis says, "The drama proper is preceded . . . by the most austere of all preludes; the infinite void and matter endlessly, aimlessly moving to bring forth it knows not what."[1] Lewis eulogizes the entire myth of materialistic evolution. The funeral I have in mind for materialism is less dramatic. The funeral I'm imagining is a lonely one, where materialism's coffin is simply hammered shut with a few solid rationally argued nails. Here are a few of them.

7.1 MATERIALISM AND EXISTENCE: AN ARGUMENT FROM MORELAND

Here is a good reason to think that materialism as a view of existence is self-refuting. J. P. Moreland writes, "It is self-refuting to *argue* that one *ought* to *choose* physicalism *because* he should *see* that the *evidence* is *good* for physicalism."[2]

Moreland's argument looks something like this:

Premise 1: If you argue for physicalism, then you must: (a) argue, (b) maintain "oughts," (c) choose, (d) see, and (e) hold good evidence.

Premise 2: Physicalism denies that one can a–e.

Therefore: one cannot argue for physicalism.

If premises 1 and 2 are true, then the argument is sound. Physicalists can of course claim that premise 2 is false, but then of course a–e are all going to be material things, since according to physicalism, that is all that there is. But then of course, logic itself will have to be something material, and presumably identified with brain states or something material. But then, the problem is that modus tollens (as expressed above) is *ontologically materially* no different than the fallacy of affirming the consequent. In other words, if logic is material, and if there are no reasons why we should pick one material thing over another (in this case, the material state of affairs of brain states in the configuration of modus tollens versus the brain state of the configuration of affirming the consequent), then modus tollens and affirming the consequent are materially ontologically equivalent. But are they really ontologically equivalent?

---

1. Lewis, "Funeral for a Great Myth," 86–87.
2. Moreland, *Scaling the Secular City*, 96.

Imagine dealing with someone who reasons that way. Suppose that your friend who is down and out understands that "if someone buys him a Ferrari, then someone has bought him a car." This is a very reasonable assumption. All Ferrari's are cars. So, you tell your friend, that you're going to help him buy a car. You're going to pay for it, and he can make payments back to you. So, your friend is stoked! So, you buy him a Honda Civic, and drive it to his place. But, instead of expressing gratitude, he's super disappointed and grumpy, because thought he was getting a Ferrari! He thought that since if someone bought him a Ferrari, that meant that someone bought him a car, and since you bought him a car, then it should follow that you should have bought him a Ferrari.

So, you try to explain why your destitute buddy's thinking is out of whack. But if he is a materialist who thinks that all of reality (including logical reality) is material, then he will be happy with maintaining that modus tollens and affirming the consequent are nothing but brain states or some other material state. So, he might respond by saying, "Look, since the material world is all there is, then:

If A, then B.

A.

Therefore, B

This argument is materially (physically) ontologically equivalent to:

If A, then B.

B.

Therefore, A.

"Ergo," your friend says, "you should be bringing me a Ferrari!" It's too bad that materialism about logic isn't correct. It would be nice if every time someone bought a car, they got a Ferrari! But, unfortunately, the real world and logic isn't like that. Again, we can *try* to live like that. *We* can *make* logic out to be a power trip that we force people to accept. If materialism implies that logic is like that, and if thinkers actually believe that logic is like that, then this is one more reason that common-sense realism really is the heresy of heresies.

7.2 From the Existence of Anything Material to the Falsity of Materialism

Here is another argumentative nail for materialism's coffin. If the account of the nature of existence derived from common-sense experience is correct, then this implies that the existence of anything material implies that not everything is material. If there is anything material, then not all things are material, and thus, *materialism* is false. Here is an argument for this idea. Consider the following four propositions:

M: Material things exist.

O: Material things express order.

S: Something is self-ordered.

E: All order is evolved.

Consider the following deduction:

1. If M then O.

2. M.

3. O.

7. If O, then S or E.

5. S or E.

6. Not E.

7. Therefore, S.

Premise 1 is reasonable from our discussion of existence as essential exemplification, which is known through ordinary common-sense experience. If any material thing exists, it exemplifies an essence. This involves a relation. All relations are ordered things; all ordered things express order. So, if something exists, then necessarily it expresses order.

Premise 2 is straightforward. Look, if I have to argue with you about this one, you should just put the book down. Common-sense realism takes this premises as obvious, skepticism notwithstanding. Premise 3 follows from 1 and 2 by modus ponens.

Premise 4 seems like a real (not a false) dichotomy in the consequent of the conditional. Either there is something that is self-ordered, that is ordered intrinsically, not ordered by something or due to something other than itself; or everything is ordered by something other than itself (i.e., evolved). Premise 5 follows from 3 and 7.

The evidence for premise 6 is supported by Dallas Willard's notion that there is a logical limit to evolved order. Here is what he says about this idea:

> Let us quite generally state then *that any sort of evolution of order of any kind will always presuppose pre-existing order and pre-existing entities governed by it.* It follows as a simple matter of logic that not all order evolved. Given the physical world— however much of evolution it may or may not contain—there is or was some order *in it* which did not evolve. However, it may have originated (if it originated), that order did not evolve. We come here upon a logically insurpassable *limit* to what evolution, however it may be understood, can accomplish.[3]

If Willard is right about this, then premise 6 is reasonable. The conclusion follows from premises 5 and 6 taken together.

This argument isn't new. It is part and parcel of a type of argument for theism. I am not here arguing for theism, but simply for the fact that if *material things* exist, then *materialism* is false. Materialism (and materialistic evolution) cannot explain the necessary immaterial order in material things. If it is true that existence is essential exemplification, then if anything exists, an essence is exemplified. If the rejoinders to the Bradleyan regress objection to existence as essential exemplification stand (as discussed in chapter 2), we can say that, necessarily, if anything exists then, since relations exist and order exists, materialism is false. So much for the second nail. Let's look at the third and final nail.

7.3 NATURAL EXISTENCE MONISM IN LIGHT OF EXISTENCE AS ESSENTIAL EXEMPLIFICATION[4]

In this next section, I want to provide a rather technical argument against materialism, which puts a third (and hopefully final) nail in materialism's coffin. The argument is that if existence is essential exemplification, then natural existence monism (materialism) cannot be true. The two are incompatible. And since we have good reasons from common-sense experience to believe that existence is essential exemplification, then we shouldn't be natural existence monists (materialists). It's time to say our final goodbyes to this notion of reality.

Consider the following five ideas.

3. Willard, "Language, Being, God," 209.

4. Logic Alert! The next two sections are fairly technical and a little bit wonky. If you feel like you've had a good introduction to some of the problems with materialism, then skip to section 7.5.

1.1 Existence is essential exemplification.

1.2 Only one concrete material object (the blobject) exists.[5]

1.3 Existence monism is understood as: $\exists x \, (Cx \, \& \, \forall y \, (Cy \to x=y))$.[6]

    1.3.1 Let C = the blobject.

    1.3.2 Let x = essence.

    1.3.3 Let y = existence.

1.4 Assume Leibniz's notion of the indiscernibility of identicals: $\forall x \, \forall y$ $[(x = y) \to (\forall P)(Px \leftrightarrow Py)]$.[7]

    1.4.1 Let P = any property.

1.5 The blobject has no real parts.[8]

If we take 1.1–1.5 together, then we will have at least three problems. The first problem obtains between 1.1–1.4 taken together and centers on the distinction between essence and existence. The second is due to a non-monistic view of the existential quantifier in 1.3 taken together with 1.4. The third is a problem between 1.1 and 1.5 taken together. Let us look at these problems in turn.

7.4 ONTOLOGICAL MATERIALIST MONISM: THREE LOGICAL PROBLEMS

First Problem

If 1.1. is true, if existence is essential exemplification, implying that for anything that exists, it exists because it exemplifies an essence, then for any metaphysically monistic view of nature, the one thing that exists (the

---

5. There are two "Blobjectivist Ontological Theses" according to Horgan and Potrč: 1) "There is really just one concrete particular, namely, the whole universe (the blobject)."
and
2) "The blobject has enormous spatiotemporal structural complexity and enormous local variability—even though it does not have any genuine parts" (Horgan and Potrč, *Austere Realism*, 3).

6. See Shaffer, "Monism."

7. See Moreland and Craig, *Philosophical Foundations*, 194.

8. Horgan and Potrč, *Austere Realism*, 3.

blobject), exists because it exemplifies an essence. But if this is true, then there are some problems when considering how to formulate existence monism.

Consider the following formulation of existence monism. Existence monism is understood as: $\exists x \, (Cx \, \& \, \forall y \, (Cy \rightarrow x=y))$.

Let C = the blobject.

Let x = essence.

Let y = existence.

Thus, substituting x and y for essence and existence respectively, natural monism would read as follows: Natural Existence Monism (NEM): "There exists an essence such that the blobject has an essence and for all existences, if the blobject exists then existence is identical to essence." If this is a correct understanding of natural existence monism, then several problems arise.

First, NEM implies that nature's (the one thing that exists in the natural world i.e., the blobject's) existence and its essence are identical. The question immediately arises: given 1.4, are there things that are possibly true of essences (including the blobject's) that need not be true of existence (including the blobject's)? Some possible things that can be true of essences that are not true of existence are the following. First, it is at least logically possible that essences can exist un-instantiated. If this is true, then whatever the nature of the blobject's essence, it is at least possible that it exist un-instantiated. However, if we ask whether existence can exist un-instantiated, this seems to lead to an obvious absurdity. For existence to exist, something must be instantiated. The idea of non-instantiated (thus nonexistent) existence is absurd. So, if this is right, given the indiscernibility of identicals, since essences and existence are discernible with respect to the possibility of the former, but not the later existing un-instantiated, it would follow that the two are not identical for a natural object. However, if they are not identical, then NEM cannot be true.

Second, it is possible to conceive that *existence* adds something to *essence*, but *not vice versa*? For we can conceive of essences (e.g., caninity), and we can even conceive of essences being exemplified by a particular dog, Fido. However, these conceptions are distinct from the actualization of the essence caninity in a particular dog. Essences exemplified (i.e., existence) adds something to both the conception of an essence, and the *conception* of an actualized essence. Thus, existence adds something to essence.

What about the other way around? Does essence add something to existence? If existence is the actualization of an essence, then no. An essence doesn't add something to existence, rather existence is essence in act, essential exemplification. One reason for thinking this is that existence is always the existence of something (some essence); the idea of the existence of nothing (no essence) would be absurd.

A proponent of NEM would have to maintain that existence and essence are identical. Given the law of the indiscernibility of identicals, if the two are identical, then there is no discernibility between existence and essence. However, it appears that existence adds to essence, but essence does not add to existence. Thus, since essence and existence are discernible, they are, contrary to the natural existence monist, not identical. Thus, if essence and existence are not identical, then NEM cannot be true.

Second Problem

To what extent does the expression of monism in 1.2 above rely on a non-monistic view of the existential quantifier? If the existential quantifier in 1.3 is understood following Frege as "explicitly analyzed quantification in terms of predication"[9] then what can predication amount to if 1.1 is the case?

Let us revisit the following formalization of existence monism as: $\exists x\,(Cx$ & $\forall y\,(Cy \rightarrow x = y))$.

Let C = the blobject.

Let x = essence.

Let y = existence.

Natural Existence Monism: "There exists an essence such that the blobject has an essence and for all existences, if the blobject exists then existence is identical to essence."

The problem that appears here is how one reconciles a Fregean understanding of existential quantification in terms of predication given the identity of essence and existence in this formalization of natural existential monism. If the existential quantifier is understood in terms of predication, and if predication is always the having of a property p by some subject S, then if monism were true, predication would be a relation, not of the *having* of a property p by subject S, but rather of *identity*. The essence predicated and the subject of predication would thus be identical. However, in addition to the arguments raised in 2.1 against the identity of essence and existence for NEM, there are some fairly common-sense reasons to disbelieve that predication is a relation of identity. Three problems arise here.

---

9. Uzquiano, "Quantifiers and Quantification."

First, consider the distinction between accidental and essential predicates. The predicate of being brown, when predicated of a dog, is surely non-identical to the predicate of being a canine. A particular dog, e.g., Fido could lack the predicate of being brown, still exist, and still exist as Fido. But surely Fido could not lack the predicate of being a canine and still exist as a dog, even if he could exist as Fido.

Second, if predication is a relation of identity, then any two predicates would be identical. However, this also seems absurd when one considers the logical relations obtaining between various predicates such as: the predicate of being trilateral and the predicate of being green. Being three-sided is identical with being a color?! Surely, this is absurd.

Third, if predication is nothing more than a relation of identity, then non-monadic relations themselves become impossible. This would imply that predication itself and all other relations just are the monadic relation of identity. However, the formalized expression of NEM $\exists x$ (Cx & $\forall y$ ($Cy \rightarrow x=y$)) relies not just on the existential quantifier, but also on the logical relations of conjunction and material implication. However, if NEM is true and if the existential quantifier is understood in terms of predication then these together imply that existential quantification is a monadic relation of identity. In that case, the conjunction and implication are also monadic relations of identity.

However, this would imply that the truth tables for both conjunction and implication are identical, but surely they are not. A conjunction can be true in only one way (when both conjuncts are true) and false in three ways, whereas an implication can be true in three ways and only false in one way (when the antecedent is true and the consequent is false). Thus, if NEM were true, then conjunction and implication are both relations of identity. However, a common-sense understanding of these logical operators would imply otherwise. And if the common-sense understanding of these operators is correct, then NEM cannot be true.

Third Problem

1.1 (existence should be understood as the actualization of an essence) and 1.5 (the blobject, the one thing that exists on the view that nature is NEM) entail the following dilemma: Either existence and essence are identical or existence and essence are non-identical. If they are identical, then we are faced with all of the problems addressed in Problem 1 above. However, if they are non-identical, and if natural existence monism requires that the blobject (the one natural thing that exists) has no real parts, then natural existence monism must be given up.

7.5. CONCLUSION: MATERIALISM OR COMMON SENSE

I have argued that existence should be understood as essential exemplification, following Thomas Aquinas. The knowledge of this comes from our ordinary common-sense experiences of the natural world, both exterior and interior. If this view is reasonable, then it implies the falsity of NEM and thus materialism. We can add this view to the list of ideas that Chesterton considered at the beginning of this work which run contrary to common sense.

CHAPTER 8

Idealism
Collapsing Kantianism

8.0 AN IDEAL INTRODUCTION TO IDEALISM

I arrive at the beach. I feel the cool, wet sand at my feet. I taste the saltiness of the ocean water on my lips. I hear the sound of the crashing surf. I smell the freshness of the sea air. I see waves breaking offshore. These things are real. Every person knows what is real from ordinary common-sense experiences like these. They also tell us more. They tell us about the nature of reality itself, about existence itself.

When I consider my experiences, I have to wonder, what exactly am I experiencing? Sometimes, especially during a particularly clear, off-shore Santa Ana wind, sunset surf session, I wonder if I'm not in a movie, and the things I'm looking at are really on a screen in front of me. Maybe what I'm experiencing is just the stuff on the screen? Maybe there's something behind the screen that I can't get to? Maybe all of my experiences of reality are just made by my mind? Maybe the stuff beyond my mind is real, but I can never know it? Is reality like a movie in my head?

This chapter will consider the central problems of a form of idealism that stems from Immanuel Kant. We will look at Kant's epistemology and metaphysics and their application to ethics. I will argue that Christian common-sense realism and the ethics which flows from it is more reasonable to a Kantian ethics based on Kantian metaphysics and epistemology. Kant is the starting point of the "idealisms" that flow through the nineteenth, twentieth, and into the twenty-first centuries (e.g., Hegel, Fichte, Schopenhauer, Heidegger, Brandom). Here I will argue that any metaphysics that flows from the Kantian distinction between noumenal and phenomenal "worlds" is fated to have serious problems for living life well.

Kant's epistemology and metaphysics yield an ethical system that is unable to ground morality as satisfactorily as Christian realism is able to. I will argue that Kant's epistemology and metaphysics logically cannot meet the epistemic requirements for taking seriously the kinds of ethical realities that are expected of human beings, especially given Christian revelation. First, I will focus on the connections between Kant's epistemology, metaphysics, and the categorical imperative in order to show how Kant's deontology rests considerably on his epistemology and metaphysics. Second, I will show what an application of Kant's epistemology and ethics would have for our understanding of Jesus' moral teachings. Third, I will consider whether or not the epistemic requirements for Jesus' ethics are such that they allow for an ethics consistent with Kant's. Fourth, I will argue that Jesus' moral commands can best be understood on a broadly realistic non-Kantian metaphysics, epistemology, and ethics, with a heavy emphasis on the teleological structure of our intrinsic epistemic and ethical essences as human beings made in the image of God.

8.1 KANT'S ONTOLOGY, EPISTEMOLOGY, AND ETHICS: NOUMENA AND PHENOMENA

Kant's metaphysics and epistemology are inseparable. They rest upon the idea that we only have knowledge of two things: (1) the "phenomenal world" of experience and (2) the structure of the categories of the understanding also inside of us. Apart from this, we know nothing of the noumenal world, of the world as it is apart from our experiences. Thus, metaphysics is simply the study of what is internal to the mind's categories and structures. This epistemology limits our knowledge to what is internal to our experiences and makes metaphysics a study of these structures, with anything beyond them simply unknowable.

This is the historical starting point for the various "idealisms" from the early nineteen-hundreds to the present. Idealism in its various forms denies the common-sense realist notion that the qualities of an object can be present before the mind. Idealism denies that "there is a real bridge between the mind and reality" as Chesterton argued. Given the denial of common-sense realism, there are important ramifications and consequences for the other areas of philosophy, especially ethics. Kantian and idealist metaphysics and epistemology apply to how we live our lives. If the idealists are right, then ethical knowledge will necessarily be limited to the realm internal to the self, including knowledge of one's own actions as they are known to affect the noumenal world internal to one's own experience.

Kant's task at the beginning of the *Groundwork of the Metaphysics of Morals* is to "know how much pure reason can accomplish in both cases and from what sources it draws this a priori teaching of its own—whether the latter job be carried on by all teachers of morals."[1] The "supreme principle of morality"[2] ends up being that to which a perfectly good will conforms in its reflections upon the understanding *a priori*, namely the categorical imperative: "act only in accordance with that maxim through which you can at the same time will that it become a universal law."[3] So, Kant's epistemology, and the metaphysics that underpins it, seems to logically entail that the categorical imperative is internal to the self. Kant's epistemology, metaphysics, and ethics are internal to reason and its capacities for reflection upon itself. They are dependent for their existence on the structure of experiences through the categories of the understanding. The good life is ontologically found only within yourself.

Thus, Kant's answers to the main questions of ethics are these.

Question: What is the good life?

Answer: The good life is a life of the conformity of reason to the moral law through rational reflection upon the categorical imperative, entailing actions that follow this supreme principle of duty.

Question: Who is the good person?

Answer: The good person is the one whose will is good in so far as it conforms to the moral law.

1. Kant, *Groundwork*, 2.
2. Kant, *Groundwork*, 5.
3. Kant, *Groundwork*, 31.

Our task is to take a look at whether Kantian-based idealism is a reasonable approach to metaphysics, epistemology, and the ethics that flow
from them. Before we look at Kant's idealism, let us reexamine Christian
common-sense realism, as a way to evaluate Kant's views.

8.2 CHRISTIAN COMMON-SENSE REALISM AS AN ALTERNATIVE TO KANTIAN IDEALISM

In chapter 2 section 2.2.3, in the discussion of realism and the New Testament, I argued that realism is presupposed through the Bible. In chapter 4, I
argued that Jesus is the foundation of being itself. Thus, Jesus was not only a
realist, he is the foundation for realism! If this is right, then Jesus, the moral
teacher, will teach us from the perspective of a realist.

Jesus has a clear view on ethics and also presents us with answers to
the two main questions that any ethics will ask. What is the good life? Who
is the good person? While Jesus dealt with these questions, his answers to
them differ from other philosophers. Jesus' answers are wrapped up in his
identity as the Son of God, as the one who is the great "I Am." The good life,
according to Jesus, is one conformed to the will of the Father, and the good
person is one who adequately reflects Jesus' character. The ontology of Jesus'
ethics is internally linked to Jesus' identity. Value properties are from him
and for him and through him. Ethical knowledge comes to its proper *telos*
by being born anew in Jesus' kingdom. Jesus also provides a specific plan to
become well off. His "way" or path to well-being and well-doing involves
various practices or disciplines that have been well recognized and well established as being practically successful in the lives of millions throughout
history.

What I want to emphasize here is not only what Jesus' ethic involves,
but that it is grounded in reality, in who Jesus really is. Ethics is determined
by Jesus' essence. Jesus' ethic, unlike Kant's deontological system, is not
merely a system of ideas developed, like Kant's, through rational reflection
internal to the mind, cut off from what is outside the self. Jesus' ethics is
part and parcel of *who he is*. Jesus' ethics stands in an internal relation to his
person and identity.

The Scriptures bear witness to this internal relation. John 1:4, "In him
was life." The good life is not merely in the system of ideas presented by
Jesus; it is *in him*. John 10:10, "I have come that they may have life and have
it to the full." Again, Jesus is *identifying* himself as the source of the good
life. Note well the scope of this life: it is full. The Apostle Paul recognizes
this intimate connection between the person of Jesus and ethics, when in

Philippians 1:11 he prays for the believers in Philippi, that they would be "filled with the fruit of righteousness that comes through Jesus Christ." The New Testament Greek word for "righteousness" is the same word that Plato uses in the *Republic*, where it is most often translated as "justice." Truly living well and being well comes through being properly related to the person of Jesus. The Apostle Peter also recognizes this truth when he writes in 2 Peter 1:3, "His [Jesus'] divine power has given us everything we need for life and godliness through our knowledge of him who called us by his own glory and goodness."

So now we have a puzzle. Is Kant's supreme principle of morality, really becoming a good person or having a good life, found merely through rational reflection and conforming one's will to the categorical imperative? Is ethics determined by a metaphysics that is cut off from the world outside the self? Or, does becoming a good person and having a good life depend on the relation of one's soul to the person of Jesus, the God-man who was really seen, heard, and touched? Kant answers the question this way:

> Even the Holy One of the Gospel must first be compared with our ideal of moral perfection before *he is cognized as such*; even he says of himself: why do you call me (whom you see) good? None is good (the archetype of the good) but God only (whom you do not see). But whence have we the concept of God as the highest good? Solely from the *idea* of moral perfection that reason frames a priori and connects inseparably with the concept of a free will.[4]

Kant seems to be saying that Jesus' ethic is recognized to be good because it conforms to the ethics of the categorical imperative (CI). The CI is generated by the operations of reason internal to the mind, cut off from the real common-sense world (which Kant calls the "noumenal world"). It is all *a priori* and in your head! Common-sense experience is irrelevant to the ethics at hand. Only the structures of the human mind are needed to derive the nature and reality of the CI.

Here is where the trouble begins. The CI (and the metaphysics that determine it) is logically antecedent as a condition for bringing about the good life. If the CI is a logically antecedent or prior to the good life, this implies that the CI would be a sufficient condition for the good life. If this is the case, then it would appear that the CI is really all that we need for true well-being, and Jesus' ethic (and the metaphysics of Jesus' identity that ground it) is merely an instance of the CI. As an instance, of course Jesus' life and teaching would conform to the CI. So, perhaps Jesus' moral commands

4. Kant, *Groundwork*, 21 (emphasis mine).

simply imply that we are really to conform ourselves to the CI in the way that Jesus did? This cannot be the case.

Jesus' ethics rests on an epistemology and metaphysics behind it, as does Kant's, and indeed as does any possible ethics. But Jesus' ontology and epistemology are radically at odds with Kant's. Thus, their ethics are incompatible. What type of epistemology does Jesus have? With respect to truth understood as correspondence to reality, Jesus is the foundation for both truth makers and truth bearers.[5]

Now Kant also maintains a kind of correspondence view of truth. In the *Critique of Pure Reason* Kant states that truth is "the agreement of knowledge with its object" (A191), but he seems to accept rather than argue for the view that "truth consists in the agreement of knowledge with the object" (A191).[6] In the "Appendix to the Transcendental Dialectic: The Regulative Employment of the Ideas of Pure Reason," he concludes, "The categories lead to truth, that is to the conformity of our concepts with the object" (A642).[7] The problem for Kant, however, is that the conformity of concept with object is never with the object as it is in itself, but only with the object as experienced, shaped through the categories of the understanding. For Kant, correspondence is never between our minds and the way things are, only between our concepts and the way objects appear in experience. Kantian "correspondence" is an "internal-to-the-mind" correspondence and is not a correspondence *between* the mind and common-sense reality.

Jesus' epistemology was a "common-sense realist" view, according to Doug Groothuis, as Jesus "would often invoke the reality of the external world to make various theological points."[8] Thus, common-sense realism in this sense runs contrary to Kantian idealism. The realist would maintain that we do have access to the way things are independently of any intermediate categorical "filter," and thus we can know things in themselves. A Jesus-centered epistemology is at radical odds with any type of Kantian "Midas touch epistemology."[9] This implies the possibility of an ethics that is grounded in common-sense reflection on our direct knowledge of Jesus' teachings and life, and not necessarily on merely rational transcendental principles like the categorical imperative.

Jesus' epistemology is deeper than a mere account of what type of knowledge we have. Jesus not only has an epistemology and metaphysics

5. See Mosteller, *Theories of Truth*, 33.
6. Kant, *Kant's Critique of Pure Reason*, 220.
7. Kant, *Kant's Critique of Pure Reason*, 532.
8. Groothuis, *On Jesus*, 51.
9. I owe this idea to Dallas Willard.

but is the ground for any epistemology and metaphysics whatsoever. The Apostle Paul also indicates that Jesus has some connection with the discipline of epistemology in Colossians 2:3 where he writes that Jesus is the one "in whom are hidden all the treasures of wisdom and knowledge." Paul gives great scope to Jesus' connection with knowledge. It is exhaustive. Note the axiological component of Paul's claims. Knowledge present in Jesus has value, and Paul indicates the internal relation of epistemology and ethics in Jesus. So, Jesus' moral commands are rooted in an epistemology and an ontology that is both realistic *and* grounded in Jesus' identity.

8.3 JESUS AND ARISTOTLE CONTRA KANT

Kant's deontological ethics is grounded on rational reflection upon the universal principles contained in the categorical imperative. If Jesus' moral claims were to be grounded on a Kantian foundation, then our obedience to Jesus' commands wouldn't really even need Jesus. They could be done purely through rational reflection. We would not need Jesus' incarnation, virgin birth, life, teachings, death, resurrection, ascension, future return in glory, and the giving of the Holy Spirit to infuse and help us with a remembrance to our minds and power to our wills. Yet it is just these very things that Jesus has done for us, which militate against the Kantian notion that becoming a good person or living the good life can come about through the mind's internal idealistic reflection. If the categorical imperative is all we need for life and godliness, then what's the point of the incarnation in the first place? Why have a real God-man born in a stable in Bethlehem? Why the blood, torture, and suffering of the cross? Why the death by crucifixion of the Jesus? Why the physical, real resurrection? Why the bodily ascension into heaven? Why come again in glory to judge the living and the dead? Why a kingdom that will have no end? These are all common-sense realities. Why do we need them if true human goodness can come from inside our own heads? The reality of each of these falsify idealist philosophy.

The incarnation gives us knowledge of God, and through Jesus' epistemology, we have direct immediate access to and knowledge of God. However, on Kant's view (as expressed in his *Prolegomena to Any Future Metaphysics*) our knowledge of God, "the theological idea," and other transcendental ideas are "nothing but pure concepts of reason which cannot be given in any experience, the questions which reason asks us about them are put to us not by the objects, but by mere maxims of our reason for the sake of its own satisfaction."[10] These concepts are "merely regulative" for human life.[11] Kant adds:

> We must therefore accept an immaterial being, a world of understanding, and a Supreme Being (all mere *noumena*), because in them only, as things in themselves, reason finds that completion and satisfaction, which *it can never hope for it can never hope for* in the derivation of appearances from their homogenous grounds. . . . But as *we can never cognise these beings of understanding as they are in themselves*, that is, as definitely, yet we must *assume them* as regards the sensible.[12]

In addition, Kant states, "We thereby acknowledge that the Supreme Being is quite inscrutable and even unthinkable in any definite way as to what he is in itself."[13] Jesus' claims about his relation to the Father run radically at odds with Kantian philosophy, and all forms of idealism that derive from it. To see this, take one of Jesus' more straightforwardly simple claims, "He who has seen me has seen the Father" (John 14:9). Really seeing Jesus in the common-sense, ordinary way means to observe him directly. Really seeing Jesus puts our minds in direct contact with *what is*. Really seeing Jesus gives us good evidence for who he is, what he taught, how he acted, and what he did. This is simple observational evidence. It is common sense. Really seeing and accepting Jesus is the greatest fear of those who accuse common-sense realists of committing the heresy of heresies, for "He's the highest personality in philosophy."[14]

According to Kant, we have never even see Jesus as he is. We only see our experiences of him. Jesus, contra Kant, relies on this simple notion of seeing him, which involves a very simple notion of direct immediate awareness, which common-sense realism maintains. Simple direct realism regarding our knowledge of God through Jesus is something quite different from Kant's positing the notion of God as a regulative notion for our actions, and that God and Jesus with him are mere "noumenal-we-know-not-what."

Things seem to get even worse if we speculate what Jesus' own knowledge of God would be like, if Kant's epistemology were correct. Could Jesus even make the claims that he made about his own knowledge of God? When Jesus claims that he has seen the Father (John 6:46), what could this mean on a Kantian epistemology? Jesus couldn't claim to have direct access to

10. Kant, *Kant's Prolegomena*, 118.
11. Kant, *Kant's Prolegomena*, 118.
12. Kant, *Kant's Prolegomena*, 131.
13. Kant, *Kant's Prolegomena*, 131.
14. Lockridge, "My King."

the Father. Since Jesus was fully human, he would only access the Father through his human experience. The Father would merely be known to Jesus as a "regulative ideal."

Imagine if you said that about your own dad. Imagine if one of your friends you grew up with, who spent a lot of time at your house with your family, runs into you one day after not seeing you for a few years. Suppose he asks about your dad. Would you respond by saying: "I can never definitely really know my Dad or how he is really doing; I can only assume whether he is or how he is doing"? Given our real experiences of our family members and their well-being, no one could reasonably answer in a Kantian way.

One might object that Jesus' "seeing" the Father isn't done as a human being with the cognitive structures of the understanding that make possible human experience, on a Kantian epistemology. However, in John 5:19 Jesus claims *to do what he sees* the Father doing, and this implies that his own knowledge of the Father is completely present to him as a human being, and not merely as a nonhuman divine person.

Because Jesus' ethics, and thus his moral commands, require a realist metaphysics and epistemology that give us direct and epistemically secure knowledge of God, a Kantian metaphysics, epistemology, and ethics are radically at odds with Jesus' moral commands, and ultimately collapse. So, if we want to reason about Jesus' ethics from a secure metaphysical and epistemological standpoint, we should look elsewhere than Kant.

But shouldn't we use philosophy to help our Christian worldview, as Origen wrote, "I wish to ask you to extract from the philosophy of the Greeks [or Prussians in Kant's case] what may serve as a course of study or a preparation for Christianity" just as "by spoiling the Egyptians, they [the Hebrews] might have material for the preparation of the things which pertained to the service of God."[15] Yes! But only if there's something worth taking! In Kant's case, as we saw with relativism, it appears that there is nothing worth plundering.

If Christians must plunder the pagans, there might be some things worth looking at over in Aristotle's camp. His ethics, which is closer to Jesus', might provide philosophical resources for an elaboration of Christian realist philosophy. In the *Nichomachean Ethics*, Aristotle grounds human well-being or happiness in a direct account of our understanding of human nature and especially our human *telos* or end as rational animals. Happiness there is something like: human function (i.e., the rational activity of the soul), plus virtue (i.e., a mean between extremes relative to the individual), plus a complete life (i.e., a life involving temporal consistency of character and

15. Origen, "A Letter from Origin to Gregory," 393.

certain external goods, e.g., political life and basic material goods). Jesus' ethics is much more consistent with this Aristotelian way of understanding the good life and being a good person than it is with Kantian idealism.

8.4 CONCLUSION: IDEAL REALITY

Jesus understood real human nature as both its author/creator and as an inhabitant in it. Jesus took on humanity in the incarnation. Unfortunately, Kant maintained that we can have no knowledge of ourselves as we are in ourselves. Jesus, on the other hand, knew what was in man (John 2:25) as well as who he was in himself. This allows Jesus to be able to pinpoint the telos of man as a being made in the image of God. Jesus states, "Therefore, you are to be perfect as your heavenly father is perfect," and this notion of perfect (*teleioi* in Greek) is at its root a teleological notion. It is the *goal*, the "that for the sake of which" we are to live and be in right relationship to Jesus and to the Father. Thus, our following of Jesus' moral commands ought to be done on non-Kantian and more broadly Aristotelian, but essentially Christian common-sense, metaphysics, epistemology, and ethics.

CHAPTER 9

Pragmatism
How to Slide from Reality

9.0 INTRODUCTION: A SLIDE FROM REALITY

I arrive at the beach. I feel the cool, wet sand at my feet. I taste the saltiness of the ocean water on my lips. I hear the sound of the crashing surf. I smell the freshness of the sea air. I see waves breaking offshore. These things are real. Every person knows what is real from ordinary common-sense experiences like these. They also tell us more. They tell us about the nature of reality itself, about existence itself. Sometimes at the beach, I only notice what's important to me, what works for me, what matters to me, and what is in my own interests. There's a lot here, after all. Maybe what is real just is what makes a practical difference to my life. Everything else is just not practical for me, if real to me at all.

This chapter introduces a brief survey of pragmatic views of reality. Pragmatic views of reality usually consider metaphysics to be a matter of speculation with very little value or utility. The main figures and theories addressed in this chapter will include, C. S. Peirce, William James, John Dewey, and Sidney Hook. I argue that relegating metaphysical reflection for pragmatic reasons cuts human inquiry off from the main data by means of which human life can be practically lived.

9.1 C. S. PEIRCE: GETTING CLEAR ON REALITY

In 1877, C. S. Peirce wrote about how to think carefully about philosophy. The way that Peirce tried to help us to get our ideas clear is not far from the kind of realism defended in this book. Peirce wrote:

> Its fundamental hypothesis, restated in more familiar language, is this: There are real things, whose characters are entirely independent of our opinions about them; those realities affect our senses according to regular laws, and, though our sensations are as different as are our relations to the objects,[1] yet, by taking advantage of the laws of perception, we can ascertain by reasoning how things really are, and any man, if he have sufficient experience and reason enough about it, will be led to the one true conclusion. The new conception here involved is that of reality.[2]

Peirce indicates that it is through the method of experience (he calls it the "method of science"), as opposed to other methods of belief-formation (tenacity, authority, and *a priori* methods), that we can come to have clear

---

1. What Peirce means by "different" here is crucial. For common-sense realism, the mind (our soul) receives the forms/qualities had by objects. Of course, there is a distinction between a quality present in an object and the quality as it is in the mind. The way in which the quality is instantiated in an object is different than the way in which the same quality is present before the mind. However, the quality is the same. What is received by the mind is the quality of an object. The mind instantiates the qualities of objects in an *intentional* way, what is present to the mind is *about* the qualities of the object. The qualities instantiated in the object are the same qualities that are intentionally instantiated in the mind. They are related by the reality of the same quality which is identical between object and what is received in the mind. Richard Rorty, an heir of early twentieth-century pragmatism, has a book called *Philosophy and the Mirror of Nature*. The analogy, which Rorty critiques, assumes that the mind "mirrors" nature. When Peirce says the two are different, he could be assuming this sort of analogy. On the other hand, he could mean, following common-sense realism, that the mind receives the forms present in objects. So, the question is crucial: By "different," does Peirce mean "mirror" or "receive"?

2. Peirce, "The Fixation of Belief," 11–12.

ideas of reality. There are perceptual laws by which, with the aid of reason, we can come to have true beliefs about how things are. This is in broad and general agreement with the kind of Thomistic realism that was discussed in chapter 2. It is through sense experience and our judgments that we can come to see clearly the nature of reality. However, there are significant differences with Peirce, and even more significant differences between Peirce and other pragmatist philosophers.

In dealing with questions about the nature of reality in "How to Make Our Ideas Clear," Peirce distinguishes between three increasingly clear grades or levels of clarity: 1st familiarity, 2nd definition, and 3rd practical/ pragmatic. In dealing with existence, Peirce says: "Thus we may define the real as that whose characters are independent of what anybody may think them to be."[3] This seems perfectly at home with common-sense realism: reality is indifferent to what we think about it.

However, Peirce seems to connect reality to epistemology in the following way. He writes: "The opinion which is fated to be ultimately agreed to by all who investigate, is what we mean by the truth, and the object represented in this opinion is the real. That is the way I would explain reality."[4] There is some ambiguity in the phrase "the object represented in this opinion is the real." If taken epistemically, it could mean that what is the real just is the object represented, i.e., the reality is the representation itself, but not the object itself. Given what is said above, it more likely means that the reality is not the same as the representation, but that reality just is what is represented by "final agreement." Still, the worry of making reality connected to opinion (to epistemology), whether linguistic or mental, is worrisome for the common-sense realist.

Later in the same paper Peirce deals with this ambiguity: "But the answer to this is that, on the one hand, reality is independent, not necessarily of thought in general, but only of what you or I or any finite number of men may think about it; and that, on the other hand, though the object of the final opinion depends on what that opinion is, yet what that opinion is does not depend on what you or I or any man thinks."[5] This is really worrisome. How is reality not independent of thought in general? Was there oxygen before there were human beings to think about it? Of course, from what Peirce says above, this seems to be a fairly obvious, "Yes." But how is it *dependent* on thought in general? There seems to be a metaphysical tension in Peirce's work here.

3. Peirce, "How to Make Our Ideas Clear," 298.
4. Peirce, "How to Make Our Ideas Clear," 300.
5. Peirce, "How to Make Our Ideas Clear, 300.

In a later work from 1893, "Immortality in Light of Synechism," Peirce writes that his view of metaphysics, which he calls "synechism," is a metaphysics that "flatly denies" the Parmenidian saying "being is, and not-being is nothing."[6] He says, "Being is a matter of more or less, so as to merge insensibly into nothing."[7] The reason that Peirce gives for this is consistent with his pragmatic understanding of reality from the works discussed above. He writes, "To say that a thing *is* is to say that in the upshot of intellectual progress it will attain a permanent status in the realm of ideas. Now, as no experiential question can be answered with absolute certainty, so we never can have reason to think that any given idea will either become unshakably established or be forever exploded."[8]

The problem that appears here is threefold. First, there is the problem with claiming that being merges into nothing. It is not particularly clear how this idea is arrived at, even on Peirce's own third-grade level of scientific clarity. Perhaps it depends on what "nothing" amounts to. It is hard to imagine anything merging with "nothing" if "nothing" doesn't exist.

Second, there is the lingering question of the relationship between the metaphysical and the epistemic. Can't we say that a thing is, and make no reference to "intellectual progress" or any inquiry whatsoever?

Third, from the fact that a question cannot be answered with absolute certainty (especially one that deals with natural experience), does it follow that we don't have reason to maintain that an idea is "unshakably established"? If it is reasonable to gain from sense experience that existence is essential exemplification, it might be possible that one lacks absolute certainty of this knowledge, but there is a deep connection between existence (from what we know by way of sense experience) and the nature of logical realities. The notion of contradiction is not only known purely a priori, but it can also be understood in an a posteriori way, as we can experience the relationship of contradiction in the way that we experience the relationship of truth. Yet, the relationship of contradiction is a necessary relation, and if tied to existence, then it is not only logically necessary, but metaphysically necessary as well. So, it seems that Peirce unfairly separates logic, metaphysics, and common-sense experience. Must they be so separated? Perhaps pragmatism as a method of inquiry requires it.

6. Peirce, "Immortality," 2.

7. Peirce, "Immortality," 2.

8. Peirce, "Immortality," 2.

9.2 WILLIAM JAMES: REALITY SLIPS AWAY

It seems to me that the tensions in Peirce's pragmatism become further pronounced as pragmatism progresses historically. For example, in his *The Principles of Psychology*, William James writes, "What we need is practical reality, reality for ourselves: and, to have that, an object must not only appear, but it must appear both *interesting* and *important*. The worlds whose objects are neither interesting nor important we treat simply negatively; we brand them as *un*real." In the next paragraph, James writes, "In this sense, whatever excites and stimulates our interest is real."[9]

This view increases the way in which reality is dependent upon our interests. This seems to me to border on a kind of ontological relativism, which I have treated in chapter 6.[10] Yet, pragmatism's slide away from common-sense realism does not end with James.

9.3 JOHN DEWEY: TALKING ABOUT THE REAL

In a discussion of aesthetic enjoyment, Dewey makes a remark with deep importance for the slide of pragmatism away from common-sense realism that is hinted at in Peirce and affirmed by James. Dewey writes, "Immediacy of existence is ineffable. But there is nothing mystical about such ineffability; it expresses the fact that of direct existence it is futile to say anything to one's self and impossible to say anything to another. Discourse can but intimate connections which if followed out may lead one to *have* an existence. Things in their immediacy are unknown and unknowable."[11]

Is existence ineffable? I have argued in chapters 2 and 3 that it is quite effable. We can know and say quite a lot about existence. There is a bit of irony here in that there is a lot to be said about a metaphysical notion about which we cannot seem to say anything! However, even worse for Dewey's view of existence is its connection to "discourse." Does "discourse" give us existence? This is a case of what Dallas Willard calls a "Midas Touch Epistemology," or in this case a "Midas Touch Ontology."[12] Whatever discourse touches, it turns to reality! But what about the existence of discourse? Must we have a discourse for discourse to exist, and a discourse for discourse for

9. James, *The Principles of Psychology*, 295.

10. See also Mosteller, *Relativism: A Guide*.

11. Dewey, *Experience and Nature*, 85–86.

12. Perhaps we should diagnose any philosophical position that maintains a "Midas Touch" epistemology, ontology, axiology, or logic as suffering from the often fatal condition of "Midasitis."

discourse . . . *ad nauseum*? If discourse even exists, mustn't its existence be independent of discourse? These questions are not easily answered for the Deweyan pragmatist.

9.4 SIDNEY HOOK: PRACTICAL REALITY *AU NATUREL*

In his *Metaphysics of Pragmatism* (originally published in 1927) Hook asks: "What then is the general defining character of the phrase 'to exist'?" He answers by quoting Peirce's claim that "*existence means precisely the exercise of compulsion.*"[13] Hook takes Peirce's idea of compulsion and says, "It cannot be gainsaid that compulsions are many and diverse and that the description of the types of existence which they reflect—logical, social, aesthetic, etc.— constitutes the chief tasks of metaphysics."[14] These he takes to be "natural facts," which combined with human freedom shape metaphysics, including existence.[15]

In his essay "The Quest for Being" in the book of the same title, Hook concludes that word "being" is a word that has "no definite meaning."[16] Rather it has a "function" to remind us "of the presence of something always referred to" and "not to designate or stand for any identifiable trait but to remind us of *what* we are talking about but which at the moment cannot itself be said."[17] Ontology, instead of being a science of being, becomes then a set of statements, "ontological statements," which are "common sense statements about the world which all scientists, if not all sciences, take for granted. . . . Recognition of their truth provides the fundamental tests of normal perception and sanity of behavior."[18]

For Hook, there is a kind of naturalism about existence or being, which has pragmatic elements, especially for scientific inquiry. The common sense that Hook alludes to here is not the common-sense ontology that I defend. Hook makes ontology or the study of being simply a common place of truisms that scientists take for granted. We have looked at some of the worries of materialism in chapter 7, so we won't rehearse those here, but we need to

---

13. Hook, *Metaphysics of Pragmatism*, 70.

14. Hook, *Metaphysics of Pragmatism*, 71.

15. Hook, *Metaphysics of Pragmatism*, 71.

16. Hook, *The Quest for Being*, 159.

17. Hook, *The Quest for Being*, 159. This is very similar to views of truth that treat truth in a linguistic "pronomial" way. See Mosteller, *Theories of Truth*, ch. 1, for an argument against this view.

18. Hook, *The Quest for Being*, 169.

think about whether existence is trivial or whether existence is something substantial.

I argued in chapter 2 that an understanding of existence as essential actualization is known through direct experience of ordinary common-sense objects. This is not a priori reflection and begs no questions as to what the case with respect to ontology must be. It simply takes the data of ordinary sense experience and shows that with careful reflection on that data, one can see that existence is essential exemplification.

This is no different than a common-sense experience of truth as correspondence between mind and world. Everyone has seen the match between their beliefs (concepts or statements) and the world that they experience. The same thing applies to a common-sense theory of existence. Everyone has experience of existing things and, with some careful reflection, can judge for themselves that the existence of the thing that they experience consists in its exemplification of an essence. I will not rehash that argument again here, but what I will do is examine the main argument that Hook offers against this broadly Thomistic common-sense view and offer a refutation of it.

Hook has several arguments against "Thomistic ontology." His first argument is that there is "logical legerdemain" when "we start from a conception of Being as such or pure Being and end up with meanings or categories that are quite distinct" from this conception of being.[19] The example that he gives is from the Thomistic mode of identification of being, good, and true. His conclusions is that the identification of the good and being make "nonsense of the view that evils and disvalues are to be found in the world."[20] Hook claims that the notion of evil being a privation of the good is only acceptable if one antecedently defines being and good. So, the Thomistic argument appears circular. In addition, Hook claims that "the tiniest twinge of pain is enough to refute" the identification of being and good. His argument can be summarized as follows:

(1) If being is equal to good, then bad is equal to a privation of being.

(2) If bad is equal to a privation of being, then pain would be a privation of being.

(3) But, pain is not a privation of being. (Hook writes, "For if anything is positive in the world, if anything proclaims itself with a scream or shout, it is pain.")[21]

19. Hook, *The Quest for Being*, 149.
20. Hook, *The Quest for Being*, 149.
21. Hook, *The Quest for Being*, 149.

(4) Therefore, it is not the case that bad is equal to a privation of being.

(5) Therefore, it is not the case that being is equal to good.

I do not want to dwell too long on this valid argument. It is clearly presumptive in premise (2) to maintain the consequent of the conditional that pain is a privation of being. Pain has an essence and exists. There is some conflation between pain and evil here. Pain need not be the same as evil, although the kind of anguish of pain that is associated with evil is still real. Suffering and pain are separable concepts; and if so, then premise (2) begs the question and is false. Thus, Hook's argument is unsound.

Hook raises a more serious argument against common-sense realism when he considers the view that being involves *"an act of existing*, as that which brings a sort of fulfillment or 'perfection' to some essence which receives it."[22] Hooks seems to have a couple of arguments going at once here. First, he claims that "it is unclear how we get from the Being of *this* and the Being of *that* to Being *qua* Being."[23] I won't respond to this other than to say, see chapter 2 of this book.

Second, he claims that if existence is essence in act, then action presupposes existence of some antecedent power, and if this is not the case then it "sets a problem for inquiry" and ends in "mystification." He asks, "What acts in the act of Being or existing? Certainly not possibilities, essences or natures. The meaning of 'death' is not lethal: the nature of 'fire' burns nothing."[24] This objection can be refuted if realism about universals is reasonable, especially the assumption that universals are "self-predicating." On this view, redness itself is red, and being itself has being (existence exists).[25] Of course, universals qua universals don't causally interact with particulars unless they are instantiated in them, but that is not to say that they are not self-predicating.

Third, Hook considers a form of the regress argument discussed in chapter 2. He claims that "concepts essences, natures and meanings are obviously objects of thought" because they (according to Thomism) exist.[26] But if they exist, then they exemplify an essence; and if they exemplify an essence, then there must be an antecedent essence in need of exemplification, and so on *ad infinitum*. He states, "If essences are endowed with Being, too, they already have an appropriate fulfillment or perfection." This he claims

22. Hook, *The Quest for Being*, 153.

23. Hook, *The Quest for Being*, 153.

24. Hook, *The Quest for Being*, 154.

25. See Moreland, *Universals*, 8.

26. Hook, *The Quest for Being*, 154.

is either "a mad-hatter's metaphysical race to complete an infinite regress" or "essence and existence are no longer distinct but collapse into each other." And, all of this is "incompatible with other assertions of Thomistic metaphysics."[27]

Two things can be said about this objection. First, the idea that essences are "objects of thought" is ambiguous. It could mean (a) that we can think about essences or (b) that essences are essentially objects of thought and have no objective reality outside of our thinking. Hook seems to assume (b). If they are mere objects of thought, then of course they would need to be preceded by something else that makes them be in our thoughts. But a realist about universals (or essences) can maintain that essences (universals) have being independent of our thoughts; for example, that redness has an essence to it, it has a perfection that is intrinsically good. In addition, a realist can maintain that one of the features of the essence of redness is a potentiality of exemplifiability: the ability to be exemplified. So, while we can make statements that are true and false about essences (e.g., "redness is a color"), these statements correspond to an extra-mental reality. They are not merely "objects of thought" even though we can think about them just as we can think about any existing thing.

The second thing to be said about this objection is that there is no infinite regress. Although universals themselves have essences, there need be no infinite regress. The mere existence of finite essences may point to the existence of a being whose essence is to exist, but this is a finite regress ending in an eternal being, not a mad-hatter's never ending regress. In addition, in chapter 2 I address the general objection against the possibility of an infinite regress of relations (the Bradleyen regress problem) in an account of existence as essential exemplification.

The real problem here for Hook is that he thinks that Thomism has as its basis an "antecedent commitment to Christian theology."[28] He claims that we can only get to God from created things (e.g., tables) only if "the argument from a first cause is valid—which it is not," but even if it were, he says that it would only be a "necessary condition not a sufficient one, for the eternity of the world would be compatible with the existence of its Prime Mover."[29]

The sort of common-sense realism maintained by contemporary Thomists is that we can know what existence is from common-sense reflection on ordinary experiences. This does not presuppose any sort of theism.

27. Hook, *The Quest for Being*, 154.
28. Hook, *The Quest for Being*, 154.
29. Hook, *The Quest for Being*, 154–55.

Arguments from ordinary common-sense awareness of existence from the existence of ordinary objects to the existence of a first cause are quite reasonable, especially those based on the impossibility of actual infinites.[30] Thus, Hook has not shown that Thomistic views of existence are unreasonable, nor has he demonstrated that such views require an antecedent theology. Contra Hook, given that everyone has the experience of existence from common-sense experience, the presumptions of naturalism and pragmatism that run throughout Hook's work seem to keep the awareness of this from being really, practically, naturally recognized.

9.5 CONCLUSION: FROM COMMON SENSE TO NON-SENSE

Let us conclude this brief examination of pragmatic views of existence with some thoughts from G. K. Chesterton. I agree with Chesterton's claim that the pragmatist method, especially along Peirce's lines, can be "a preliminary guide to truth."[31] But, as Chesterton recognizes, and as the history of pragmatism unfolds, there can be "an extreme application of it which involves the absence of all truth whatever."[32] Chesterton writes,

> I agree with the pragmatists that apparent objective truth is not the whole matter; that there is an authoritative need to believe the things that are necessary to the human mind. But I say that one of those necessities precisely is a belief in objective truth. The pragmatist tells a man to think what he must think and never mind the Absolute. But precisely one of the things that he must think is the Absolute. This philosophy, indeed, is a kind of verbal paradox. Pragmatism is a matter of human needs; and one of the first of human needs is to be something more than a pragmatist. Extreme pragmatism is just as inhuman as the determinism it so powerfully attacks. The determinist (who, to do him justice, does not pretend to be a human being) makes nonsense of the human sense of actual choice. The pragmatist, who professes to be especially human, makes nonsense of the human sense of actual fact.[33]

The discussion in this book has been about a common-sense realist view of existence. Pragmatism, as Chesterton points out, overlaps with

30. See Craig, *The Kalām Cosmological Argument*.
31. Chesterton, *Orthodoxy*, 64.
32. Chesterton, *Orthodoxy*, 64.
33. Chesterton, *Orthodoxy*, 64–65.

common-sense realism in the practical starting point and application of philosophical reflection. Yet, without objective truth, especially about the ultimate nature of reality, a merely pragmatic life is not worth living. What Chesterton advocates is the importance of thinking about the Absolute. While this term is loaded with ideas borrowed from philosophical idealism, especially Hegelianism, it need not be taken solely in that way. "Absolute" might also be taken to refer to those metaphysical realities that can be known through the senses, but are themselves nonphysical, permanent realities like existence itself. The pragmatist, according to Chesterton, "makes nonsense of the human sense of actual fact."[34] The actual facts of our ordinary common-sense experiences point to the nature of existence as essential exemplification. Pragmatism makes common sense into non-sense and makes actual facts impractical.

34. Chesterton, *Orthodoxy*, 65.

Chapter 10

Existentialism
Ontological Suicide

10.0 INTRODUCTION: WHICH COMES FIRST: EXISTENCE OR ESSENCE?

I arrive at the beach. I feel the cool, wet sand at my feet. I taste the saltiness of the ocean water on my lips. I hear the sound of the crashing surf. I smell the freshness of the sea air. I see waves breaking offshore. These things are real. Every person knows what is real from ordinary common-sense experiences like these. They also tell us more. They tell us about the nature of reality itself, about existence itself. Going to the beach is a choice. We choose to experience the sand, sea, and waves. But do the things I experience become what they are because of my choices? Do they have essential natures because of my action?

While "existentialism" is a broad topic, the specific existentialist understanding of the nature of reality will be examined in this chapter. Specifically, we will examine Sartre's idea that existence precedes essence. This chapter seeks to show that existentialism always takes its own life. The ideas here only consider a few brief notions from Sartre's essay "Existentialism and Humanism" coupled with a few thoughts from his ponderously long *Being and Nothingness*. There is a great deal that can and should be said with respect to exposition and criticism of Sartre's works. This short chapter simply calls into question a few salient ideas that are central to Sartre's brand of existentialism.

10.1 SELF-MADE PEOPLE ADORING THEIR CREATORS

One of the key notions of "existentialism," according to Jean Paul Sartre, is this: "*Existence* comes before *essence* . . . we must begin from the subjective."[1] Does this mean that Sartre is a subjectivist about everything? Not necessarily. Sartre, at least according to one interpretation of his work, is not a subjectivist about ordinary objects of experience. Frederick Copleston in his *History of Philosophy* writes that Sartre appears to have a realist basis with respect to "the self in relation to its transcendent object."[2] According to Copleston, Sartre does not think that "consciousness creates the object" but that an object, (including the self) "acquires an instrumentalist meaning, standing out from its background as this sort of thing and not another, only in relation to consciousness."[3]

Sartre claims that an artifact—for example, a knife—has its essence prior to its existence, and on theistic and modern philosophy, so do human beings. But on Sartre's atheistic existentialism, "man" (or "human reality") is a being "whose existence comes before its essence."[4] Sartre says that existence precedes essence means that "man first of all exists, encounters himself, surges up in the world—and defines himself afterwards."[5]

But what about being itself? Quoting from Sartre's *Being and Nothingness* Copleston indicates that Sartre believes that "Being is. Being is in itself. Being is what it is."[6] Copleston adds that, for Sartre, "being is opaque,

1. Sartre, *Existentialism and Humanism*, 26.
2. Copleston, *A History of Philosophy*, 9:348.
3. Copleston, *A History of Philosophy*, 9:349.
4. Sartre, *Existentialism and Humanism*, 28.
5. Sartre, *Existentialism and Humanism*, 28.
6. Copleston, *A History of Philosophy*, 9:349.

massive: it simply is."[7] However, consciousness does play a role in that "all differentiation within being is due to consciousness."[8] This is what Sartre means by "existence comes before *essence*." It appears that essences, are made through consciousness, although there is existence/being prior to consciousness' activity. Copleston states, "For Sartre being in itself is logically prior to not-being and cannot be identified with it; but the table for example is constituted as a table through a negation." Without consciousness "being is gratuitous or *de trop*, as Sartre puts it in his novel *Nausea*."[9]

So, there is being prior to man's acting essence, but that even man's essence "is nothing" prior to its acts of consciousness. Sartre indicates that "man" is indefinable, because "to begin with he is nothing."[10] "Man" will be what he is by "making himself." Sartre further claims, "Man simply is."[11] The "first principle of existentialism" is that "man is nothing else but that which he makes of himself."[12] Existence precedes essence, and essence comes through a kind of making via conscious action.

10.2 EXISTENTIAL ETHICAL CONFUSION

There is some terrible confusion here. How can "man" simultaneously "be simply" *and* "be nothing." As with Heidegger, being and non-being are back together again! This contradiction on Sartre's part is real, but I'm not sure that it was intended. What he seems to be saying is that human essence flows from human action, human freedom. For the common-sense realist, existence is essential exemplification; for the existentialist of the Sartrean variety, essence is existential free-action. We "make" our own essence by our action; by our own choices, and these choices are "better" because we choose them. The individual choice is a choice for "all men." Doing so is what produces "anxiety" for Sartre, especially because of the recognition that since God does not exist, everything is permitted.[13]

The choice itself appears to be based on sentiment or feeling, but is only really determined by the choice. The performance of the action is what matters, for Sartre. He states, "We ourselves decide our being."[14] Even be-

7. Copleston, *A History of Philosophy*, 9:349.
8. Copleston, *A History of Philosophy*, 9:350.
9. Copleston, *A History of Philosophy*, 9:350.
10. Sartre, *Existentialism and Humanism*, 28.
11. Sartre, *Existentialism and Humanism*, 28.
12. Sartre, *Existentialism and Humanism*, 28.
13. Sartre, *Existentialism and Humanism*, 33–34.
14. Sartre, *Existentialism and Humanism*, 39.

tween the choice of communism and fascism, Sartre says that if fascism is decided upon, then "fascism will then be the truth of man" and that "in reality things will be such as men have decided they shall be."[15]

In emphasizing existential choice, there is a kind of general arbitrariness that existentialism ignores. If essence is determined by acting existence, then which essence (of a political economy) should I or we choose? Secular, liberal democracy? Fascism? Communism? Sharia Law? The content of choice is not able to be compared on any value ahead of time, or a priori. Sartre says, "I ought to commit myself and then act my commitment,"[16] and, "There is no reality except in action."[17]

The example that Sartre gives in his essay about the man who is trying to decide between (a) staying home to care for his mother, (b) leaving his mother and joining the resistance, or (c) shooting his mother in the head and then shooting himself in the head to make the pain go away. Ok, I added option (c) to the scenario. Sartre only offers (a) and (b). But why not (c) as well? Why shouldn't (c) be something that one can reasonably commit oneself to and then act on that commitment? Why not also consider that reality made through free action? Without essences existing in things, including ourselves and in moral reality, there is no way to compare the relative worth of any human action. But, this is not the only problem for Sartre's ideas here.

10.3 EXISTENTIAL LOGICAL CONFUSION

Here is a real logical problem. It is the same kind of problem which plagues all forms of relativism, which it seems to me, Sartre's existentialism is a type. The problem is this. Consider the existentialist claim:

EC: "There is no reality except in action."

Consider the contradictory of EC:

Not-EC: "It is not the case that there is no reality except in action."

Now, suppose I am trying to decide which of these is real. I must take the action to decide which will be real, and reality is what I decide it to be. I cannot decide EC or Not-EC *a priori*, and there is no sentiment, feeling, or authority to help. But I must decide. So, either choosing EC or Not-EC is merely *arbitrary* or there is some way antecedent (to the choosing) to decide

15. Sartre, *Existentialism and Humanism*, 40.
16. Sartre, *Existentialism and Humanism*, 40.
17. Sartre, *Existentialism and Humanism*, 41.

which is more reasonable: EC or Not-EC. If the choice is not arbitrary, then existentialism must be given up as not all of reality is determined by action, or if existentialism is to be chosen, then it is a merely arbitrary choice and has *nothing* to commend it other than it was chosen. But if someone chooses to reject EC, and accept Not-EC, then that is just as reasonable and acceptable and praiseworthy as EC. So, existentialism is as reasonable as its contradiction; hardly a reasonable view.

10.4 EXISTENTIAL ONTOLOGICAL CONFUSION

There also seems to be a glaring ontological issue here as well. Human beings seem to have specific qualities when they exist, namely the capacity of choice and freedom. How can essence be determined by anything that merely exists without an essence? This seems absurd. Reconsider Chesterton's ideas that eggs are eggs. Existentialism seems to be saying that eggs get to be eggs by being scrambled. It's the scramble that matters more than the eggs. But you can't get *scrambled* eggs, unless you start with existing *eggs*, with things that have the essence of eggs before they get scrambled.

Sartre seems to be saying that human beings exist because they exercise their freedom, but mustn't we be the kinds of things we are (have the essential qualities, at least the capacity, for the exercise of freedom) before we exercise our freedom? Unless we are essentially a certain kind of thing to begin with, then we cannot exercise any capacities at all, including human freedom. Eggs are eggs before, during, and after they are scrambled. Humans are humans before, during, and after they freely act.

10.5 FUTILITY OR FINALITY: EXISTENTIAL LESSONS FROM BELLOC

One of the lessons that existentialist philosophy purports to teach is that there is a certain anxiety (Heidegger), nausea (Sartre), or absurdity (Camus) to reality, and especially human life. Common-sense realism sees that existence is essential exemplification from common-sense experience. The realist can maintain that although there is real being that is eternal and personal, the world we live in is fallen, and all of creation seems futile. As St. Paul writes in his Letter to the Romans (Rom 8:20–22 KJV): "For the creation was subjected to futility, not willingly, but because of Him who subjected it in hope; because the creation itself also will be delivered from the bondage of corruption into the glorious liberty of the children of God.

For we know that the whole creation groans and labors with birth pangs together until now."

Common-sense realism recognizes that the world really is fallen, but instead of anxiety, nausea, and/or absurdity, we recognize that the world was subjected to its fallenness by God for the hope of a better world. Further, this hope is not in something "other" than God and the common-sense world in which we live. Rather, it is a fulfillment of our earthly home. The ordinary things of common sense will themselves be redeemed and resurrected, our souls and our bodies.

In his *The Four Men*, Hillarie Belloc offers a memorable illustration of the kind of anxiety/nausea/absurdity that seems to be part and parcel of reality according to existentialists. The discussion in this chapter of the dialogue surrounds the best and worst things in the world.

> *Myself.* "While you were speaking, Sailor, it seemed to me you had forgotten one great felicity, manly purpose, and final completion of the immortal spirit, which is surely the digging of holes and the filling of them up again."

> *The Sailor.* "You are right! I had forgotten that! It is indeed an admirable pastime, and for some, perhaps for many, it is the best thing in the world."

> *Myself.* "Yes, indeed, for consider how we drink to thirst again, and eat to hunger again, and love for disappointment, and journey in order to return. And consider with what elaborate care we cut, clip, shave, remove and prune our hair and beard, which none the less will steadfastly re-grow, and how we earn money to spend it, and black boots before walking in the mire, and do penance before sinning, and sleep to wake, and wake to sleep; and very elaborately do pin, button, tie, hook, hang, lace, draw, pull up, be-tighten, and in diverse ways fasten about ourselves our very complicated clothes of a morning, only to unbutton, unpin, untie, unhook, let down, be-loosen, and in a thousand operations put them off again when midnight comes. Then there is the soiling of things for their cleansing, and the building of houses to pull them down again, and the making of wars for defeat or for barren victories, and the painting of pictures for the rich blind, and the singing of songs for the wealthy deaf, and the living of all life to the profit of others, and the begetting of children who may perpetuate all that same round. The more I think of it the more I see that the digging of holes and the filling of them up again is the true end of man and his felicity."

The Poet. "I think you must be wrong."[18]

There is no *argument* here against the anxiety/nausea/absurdity of life when "Myself" comically claims that the digging of holes to fill them up is the best thing in the world. The Poet simply responds that he "must be wrong." Perhaps there is no argument against existential emotional feelings that motivate the existentialist's choices. However, there are facts. On the one hand, life seems to be an absurd merry-go-round of daily repetition. Vanity of vanities is a life "under the sun" says the preacher in the book of Ecclesiastes.

On the other hand, there is real being. We see it all the time, real essences really exemplified. We also see real beauty even in the simplest of things. These are real facts that show that there is more to life and to the world than the daily grind. This world and all of the beautiful things in it are really good. They make us glad, but as Belloc says, they are not our final gladness. They may seem futile, but they open the door to a final home where real life begins.

18. Belloc, *The Four Men*, 85–86.

PART 4

Reality Realized
Workaday Christian Metaphysics

CHAPTER 11

Real Ethics

Common Sense and the Good Life

11.0 REAL GOOD

I arrive at the beach. I feel the cool, wet sand at my feet. I taste the saltiness of the ocean water on my lips. I hear the sound of the crashing surf. I smell the freshness of the sea air. I see waves breaking offshore. These things are real. Every person knows what is real from ordinary common-sense experiences like these. They also tell us more. They tell us about the nature of reality itself, about existence itself. What role do the things I experience have for me becoming a good person? Even if I learn about existence from these ordinary objects of experience, what implications does this have for me living a good life? What does existence mean for the goodness of specific areas of human life, medicine, for example?

If we can know the nature of *what is*, the nature of existence itself, then this has crucial implications for ethics, how we live our lives. In this chapter I argue that common-sense realism is the best basis for understanding ethics and living one's life well. In addition, this chapter will consider specific cases of the application of common-sense realism to Christian thinking about bioethics.

First, we will look at some ideas from C. S. Lewis's *The Abolition of Man* as a paradigm case of common-sense ontological realism as it applies to ethical reality. Second, we will look at some clear-cut logical arguments as to the relationship between common-sense realism and ethics. Finally, we will consider how common-sense realism about ethical reality applies to issues bioethics, particularly genetic enhancement.

11.1 ABOLISHING COMMON SENSE

In 1943, C. S. Lewis published *The Abolition of Man*.[1] This book is an excellent example of how deep thinking about the nature of ethics can only occur from deep thinking about "what is." In *The Abolition of Man*, Lewis sounded a warning call about what happens when the human race, especially those with power, reject what he calls the *Tao*. The *Tao* is shorthand for "the doctrine of objective value."

This doctrine is "the belief that certain attitudes are really true, and others really false to the kind of thing the universe is and the kinds of things we are."[2] This is a clear-cut common-sense realist (both epistemologically and ontologically) view of the world. It maintains that the universe (all of reality outside us) and human beings (everything inside ourselves) are a certain *kind* of thing. This implies that all of reality has an essence to it. The common-sense realist view advocated in this book is that existence is *essential exemplification*. So, Lewis's doctrine of objective value is a common-sense realist view.

Although all of the ideas in *The Abolition of Man* hinge upon the truth and reasonableness of the doctrine of objective value, Lewis's book is not a

1. For an excellent overview and exposition of the themes of this book, see Mosteller and Anacker's *Contemporary Perspectives*.

2. Lewis, *Abolition*, 12.

treatise in metaphysics or general ontology. I would like to sketch briefly the argument that Lewis makes in that book. If Lewis's view is consistent with common-sense realism, then there are important lessons for how we should live our lives. In particular, there are lessons for areas of ethical reasoning in bioethical considerations like human enhancement.

I will show how Lewis demonstrates that an axiologically rudderless approach to ethics has devastating consequences for medicine and health care. Lacking a common-sense realist commitment to the objectivity of value entails that ethics, including bioethics, along with the practice of medicine and healthcare, are impossible. This is of special importance given both the current reality of powerful technologies (e.g., CRSPR/Cas9) that were unknown in Lewis's time, coupled with the likelihood of even more radical technologies unfolding in the years ahead (e.g., artificial intelligence, trans-humanism).

The argument of this chapter has four parts. First, I consider Lewis's "doctrine of objective value." I argue that it is not only a coherent common-sense realist approach to ethics, but that it is more reasonable than subjectivist approaches. Several reasons for this will be put forward. Second, I offer an assessment of Lewis's argument against those he calls "the conditioners" who by means of advanced scientific technology can mold and make our species into whatever they wish them to be, including whatever they wish our species to believe about the nature of value. Several objections to Lewis's argument will be considered and rejoinders given. Third, I offer a conceptual clarification of why a rejection of the doctrine of objective value entails the impossibility of ethical reality as applied to bioethics. Finally, I conclude by considering Lewis's own solution to the difficulty of surrendering the objectivity of value to scientific advancement. I argue, following Lewis, that the objectivity of value must apply to all areas of human inquiry (including and especially scientific inquiry) or face specific logical absurdities, and that this is especially the case when considering the flourishing of medicine and healthcare.

11.1.1 Ontological Emotivism and The Tao

I find it fascinating that Lewis begins his entire discussion of the ethical ramifications of *The Abolition of Man* with a story of two people looking at a waterfall who form different beliefs about the aesthetic qualities of the waterfall. This is an entirely common-sense approach. We've all had this sort of experience and probably have gotten into a number of arguments with people regarding our views about the natural world. It is insightful that Lewis starts with an aesthetic example that involves natural beauty, as opposed to an aesthetic example that involves a work of art. He seems to be saying, right from the beginning of his book, that there are real things in the world, like waterfalls, that we can all see and look at, and we can see the real, essential aesthetic qualities in those works of nature, and make judgments about them.

Here is the example Lewis gives. Two people look at a waterfall, and each person forms a belief about the waterfall:

Person 1: "The waterfall is sublime."

Person 2: "The waterfall is pretty."

Lewis says that in the intellectual climate of the early twentieth-century modern educators, who reject common-sense realism (especially about axiological qualities) say that P1 and P2 are not saying anything about the waterfall but are merely talking about how they feel. "It is sublime" = "I have sublime feelings" and "It is pretty" = "I have pretty feelings."

Lewis offers two very brief, very direct, very devastating arguments against this sort of axiological emotivism. The first argument goes like this:

1.1 The emotions and feeling prompting projection of sublimity (which the modern educator insists is going on) onto the waterfall are the "correlates" "almost the opposites of the qualities projected."[3]

1.2 To call a waterfall sublime is not to have sublime feelings but to have "feelings of veneration"[4] (i.e., the correlate feeling of feeling sublime).

1.3 Therefore, "This is sublime" if reduced to speaker's feelings should be "I have humble feelings."[5]

This argument is fairly straightforward. When you stand on the shore of the ocean, especially when there are large waves offshore, and you look out upon the waters and you see power and vastness of the sea, you might say, "That is awesome!" But that doesn't mean that you are having feelings of "awesomeness." Rather, you feel pretty small and frail. So, "That is awesome!" can't mean "I have awesome feelings."

Lewis's second argument goes like this:

2.1 "This is sublime" = "I have sublime feelings" leads to absurdities.

2.2 e.g., "You are contemptible" = "I have contemptible feelings."

3. Lewis, *Abolition*, 2.
4. Lewis, *Abolition*, 2.
5. Lewis, *Abolition*, 2.

2.3 e.g., "Your feelings are contemptible" = "My feelings are contemptible."

2.4 These two examples are absurd; therefore, the claim that value statements are merely statements about one's feelings is false.

When my kids were little, and I told them they were acting naughty,[6] what I certainly did not mean that I was feeling naughty! What would that even mean that my kids acting naughty means that I'm feeling naughty! Perhaps parents are often at fault for how their kids behave, but I usually don't feel naughty when my kids behave badly.

In addition to these two arguments, it is fairly clear that from the fact of aesthetic (or ethical) disagreement, it does not follow that there are no aesthetic (or ethical) truths. Consider the counterexample of directional differentiation. Mere disagreement about which way north is does not entail that there are no right answers about which way *is* north. This is a general problem of relativism. Mere disagreement about reality does not mean there is no way that reality is. Or to put it another way, when people have different opinions about the nature of reality, what certainly *does not follow* from that disagreement is that there are no right answers to the reality in question.

Suppose the people in Lewis's example differed in their beliefs about the height of the waterfall, instead of differing about the beauty of the waterfall. Would it follow that there is no right answer about the height of the waterfall, just because one person thought it was ten feet high, and another person thought it was fifty feet high? But why think that things should be relativistic simply when it comes to aesthetics or ethics, or epistemology or general ontology? Unless one is biased from the get-go, about aesthetic or ethical qualities not being real in the first place, then we should stick with the common-sense notion that the waterfall not only has a real height that can be known, but also a real beauty that can be known. Different beliefs formed about beauty occur all the time, but so do differing beliefs about height. A difference of belief about beauty or height is an opportunity to explore what is real, not to simply say, "There's no right answer!"

In response to the axiological emotivism, which is about as far from common-sense realism as you can get, Lewis puts forward the commonsensical idea that there is a reality that exists apart from us that we can know. Lewis states that the view he is to defend has been held across times, cultures, religions, and philosophies. He writes,

> This conception in all its forms, Platonic, Aristotelian, Stoic, Christian, and Oriental alike, I shall henceforth refer to for brevity simply as "the Tao." . . . It is the doctrine of objective

6. King Edmund would have called them "naught."

value, the belief that certain attitudes are really true, and others really false, to the kind of thing the universe is and the kind of things we are. Those who know the Tao can hold that to call children delightful or old men venerable is not simply to record a psychological fact about our own parental or filial emotions at the moment, but to recognize a quality which demands a certain response from us whether we make it or not. I myself do not enjoy the society of small children: because I speak from within the Tao I recognize this as a defect in myself—just as a man may have to recognize that he is tone deaf or colour blind.[7]

This passage is incredibly insightful and helpful for the common-sense realist. The analogies that Lewis uses here are of particular importance. There is a real quality of "being venerable" in the elderly, and a real quality of "being delightful" in children. The quality is real and is really in the objects that have them. This means that the qualities themselves have an essence and they exist! They exist in concrete particulars, which we can observe, know, and respond to. We can respond to them appropriately, or not! Not appreciating children at play (I often imagine if Lewis was irked by scream-ing kids outside his windows while he was concentrating on writing the *Chronicles of Narnia!*) is a defect at recognizing the real quality of delight-fulness in children. Aesthetic and moral qualities are as real as tones and colors. Now, unfortunately (see chapter 5 for a longer discussion of this), there have been several hundred years of philosophers denying that colors and sounds are really in the objects that have them. So, Lewis might have chosen a better example. But for the common-sense realist standing in the broad daylight of the brotherhood of man, the sky is really blue, and the singing of the birds really sweet.

So, what is our current situation? Or what was the situation at the time Lewis wrote? Lewis sums it up this way:

> And all the time—such is the tragi-comedy of our situation—we continue to clamour for those very qualities we are rendering impossible. . . . In a sort of ghastly simplicity we remove the organ and demand the function. We make men without chests and expect of them virtue and enterprise. We laugh at honour and are shocked to find traitors in our midst. We castrate and bid the geldings be fruitful.[8]

Have things have gotten much better morally, especially for younger people, since the 1940s? Well, the great disasters of the twentieth century have been

7. Lewis, *Abolition*, 12–13.

8. Lewis, *Abolition*, 14.

beaten back, or nearly so: fascism and communism (at least of the Soviet variety; over a billion still languish) were largely defeated by the greatest generations. But have we become more moral in the intervening years? Have we become better in helping the young develop their moral character, the part of the soul that serves as the "organ" for recognizing and acting upon moral realities? From my own experience of twenty-plus years of college-level teaching, students seem to be no better off than what Lewis is suggesting here, and perhaps a bit worse. The wholescale rejection of the objectivity of value in higher education and culture as a whole is nearly complete. Common-sense realism has an uphill task.

The consequences of a relativistic instead of a realistic view of values has real consequences to other areas of ethical life. Suppose we applied a non-realist view of ethics to medicine. Suppose we maintain that *all* value is relative to something else (e.g., personal/individual preference). This would entail that the value of medicine and healthcare are also relative to a personal/individual preference. Thus, even the value of "health" would be relative to an individual preference or desire. So, to "discriminate" between a "healthy body" or an "un-healthy body" would be to foist one set of values upon others who may not accept it. But is this reasonable? Is there no real value to health over disease? In addition to being self-defeating, axiological relativism cannot maintain itself as valuable if all value is relative, and this is absurd.

11.1.2 Innovating Onto-Ethics

Lewis considers two possible responses to the *Tao*. Accept it partially (pick and choose morality) or reject it fully (build your own morality). The former are "the innovators," the latter "the conditioners." Let us look at each of these positions in turn.

Lewis starts with the recognition of the real value of patriotism. Lewis writes, "When a Roman father told his son that it was a sweet and seemly thing to die for his country, he believed what he said. He was communicating to the son an emotion which he himself shared and which he believed to be in accord with the value which his judgment discerned in noble death."[9] Lewis then shows how the "pick and choose" moralists, the innovators, claim that values are reducible to something else like utility or survival. So, patriotism reduces to "useful for the community" (i.e., a factual proposition). But Lewis asks: Why should *I* die for others? Pick someone else!

9. Lewis, *Abolition*, 14.

Lewis says that the innovator might try to reduce patriotism to "instinct." But, if patriotism is instinctive, why must I be told to be patriotic? In fact, Lewis points out, fighting for others' lives isn't the only instinct I have. Fleeing is as instinctive as fighting. Which instinct should I obey? Fight or flight? So, Lewis concludes that patriotism isn't a value that is reducible to something more basic. It is an absolutely real value. It is an objective value, part of the Tao.

Lewis says, "Unless you accept these without question as being to the world of action what axioms are to the world of theory, you can have no practical principles whatever. You cannot reach them as conclusions: they are premises."[10] Logic and morality are on the same ontological ground. They both are real and should constrain our beliefs and actions.

The innovator is arbitrary in "picking and choosing" which part of the Tao (doctrine of objective value) he wants to keep. The innovators attempt to ground value in some more basic drive or impulse like "instinct" or try to pick and choose their values, claiming that there are some areas of human life that have objective values and others that do not. Lewis argues that this position is internally incoherent and that it must be rejected.

Think about the implications this view has for medicine and healthcare. The innovative route of rejecting the doctrine of objective value is one that hinges upon mere survival or mere utility, and it entails the impossibility of medicine and healthcare as normative disciplines. If we regard "survival of the species" as a normative goal of medicine and healthcare, but do not do so with any objective, real grounding to show the real value of this goal, then one can always ask, "Why should our species survive?"

You might think that the answer to this question is an obvious one. But I have seen responses to it which tend in the negative direction. Once, I was at a philosophy conference, and one of the topics that was being addressed was ethics and what the philosophers on the panel called "overpopulation." One of the panelists suggested that there were too many people on the planet. I wanted to ask, "Which ones do you think shouldn't be here?" But, it was a large group in a big auditorium, and I didn't want to make a scene. But suppose that I lined up my kids, and all of my nieces and nephews and told them, "The world would be better off without some of you!"

The philosophers at this conference may not have wished an end to the entire species, but they did claim that the world would be better off without some or perhaps most of the members of our species. But, if a philosopher proposes that the world would be better off without some of us, it is not a far step to add that the world would be better off without all of us. And this

10. Lewis, *Abolition*, 26.

raises the question that Lewis forces the Innovators to answer: "Should our species survive?" Common-sense realism about reality and ethics, informed with the Christian charity can answer that with reasonable, "Yes."

11.1.3 On Any Condition?

The third chapter of Lewis's *Abolition* bears the same name as the book, "The Abolition of Man." In this chapter, Lewis considers "the conditioners" who, by means of advanced scientific technology, can mold and make our species into whatever they wish them to be, including whatever they wish our species to believe about the nature of value. These people reject natural moral law entirely and maintain that the Tao, grounded in human nature, is one more merely natural object to be conquered in our "conquest of nature." Lewis speculates about the final stage of humanity's conquest of nature when, "Man by eugenics, by pre-natal conditioning, and by an education and propaganda based on a perfect applied psychology, has obtained full control over himself. *Human* nature will be the last part of Nature to surrender to Man."[11]

This view, according to Lewis, attempts to *naturalize* value. It seeks to treat values, both moral and aesthetic, as mere natural (i.e., physical) phenomena to be "conquered" in the same way we have "conquered" in the arenas of transportation (air travel), communications, (the "smart" phone), computing (the PC), genetics (mapping of the human genome), to name a few. Yet Lewis realizes that if natural moral law were naturalized (physicalized) so that human beings could be conditioned to behave or maintain some values over others, then the very motivations of the conditioners are naturalized as well. This entails that mere bodily impulses, nature in the most basic sense, would rule all decisions about human value. Lewis claims that if we reject the Tao and try to build our own morality artificially and impose it on the artificial people we produce from bioengineering, then we quit being human: "They are not men at all: they are artefacts. Man's final conquest has proved to be the abolition of Man."[12]

It seems to me that there are some fairly heavy metaphysical assumptions in background of the conditioners whom Lewis has in mind.[13] Here are a few of them:

11. Lewis, *Abolition*, 37.

12. Lewis, *Abolition*, 41.

13. The rest of this section is a little "logic heavy." If you believe that you are sufficiently convinced of the reasonableness of Lewis's view, then skip to section 11.2.

S: Only the physical exists.

Q: We should conquer nature.

R: Conquering nature just is the power of some men over others with physical nature as an instrument.[14]

The problem it seems to me is an implicit problem involving S with both Q and R. If only the physical exists, then the proposition Q that we should conquer nature is also and only a physical thing; presumably it will be identical to a brain state or function of the brain. But suppose one considers the negation of Q. Let us call this "Not-Q," which states, "We should not conquer nature." A scientist or healthcare worker or physician could entertain Q and Not-Q. But how is she to decide which to believe if she also accepts S? For both Q and Not-Q are going to be physical things (brain states or something else physical); and of course, any epistemic justification for Q and Not-Q will also be identical to something physical (brain state or otherwise). So, how does one pick Q over Not-Q if one also accepts S? One cannot appeal to *good* evidence or *good* reasons or moral realities like duty or whatever. There will only be physical things; and any choice will not be determined by anything other than some physical process. Thus, the attempt to conquer nature while simultaneously accepting Q stultifies the whole process and especially the process of "designing" future progeny. Thus, the view of the conditioners should be rejected.

But, S isn't the only ontology available to healthcare workers or medical professionals or physicians. One could deny S and accept R and be guided, non-arbitrarily by real objective values. This is the main point of *The Abolition of Man* and the main point of defending Christian common-sense realism.

If medicine and healthcare as normative and intrinsically good disciplines are to exist at all, they can only do so on the basis of objective reality and objective value and especially so in our "conquest of nature." This is especially needful the more that we "conquer." For example, improvements in gene editing hold great promise to improve the lives of millions, but also hold the nightmare of their use for the creation of human beings for slave labor or for cannon fodder or whatever form of high-tech human trafficking wicked minds can invent.

Since the anti-common-sense views of both the innovators and the conditioners with respect to morality fail, how should we move forward? The following illustrates the vision of scientific inquiry that Lewis presents at the close of the lectures. Lewis states, "The regenerate science which I

14. Lewis, *Abolition*, 45.

have in mind would not do even to minerals and vegetables what modern science threatens to do to man himself. When it explained it would not explain away.... In a word, it would conquer Nature without being at the same time conquered by her and buy knowledge at a lower cost than that of life."[15]

This sort of scientific inquiry would have a specific commitment to the objectivity of value. If the subjectivistic, innovative, and reductive approaches to the doctrine of objective value have failed, and if no other alternatives are available for scientific progress to move forward, then acceptance and integration of the objectivity of value into the very nature of scientific progress seems to be the most reasonable course to take. This idea can be strengthened considerably if it is the case that science qua science requires a commitment to the objectivity of value with respect to the value of scientific inquiry taken as it is in itself.

11.2 COMMON-SENSE MEDICINE AND BIOETHICS

I would like to turn now to a few arguments regarding how the common-sense realism developed in this book, and in Lewis's *Abolition of Man*, applies directly to our thinking about the discipline of medicine. Here is a simple argument:

3.1 All things that exist are things that exemplify an essence.

3.2 Medicine exists.

3.3 Therefore, medicine exemplifies an essence.

The first premise was established in chapter 2 of this book. It can, of course, be challenged. Such challenges might include the following: defense of a what Dallas Willard called the "Midas Touch" epistemology with a concomitant view of perception. If we can't get at things as they are on the appropriate basis of thought and experience, then of course we can't get at existence either. Yet, we do find things as they are on the appropriate basis of thought and experience all the time. To deny this is simply to deny the obvious.

The second premise is true. But is there an equivocation or a fallacy of division going on here? Is the notion of "exists" and/or "exemplifies an essence" equivocal between the first two premises? I don't believe either of these notions is equivocal. The mode or manner of the existence of medicine may be categorized differently than the existence of other things (stars, dogs, atoms, souls, governments), but the existence of each of these is univocal.

15. Lewis, *Abolition*, 49.

The notion of exemplifying an essence might be thought to be equivocal, but again there being different manners in which an essence is exemplified or different kinds of essences that are exemplified does not entail that an essence is not exemplified in all existing things.

There doesn't seem to be a fallacy of division similar to: "All salt is tasty; Sodium and chlorine are salt. Therefore, sodium and chlorine are tasty." The argument above is not meant as a whole to parts, but as a move from general to specific. If these ideas are sufficient as a defense of this argument, then we have good reason to maintain that the argument is sound.

11.2.1 The Essential Telos of Medicine

Let us now consider the reality of a natural purpose or *telos* to medicine by defending the following argument:

4.1   All things with essences have a *telos*.

4.2   Medicine exemplifies an essence.

4.3   Therefore, medicine has a *telos*.

4.4   If something has a *telos*, then the *telos* is either natural or artificial.

4.5   Medicine has a *telos*.

4.6   Therefore, the *telos* of medicine is either natural or artificial.

4.7   The *telos* of medicine is not artificial.

4.8   Therefore, the *telos* of medicine is natural.

The key premises of this argument are 4.1 and 4.7. Let us look briefly at these in turn.

Regarding 3.1, can we derive essential teleology from the real experience of existence as essential actualization? I believe that the answer is, "Yes!" Here is why. When we experience an essence in act, we know what the essence is for, even if we do know what the essence is. We at least know that the essence is *for* the full actualization of the qualities of the essence itself. And full actualization is exactly the notion of teleology. Thus, existence as essential actualization is necessarily teleological.

Regarding 4.7, the telos of medicine is not artificial because medicine is directed toward the actualization of human essences, which necessarily are teleological. Thus, although medicine as an art is artificial, in the sense that it does not occur without an "artist" (rational actor), its telos is not artificial, as it pertains directly toward human teleological existence.

11.2.2 From the Teleology of Medicine to the Good of Medicine

Now I would like to turn to an argument for the conclusion that the goodness of medicine flows from the realization of its *telos*. The goodness of a thing must be realized in the existence of the thing. There is no such thing as the goodness of *x* simultaneous with the non-existence of *x*. But if the goodness of *x* is realized in the existence of *x*, and the existence of *x* just is the essential exemplification of *x*, and if the essential exemplification of *x* is necessarily teleological, it follows that the goodness of *x* flows from its telos.

Thus, the realization of a natural *telos* of medicine is an actualization of the goodness of medicine with respect to its *telos*. Therefore, the realization of the natural *telos* of medicine is the actualization of the goodness of medicine. So, since medicine has an essence, a *telos*, and a good, let us apply this idea to a particular case of the ethics of human enhancement.

11.2.3 Realist Cures for Chronic Cases of the Fuzzies

Unfortunately, medical human enhancement is chronically "fuzzy"; it is often difficult to figure out how we should think about many cases of human enhancement. Consider a recent example.

> Ted Richards loves parrots. In fact, the resident of Bristol, U.K., is so batty for the birds that he has gone through extensive and extreme body modification surgery to look like them. First, the self-described "Parrotman" had his face tattooed to look like he has feathers in the five colors of his parrots. Then he risked going blind by having his eyes colored with tattoo ink. After that, he had his ears cut off—a process that helped him better resemble the birds but impaired his hearing. . . . "Parrots only got little holes anyways, so I had them cut off," he said in the preview clip above. "You know, it's your body at the end of the day. You should be able to do whatever you want with it."[16]

Body modification and genetic enhancement (extreme or otherwise, low-tech surgery or high-tech CRSPR) is an activity that overlaps with medicine. It requires medical technique, medical knowledge, and medical risks for one's health. Consider this argument:

5.1 "Modification" as an activity that overlaps with medicine either hinders or helps or neither helps nor hinders the realization of the natural *telos* of medicine.

16. Moyce, "Man Goes under Knife."

5.2   It is not the case that modification helps realize the natural *telos* of medicine.

5.3   It is not the case that modification neither helps nor hinders the realization of the *telos* of medicine.

5.4   Therefore, modification hinders the natural *telos* of medicine.

5.5   The realization of the natural *telos* of medicine is the actualization of the goodness of medicine.

5.6   Therefore, any activity (*viz.* modification) that hinders that good will not be a good act with respect to the goodness of medicine.

5.7   Therefore, modification is not a good act with respect to the goodness of medicine.

If this argument is sound then how should we think about this issue of modification? Some acts might help realize the good of medicine (*viz.* human essential actualization with respect to human health). There are very clear cases of this even with respect to "modification," e.g., amputations for gangrene (to prevent a worse loss). The purpose or *telos* of the act will have a moral component to it with respect to the *telos* of medicine, which is again pegged to human essence, which is directly connected to existence as such.

So, any act that helps to realize the good of medicine will be a good act with respect to the goodness of medicine, and any act that neither helps nor hinders the realization of the natural *telos* of medicine should be considered good on its own merits and possible consequences to the *telos* of medicine. Such acts would need to be evaluated on a case-by-case basis. But we must not forget that some acts are really a violation of the inherent goodness of medicine. Such acts violate the real common-sense objective value that essentially exists in all of *what is*.

11.3 CONCLUSION: REAL VIRTUE FOR REAL LIFE

In *The Abolition of Man*, C. S. Lewis wrote, "For the wise men of old the cardinal problem had been how to conform the soul to reality, and the solution had been knowledge, self-discipline, and virtue."[17] The cardinal problem of the wise of yesteryear is not even on the radar today. Conforming the soul to reality? Rather oppressive that!

But it nevertheless remains a pressing problem, and we all know this, especially in mundane matters. What happens if I don't conform my beliefs

---

17. Lewis, *Abolition*, 48.

with the reality of how much gas is in the tank of my car? Or how much money is in my bank account? Lewis recognizes that the key to conforming our souls to reality is knowledge, self-discipline, and virtue. It is here that the foundation of ethics, especially the ethics of medicine and healthcare should begin and have its proper end. In addition, in chapter 4 I argued that existence is personal, and if this is right, then goodness (ethics) is too. In order to conform our souls to reality, we may need help to restructure ourselves in order gain real knowledge self-discipline and virtue. The Christian personalist view of reality maintains that since Jesus is the ground of created reality, then he is the only way for such a restructuring of our souls to occur. This is a longer story which is introduced in chapter 4, but it must be considered carefully.[18]

18. See Koukl, *The Story of Reality*, for an excellent overview of the Christian story of reality.

CHAPTER 12

Real Religion and Politics

Common Sense for Church and State

12.0 REAL CHURCH AND STATE

I arrive at the beach. I feel the cool, wet sand at my feet. I taste the saltiness of the ocean water on my lips. I hear the sound of the crashing surf. I smell the freshness of the sea air. I see waves breaking offshore. These things are real. Every person knows what is real from ordinary common-sense experiences like these. They also tell us more. They tell us about the nature of reality itself, about existence itself. The reality that I experience while surfing is both here and now, but also points to something transcendent; something beyond the here and now. What does the content of what I learn about the nature of existence from common-sense experience teach me about religious beliefs and practices as well as the social/political environment in which they occur? What does ontology, understood as a theory of existence, have to do with the conjunction of religion and politics? This chapter presents an evaluative framework of connections between various answers to the broadest question of ontology regarding the nature of existence and our understanding of theology and politics.

12.1 FROM ONTOLOGY TO CHURCH AND STATE

General ontology is an attempt to describe and give the most general account of being *qua* being. It answers the broadest question that can be asked: What is existence? The way in which one answers the question of ontology has bearing on how one answers all other questions in philosophy and outside of philosophy. For example, if one maintains that existence is physical or material, that all of reality is captured in the categories of physics, then this implies an epistemology that is empirical; knowledge is found only by sensate means. A physicalist ontology implies hedonistic ethics (bodily pleasure is the only good) as well as a sensate aesthetics (beauty is really only skin deep). Ontological physicalism would also have ramifications for logic. Logic under such an ontology could not be the study of the necessary relations that obtain among formal propositions but would have to be nothing more than some sort of language game reduced to physical causation.

If it is correct that general ontology has profound implications for the other areas of philosophy (epistemology, ethics, aesthetics, and logic), and if it is true that philosophy informs both theology and politics, then it follows that ontology has profound implications for politics and theology. Do philosophical questions about epistemology, aesthetics, and logic inform politics and theology? The answer is fairly clearly "yes." Politics, understood as the study of the normative structure of communal governance, must presuppose or have an account of the following things: How and what do we know about politics (epistemology)? What is good governance (ethics and aesthetics)? What are the reasons we have for organizing our body politic one way versus another (logic)? Similarly, in religion, theology understood as the rational study of God must give an account of whether or how one knows God (epistemology), whether God is good (both ethically and aesthetically), as well as give arguments as to both God's existence and attributes (logic). Thus, since philosophy is informed by ontology, and both politics and religion are deeply informed by philosophy, it follows that politics and religion are deeply informed by ontology.

In addition to this little syllogism, this seems fairly obvious when we reflect on the deeper questions of both politics and religion. For example, the political question "What is the state?" and the religious question "Does

God exist?" both involve ontological questions about existence regarding particular things (the state or God). In addition, how one answers questions in general ontology will affect how one answers these questions. To continue with our example of materialism, if the real is the physical, then the state will be best understood as some sort of physical entity obeying physical laws. Similarly, if physicalism were true, then an immaterial God could not exist; God would either not exist at all or God would be a physical being. Understanding that ontology informs philosophy and in turn politics and religion implies that if one wants to understand the relationship between politics and religion one must first have a clear account of *what is* (give an answer to the question: what is existence?). The way one answers this question will provide an initial relationship between politics and religion, namely that both of these areas of inquiry are understood in terms of the answers given to the question of ontology. Theoretical consistency would require as much. Again, from our example, if physicalism were true, both religion and politics would be understood in physicalist terms, and thus all relations between them must also be understood in these terms. The purpose of this chapter is to point out this foundational relation between religion and politics, and to examine two possible answers to the question of ontology, showing the implications for religion and politics. Let us now turn to that task.

12.1.1 Essential Exemplification (Again)

The common-sense view defended in this book is that existence is "essential exemplification." In chapter 2, I argued we can know this from a careful phenomenological reflection on the process of observation of contingent particulars in ordinary sense experience. It is from our acts of simple apprehension that we ground a theory of existence. We take those acts of simple apprehension, and we hold them before our "mind's eye" and consider what those simple acts tell us about the nature of existence.

12.1.2 Natural Existence Monism (Again)

In chapter 7, on materialism, we considered the materialist monist view of blobjectivism. Because there is only one thing, and given the formalization of natural existence monism, the only relation that exists is the relation of identity. This does not produce an *ontological* pluralism (a *plural* category with one member would be odd indeed). However, it seems to entail an *epistemic* pluralism. Consider the blobjectivist claims: "Truth is semantic correctness under contextually variable semantic standards"[1] and "numerous posit-wielding statements of physical theory are true even if the posits are mere constructs of the theoretical framework and are not genuine denizens of reality."[2]

Blobjectivism does not make a difference between things and their existence. There is nothing but one thing: nothing but the blob. So, talk about the existence of the blob is just to talk about the one thing that is. This is an extreme monism. So, within blobjectivism (monistic materialism), we have both a monism on the ontological level and a pluralism on the epistemic/semantic level.

12.2 A CLASH OF ONTOLOGIES

So, now we have a major contrast between two very different ontologies: common-sense realism and materialist monism. What I would like to suggest is that these two ontologies imply two very different approaches to politics and religion (as well as other areas of ethics). Let us consider three metaphysical features that can be applied to these two very different ontologies, common-sense realism (CSR) and monist materialism (MM). Then we will examine what the implications are for politics and theology.

First, consider the level of *being qua being*. Consider each ontology as a general approach to existence. For CSR, the key aspect here is relationality. If existence is essential exemplification, then there is some relationality involved in the nature of reality. For the Christian common-sense realist, this is especially important in the doctrine of the Trinity. Relationality, as part of the nature of reality can imply *community* in terms of both politics and religion. Thus, democracies as political communities and churches as faith communities are possible.

For materialist monism, existence is mere self-identity. This implies a kind of isolation. Is it any wonder that the political ideologies and religious approaches based on materialism are very lonely? On the political side, I have in mind here the Marxist materialist totalitarianism that ruled large swaths of the planet (and still does for at least over a billion people). Those systems of politics are tyrannical! There is usually one lonely person (or a few) ruling over millions or billions. On the religious side, I have in mind Bertrand Russell's "A Free Man's Worship" when he wrote: "All the loneliness of humanity amid hostile forces is concentrated upon the individual soul, which must struggle alone, with what of courage it can command, against

1. Horgan and Potrč, *Austere Realism*, 164.
2. Horgan and Potrč, *Austere Realism*, 171.

the whole weight of a universe that cares nothing for its hopes and fears."[3] This is loneliness bordering on solipsism.

Second, consider the relational aspects of ontology. For CSR, there is duality: essence and exemplification. This implies a kind of subsidiarity in politics and religion. Political systems derived from common-sense realism have a determinate order to political life, with things like "the consent of the governed" or "self-evident truths" being the basis for good governance.

For, MM, there is only singularity in any relationality. This is a kind of solipsism. Only the self is important. This is a factual question that could be considered by the disciplines of political science or anthropology or sociology: are social institutions healthier in political systems based on an MM or CSR ontology? Or you could just travel to your favorite totalitarian state and see the answer pretty obviously.

Third, consider the level of the epistemic. For CSR there is objectivity. The mind and the world can connect, and we can know the essences which are exemplified in the objects that have them. This gives us the objectivity of knowledge, including political and theological (as well as ethical and aesthetic) knowledge. The Christian tradition is a knowledge tradition. The Nicene Creed tells us that Jesus was crucified "under Pontius Pilate." Why does Pilate's name get recited in the creed? It is a reminder that the Christian religion is really historical. It can't be any way you like. Politics too for the realist can't be just any way we please. Political systems that ignore reality, especially human nature, usually end badly.

For MM, there is indeterminacy. There is only "the blob." It can be carved up any way you like. This implies subjectivism and mere opinion. Reality can be however you like! But is reality like that? Are religion and politics just language games? Was Jesus really crucified under Pontius Pilate? Was the resurrection developed as a way for the early church to "cope"? Are Christians above all the most to be pitied for believing something that never really happened? Is politics just a matter of power agreements? Is there no real truth or real nature or nature's God that we ought to conform our political lives to? Are the killing fields and gulags just one way to slice up political life, equal among others? Are eggs really eggs?

12.3 CONCLUSION: COMMON SENSE IN RELIGION AND POLITICS

Common-sense realism has the advantage of being understood from common-sense experience and easily known to be true. While it does imply

---

3. Russell, "A Free Man's Worship," 54.

something over and above the physical world, this is only a problem if one is already committed to monistic materialism. Blobjectivistic natural monism might have the advantage of cohering with the ways in which "we make the world" of culture and human art, including religion and politics. Yet, I argued in chapter 7 that, given the law of indiscernibility of identicals, if there is discernibility between existence and essence, then the two are identical. However, it appears that existence adds to essence, but essence does not add to existence. Thus, since essence and existence are discernible, they are, contrary to MM, not identical. Thus, if essence and existence are not identical, then MM cannot be true. If it cannot be true, then it will not be a real basis for philosophy of religion or politics. The real basis for religion and politics can be found in common-sense realism.

CHAPTER 13

Real Economics

13.0 COMMON-SENSE REALISM AND ECONOMICS

I arrive at the beach. I feel the cool, wet sand at my feet. I taste the saltiness of the ocean water on my lips. I hear the sound of the crashing surf. I smell the freshness of the sea air. I see waves breaking offshore. These things are real. Every person knows what is real from ordinary common-sense experiences like these. They also tell us more. They tell us about the nature of reality itself, about existence itself. The ordinary sense experiences of things like being at the beach point to reality that is independent of me and is common to others, as well. Reality is not just mine; it is ours. Our lives are lived in a community that involves economic activity. If you are a surfer who has purchased a surfboard, or even made your own, there is a great deal of economic activity that goes into this craft. How does economics connect to a theory of reality?

If it is possible for us to come to know what existence is by the interior and exterior routes described earlier in this book—namely that existence is essential exemplification, and that anything that exists does so because it is identical with its existence (in the case of God) or exemplifies an essence (for any being other than God)—then this provides the basis for further reflection on any existing thing as well as existence as such. This is to say that if we want to understand any real thing, we must begin with an understanding of what existence is (essential exemplification) and what it is for things to exist (to exemplify their essences). This will apply to our own existence as human beings and to all of our actions in so far as they exist. So, if we want to understand what we are, we must understand *that* we are *because of* the exemplification of our essence as human beings.

Earlier in the book, I argued that the ability to see what existence is can be done by a process of abstraction, separation, and judgment from any experience, either from the senses or of one's self. The rest of this chapter will show a path that leads from our knowledge of what existence is, and what it is for us to exist, in order to extend that knowledge from this basic ontological starting point outward to economic activity.

This discussion is not meant to be exhaustive. It is an attempt to consider how the central question of metaphysics—"What is existence?"—plays out in economic life. The purpose here is to show how a common-sense realist theory of existence informs economic thinking and to show how this can be put into practice.

13.1 HUMAN EXISTENCE AND HUMAN PERSONHOOD

If it is true that existence is essential exemplification, and if it is possible by means of abstraction (by means of the mind's powers to abstract from concrete acts of experience of particulars) to reflect upon those essences experienced in those acts, then one can come to have knowledge of essences. Such knowledge will be of those qualities of an essence that make the essence what it is and not another essence and will allow one to consider the possible relations of an essence to other things outside of itself. For example, it is possible to know that a blue thing exists as a blue thing because it exemplifies the essence of blueness. By means of abstraction, once can consider the essence of blueness apart from the particular that has it in order to know what blue is, and how it differs from other colors (e.g., red or yellow) or other qualities (e.g., extension or sound). One can see that to be blue is just to be a particular color with a particular phenomenal quality of blueness. Further, one can consider how blue relates to other things (e.g., blue stands in a relation of "darker than" to yellow). This knowledge of essences is quite simple, and like our knowledge of existence, can be tried by anyone who will take the time to engage in an act of simple apprehension of an ordinary sense experience, abstract the essence from the particular in an act of abstraction, and then reflect upon the essence that one has before one's mind.

One can try this simple procedure with one's own self. One can consider oneself as a particular. Through the means described in chapter 3, one can come to know that one exists because one exemplifies an essence. One can consider that essence in abstraction and reflect upon what make one's human essence what it is (i.e., the qualities that distinguish it from everything else) and the possible relations that this essence can stand to other things.

It does not take very much reflection along these phenomenological lines to see the broad features of what makes one's human essence what it is and distinct from all other things. Through such acts of mental reflection, one can see at least three features of human essence. First, we are embodied rational beings. Second, we are volitional (we have free will). Third, we are communal.

It is logically possible that these things simply are not real features of human essences. However, apart from philosophical arguments defending the realities of these features, which are substantial across the history of philosophy, you simply should ask yourself, have you ever experienced the following things: your own body, the use of your rational faculties, your free will, and other persons? It is logically possible than none of these things are real, but because this mere possibility exists, it should not by itself dismiss the real experience of these things in ordinary human life. Probably a greater challenge to the approach to our knowledge of human essence that I am describing here comes in the form of a crude materialism or physicalism in which essences are mere posits of an experiencing "mind" upon the material reality that one "experiences." I have addressed some of these problems in chapter 7.

If these things are true of us, and if we are interested in dealing effectively with human reality, then to live as a human being, in all areas of our lives, will be to use these realities as a guide for our actions. This will of course include economic actions. So, economic life will be one that recognizes the essence of human bodies and material realities lived in light of our rational faculties. Thus, economics in so far as it reflects what human beings are will be a discipline in which the concern for human material welfare is paramount. But, economic life will not merely be material, for we are not merely material beings. We have "higher" faculties of reason. Thus, economic life will be ordered in such a way that reason plays a central role. Economic life will be engaged by the mind, by reflection, by logical consideration of those things super-material or even super-natural.[1] Third, economic life will be free, allowing the reality of free will to exemplify itself in our social exchanges.

13.2 THEOLOGICAL KNOWLEDGE OF HUMAN PERSONHOOD: THE *IMAGO DEI*

I would like to add three additional features to human essence. These are items of knowledge—which can inform a view of economics—that are known by revelation apart from human reflection on particular cases of existing things. These three features are consistent with such reflection and extend our knowledge of what it means to exist as a being exemplifying a human essence in such a way as to compliment (or complete) the sketch of human essence given by rational experience alone. These three items are part of a Christian view of economics and can be tested for their viability by means of human experience.[2]

On a Christian view of the human person, human beings are made in the image of God. The implications of this are numerous, but the concept involves an understanding of theology proper: what is God like on a Christian view? First, God is a rational being. Second, God is a volitional/creative being. Third, God is a Trinitarian being, which implies his relationality. If these revelation claims are true, they are consistent with rational reflection on human essence by means of which we can see our rationality, will, and relationality.

Although some of these features appear consistent with rational reflection, they go beyond such natural rational reflection. For example, the Trinitarian nature of God with respect to our existence as contingent beings implies that God's existence as that which is identical to his essence is also Trinitarian, or relational in nature. By analogy with respect to being made

---

1. This is an overly broad claim here, and I will try to narrow down this concept further in the next few pages.

2. This is not an argument for theism. I am simply considering what follows for economic theory if these claims are true. One can test these claims to see whether they are true by putting them into practice and seeing the results.

in God's *image*, our essences, although distinct from our existence, contain a relationality that goes beyond human relations and connects with God himself. A view of human essence from a Christian perspective entails that human essence is not only dependent on God for its existence,[3] but enters into an interpersonal relation with its creator that *images* the Trinitarian nature of God himself.

Given the truth of human essence reflecting the image of God, the implications for economics are many. First, given our rational faculties embodied in the material world (which was created as essentially good on a Christian view), our economic life will be one that begins with our thought of how to engage the world economically by rational means. Second, given God's volitional/creative abilities present in us as an image of God's will and creative powers, we become "sub-creators" and are given charge of the material cosmos as a gift to be cultivated like one cultivates one's own garden. Thus, one can use this notion of the world as a gift to be subdued, cultivated, and used toward human flourishing as a basis for further reflection on economic activity. Third, our relationality is twofold. There is first of all our relationship with God, and our economic life ought to be ordered toward the glory of the One on whom we are dependent such that all economic activity attempts to exemplify the good-making qualities of God's nature. Second, there is our relationship with others. This relationship will mirror the Trinitarian nature of God's essence, which is one of self-giving love. This concept should enter into any robust Christian consideration of economic life and activity.

13.3 THEOLOGICAL KNOWLEDGE OF HUMAN PERSONHOOD: THE FALL AND ESCHATOLOGY

Thus far I have only been considering how we can understand human essence as such from both rational reflection on particular experiences of being human and Christian revelation. I would like to add two things to these ideas that are not part and parcel of the essence of being human, but that nevertheless are attendant realities that are part of the human experience and that theological knowledge can explain. While our knowledge of human essence from rational reflection does not entail the fact that there is something "not quite right" with human life, one can by just thinking about one's own life see that human life is far from perfect.[4] The consequences

3. Attempts at natural theology from reason apart from revelation may also be successful in minimally demonstrating this point rationally.

4. If you are overly optimistic about human goodness, read Rummel's *Death by Government*, which chronicles the genocides of the twentieth century.

of human sin are quite obvious to common-sense experience. Christian revelation concurs with this obvious item of knowledge gained from human experience and offers both an etiology and corrective eschatology that seem to have implications for economic philosophy.

The Christian etiology of human sin (brokenness, bentness, or something's-not-quite-right-ness) begins with the free exercise of the human will. One could explain this by an account of God's essential perfect nature creating beings that are themselves perfectly good with respect to their contingent, finite essences, where one necessary feature of any perfectly good contingent rational being capable of entering into a loving relationship with God (a being incapable of such a relation would not be as perfect as a being who could) is the ability to freely exercise their will. This could be described as the ability to do or to forbear any particular volitional act, including one that would allow one's essence to be fulfilled in future actions or one that would prohibit it from being fulfilled.

A Christian view of the fall of human beings describes such an act in the context of a drama of great cosmic spiritual personal realities and accounts for our brokenness by means of the exercise of our wills away from God's design for our lives, including our economic lives. While necessarily a perfect being creates only good things, necessarily if God creates free beings, then it is possible (but not necessary) that the exercise of free will entails the privation of the full actualization of our *imago Dei* essential nature. Christian revelation chronicles this account of the fall as both initial, for God's first created human beings, and perpetual, for all human beings with clear economic consequences. Work was created by God as an essential good and part of our human essence in the Garden of Eden as part of God's economic plan for our lives. However, after the fall, work becomes fraught with toil, labor, and ultimately vanity as human beings live, flourish, return to the dust in death, while retaining the hope of a new heaven and new earth in the resurrection.

This brings me to the second attendant reality informed by Christian theology, which complements our rational and theological reflection on what it means to be human. Christian revelation regarding human essence is eschatological. That is, it pertains to the ultimate ends of being human. By means of rational reflection we can see that human essences are teleological, that is they actualize their essences in order to produce human well-being. But Christian theology goes beyond this rational reflection, and supplements it with knowledge of both the corrective measures needed to "straighten" human brokenness and gives an account of human life—individual, social, and economic—that goes beyond the created order as we know it now. Such an eschatology goes beyond this life and gives us a glimpse of the afterlife and an eternal economy of human beings made in God's image fully restored in a new earth. This eschatology is informed for Christians in at least two ways: (1) in the incarnation of Jesus Christ; (2) in the passion of Jesus, including his suffering, crucifixion, resurrection, ascension, and second coming. A full discussion of how these items of historical revelation give us knowledge of the solution for the human condition is beyond the scope of this chapter, but let us consider just one example as applied to economics.

If it is true that human essences, which appear in concrete individuals, are restored because of Jesus' life and resurrection, then this will have at least three implications for economic activity. First, it will allow an economic thinker to recognize the broken and fleeting nature of this life to be lived as fully as possible toward that which is good. Second, it will recognize that what is done in this life has eternal implications and consequences. Thus, our economic attitudes will be realistic in their attempts to organize into specific economic structures. We might call this Christian economic realism. It recognizes both the goodness and the terribly marred features of human nature. We are not perfect angels that just need the right material conditions to be perfect.

Third, it recognizes that utopia here and now cannot be created, but there is a perfect world that will be realized in the future. Thus, Christian economic realism will engage with human realities as they are, avoid utopianism, but place one's ultimate economic citizenship not in this life but in the next. The image one might see here is one of an economic pilgrim on a journey through this present age dealing economically with things as they really are based on an appropriate experience of this life. We pilgrims journey toward our true home, a home that will have an economy with a full and complete exemplification of restored and renewed human essence in right relationship with other like-minded human beings in a fully restored relationship with God. It is this type of Christian realism that can not only guide our thinking, but guide our *doing*, as I believe it has been attempted in the case of the Mondragon Cooperative.

13.4 MONDRAGON COOPERATIVE: CHRISTIAN METAPHYSICAL REALISM AT WORK[5]

Sometimes there arise individuals who take ideas sufficiently seriously and have been given a particular gift and perhaps the right circumstances to be

5. Special thanks to Leire Uriarte Zabala, Universidad de Mondragon—LANKI (an expert on cooperatives), Carlos García de Andoin, Instituto de Teología, Diocese of Bilbao (an expert on Mondragon and its relation to the church), and Fernando Molina

able to try to put those ideas into practice. One such man was José María Arizmendiarrieta Madariaga (1915–76).[6] Arizmendi (as he was commonly known) founded the Mondragon Cooperatives in the 1940s and '50s.[7] From its humble beginnings as a center for training and manufacturing for Basque youth after the Spanish civil war, Mondragon has grown to a multinational organization to include over seventy-four thousand workers with a total income of nearly twelve billion euros (approx. 13.5 billion USD) as of 2013.[8]

The Mondragon cooperatives were founded on four principles held dear to Arizmendi: (1) The dignity of the human person, (2) solidarity, (3) the goodness of work, and (4) education.[9] While these are not the only values of the Mondragon Cooperative, they are central to the history of this particular organization.[10] Before we turn to each of these values and see how they are connected with a Christian realist ontology, a word must be said about the philosophical roots of these ideas in the founder of Mondragon.

There is a key historical connection between the founder of Mondragon, Father Arizmendi, and the common-sense ontological realism defended in this book. In chapter 2, I discussed the process by means of which the human mind moves from a direct, immediate awareness of things as they are in themselves in ordinary sense experience (epistemic realism), to knowledge of not only what it is for something to exist but also to knowledge of existence itself. These ideas were defended and elaborated by Arizmendi's contemporaries, such as Jacques Maritain.

Maritain is the key intellectual bridge between epistemic and ontological realism and the values of the Mondragon cooperative held by Father Arizmendi. Arizmendi was not a systematic philosopher, but he was influenced by those who were, such as Maritain.[11] Biographer Fernando Molina

Aparicio, Universidad Pais Vasco (a biographer of the founder of Mondragon) for taking their time to meet with me to discuss Mondragon during my first visit to the Basque region. Thank you as well to the Praxis Peace Institute for arranging a multi-day group tour of the Mondragon Cooperatives during my second visit to the region.

6. For a thorough and recent biography (in Spanish) of Arizmendiarrieta see Molina, *José María Arizmendiarrieta, 1915–1976 Biografía*. For a lengthy treatment of the thought of Arizmendi (in Spanish) see Azurmendi, *El Hombre Cooperative*.

7. For book-length treatment and overview of Mondragon see Whyte and Whyte, *The Making of Mondragon*. For a narrower look at the Christian influences of Mondragon, see Molina and Miguez, "The Origins of Mondragon."

8. See Mondragon, *Annual Report*.

9. These ideas were presented to me in a presentation given by Ander Etexeberria during my visit to Mondragon.

10. For a longer consideration of the original values of the founding of Mondragon see Altuna, *La Experiencia Cooperative de Mondragon: Una Síntesis General*.

11. "Las fuentes de Arizmendiarrieta pueden dividirse fundamentalmente en

claims that it was the thought of Maritain that functioned like a religious conversion in the establishment of Mondragon, which was a direct expression of the Christian gospel of Jesus in an industrial society.[12] Mondragon emerged from an ontological realism emphasizing that reality is essential exemplification, and that human essence should be seen as the foundation for economic life. However, this foundation is not purely secular for Arizmendi. It is informed theologically, grounded in special revelation. "In Arizmendiarrieta's humanist view of society, man was created in the image of God and should not live enclosed in egocentric individualism, turning his back on Christian solidarity."[13]

Let us consider these four values in turn: (1) dignity, (2) solidarity, (3) work, and (4) education. Let us begin with human dignity. Human dignity is grounded in realism. From ontological realism flows an understanding of the nature of essences exemplified. From an analysis of human essence flow certain realities that are part and parcel of *being* human. Human *dignity* reflects the intrinsic goodness of human beings as part of the created order. *Solidarity* flows from the communal nature of human beings reflected in the image of God understood as a Trinity. The goodness of *work* flows from Judeo-Christian revelation, which views this earth as a place over which human beings have stewardship. Work is neither a result of the fall of man (it existed before this event), nor is work something to be avoided. It is the expression of the soul of the worker, in the way that the created order is the expression of the soul of God.[14] And finally *education* recognizes the

---

cuatro grupos: 1) la doctrina social cristiana, 2) los pensadores personalistas, ante todo Maritain y Mounier, 3) la tradición social vasca, destacando en ella la tradición social-cristiana de los «sacerdotes propagandistas», por un lado, y de los ugetistas y socialistas, por el otro, especialmente del llamado «socialismo eibarrés», y 4) los clásicos del cooperativismo (P. Lambert, etc.)" (Azurmendi, *El Hombre Cooperativo*, 37).

12. "Apoyado en Maritain y Mounier, planteaba una revolución interior equiparable a la conversión religiosa, no en vano estaba sustentada en una espiritualidad que preconizaba la austeridad y compromiso con el prójimo. Presentaba el cooperativismo como una expresión del cristianismo evangélico de Jesús en una sociedad industrial en la que, más que nunca, lo humano había quedado injertado en lo económico" (Molina, *José María Arizmendiarrieta*, 451). Apparently Arizmendi would give away books by Maritain to his students to read (Molina and Miguez, "Origins of Mondragon," 293–94).

13. Molina and Miguez, "Origins of Mondragon," 294. After visiting Mondragon and interviewing both employees and academic experts on Mondragon, it seems to me that whether or not a purely secular (with neither transcendent epistemic or ontological grounding) understanding of Arizmendi's values can sustain itself intellectually or in practice is questionable. In fact, I do not believe that Mondragon could have been possible on the secular ontology that now dominates the Basque region, Spain, Europe, and the West. For an exploration of secularism in all areas of life, including economic life see, Poplin, *Is Reality Secular?*

14. For a delightful defense of the goodness of work, see Sayers, "Why Work?"

rational creative and volitional aspects of human nature understood as the *imago Dei*.

The Mondragon cooperative attempts to live out these core theologically rooted principles to this day. However, it competes in a global capitalist free-market system, and has managed to survive many crises in its history. In the remainder of this chapter, I will consider how the values of Mondragon are consistent with supporting global free markets. I will do this by considering some basic principles of free-market economics and then considering how these stand in relation to the values of Mondragon, which are ultimately grounded in a Christian ontology.

13.5 FIVE FREE-MARKET PRINCIPLES, FIVE FEATURES OF HUMAN EXISTENCE, AND FOUR VALUES OF MONDRAGON

Throughout this book, I have argued that we can come to know that existence is essential exemplification and that from this knowledge, we can consider a knowledge of essences, including human essence. From our knowledge of human essence considered both from reason and revelation, I claimed earlier in this chapter that the following general facts of human essence (E) were plausible, namely that to be human means to be a being with:

E1   Rationality

E2   Freedom

E3   Relationality

E4   Fallenness

E5   Redeemability

I then considered that one example of the implementation of such a vision of human personhood was found in the Mondragon Cooperative movement based on the following "Mondragon Values":

MV1   Human Dignity

MV2   Solidarity

MV3   Goodness of work

MV5   Education.

Sayers quotes from Maritain in this essay.

I then considered that not only are E1–5 compatible with MV1–5, but that MV1–5 are ontologically dependent upon E1–5. Now I would like to consider whether E1–5, together with MV 1–5, are compatible with free-market economics. I begin by listing a few key principles or ideas that are part and parcel of a free-market perspective on economics.

The Foundation of Economic Education (FEE) is an excellent example of an organization that supports, defends, and educates regarding the practices of global free markets. They have published or hosted public lectures from thinkers such as Ludwig von Mises, F. A. Hayek, Henry Hazlitt, Milton Friedman, and Walter Williams. These are key thinkers who defend free markets. In 1993 FEE published a series of articles entitled "The Economic Way of Thinking" by the late Ronald Nash as an overview and introductory defense of free markets held by thinkers like Von Mises, Hayek, and Friedman.[15] It is from these articles that I will consider a brief list of concepts and values to consider their relation to the ontology considered in this chapter and its exemplification in the Mondragon cooperative. Nash's summarizes the core concept and values of a free market (FM 1–6):

FM1. *Scarcity and Choice.* Economics is the study of "the choices human beings make with regard to scarce resources. If there is any such thing as bedrock in economics, it rests in these two fundamental concepts: scarcity and choice."[16]

FM2. *Relativity of Economic Value.* "Economic value is always in the eye of the beholder."[17] Nash writes, not "all economic choices are equally good in a moral or religious sense. Anyone is within his philosophical and theological rights to criticize particular economic choices. No defender of the market economy is required to defend all the goods produced by the market. It seems clear, therefore, that any objection to the theory of subjective economic value on theological or moral grounds is mistaken. In fact, it is from Christian theology that economics borrowed its central concept of imputed value."[18]

FM3. *Market Spontaneity.* The market "is a spontaneous and impersonal order of arrangements that serves as the framework within which

---

15. Nash has been called "the most zealous Christian advocate of Austrian economic theory" (McDaniel, *God & Money,* 146).

16. Nash, "The Economic Way of Thinking, Part 1."

17 Nash, "The Economic Way of Thinking, Part 1."

18. Nash, "The Economic Way of Thinking, Part 2."

individual human beings make economic choices"[19] and it does the following four things:

3.1 "permits people to specialize in those things they do best";[20]

3.2 allows people to "alter their choices in response to changing incentive";

3.3 "supplies important information via changes in the relative prices of goods";

3.4 "makes people accountable for their economic activities."[21]

FM4. *Political Liberty.* There are "necessary conditions for free markets," including:

4.1 "an enforced right to own and to exchange property";

4.2 "an enforcement of contracts";

4.3 "laws that forbid the use of force, fraud, and theft";[22]

4.4 "the existence of inherent human rights, such as the right to make decisions";

4.5 "the right to be free";

4.6 "the right to hold property";

4.7 "the right to exchange what one owns for something else."[23]

FM5. *Private Property.* "The best way to mitigate the effects of evil in the human heart and the subsequent pursuit of unlimited power is to disperse and decentralize power. . . . Private ownership of property is an important buffer against any exorbitant consolidation of power by government."[24]

FM1–FM5 are not the only values that Nash considers in his series of articles, but I think that these are the salient ones for a consideration of the compatibility of E1–5, MV1–5, and FM1–5. Let us now turn to see how

---

19. Nash, "The Economic Way of Thinking, Part 3."
20. Nash, "The Economic Way of Thinking, Part 1."
21. Nash, "The Economic Way of Thinking, Part 3."
22. Nash, "The Economic Way of Thinking, Part 3."
23. Nash, "The Economic Way of Thinking, Part 1."
24. Nash, "The Economic Way of Thinking, Part 1."

these values are compatible with what we know about human nature and the values of the Mondragon cooperatives.

13.6 THE COMPATIBILITY OF FREE MARKETS, HUMAN EXISTENCE, AND MONDRAGON VALUES

Let us consider FM1–5 with respect to E1–5 and MV1–5. I will show how each of these free-market principles is both consistent with the features of human existence discussed above, and how they can help exemplify the values of Mondragon. I will consider FM1–5 each in turn.

FM1 (Scarcity and Choice) is simply an understanding of what economics is. It is a principle consistent with both E1-Rationality and E3-Relationality. It seems to me not incompatible with MV1–5 and may be consistent with MV1-Human Dignity insofar as FM1-Scarcity and Choice recognizes that part of human dignity that just is our freedom and rationality. Thus FM1-Scarcity and Choice is probably neutral with respect to MV1–5 and compatible with other related values other than MV1–5.

FM2-Relative Economic Value is a view of the nature of economic value, which Nash is careful to distinguish from moral (or axiological) value. It is simply the idea that different participants in a free-market system place different relative economic values on different things. This seems consistent with E1-Rationality and E2-Freedom, and possibly consistent with E4-Falleness, if FM2-Relative Economic Value maintains the distinction that there are some things (even economic things that are of a low moral value sufficient to entail that they ought to have a low economic value). This would entail consistency with MV1-Human Dignity and MV3-Goodness of Work. There may be some types of work or some human acts that people do value economically but that are of such low moral value that this value militates against human dignity or the objective value of work. This is to say that such a thing, which is economically valued, could ruin the soul of the person and destroy their intrinsic dignity. It could stunt the exemplification of their human essence and thus stunt the natural telos of being human. It implies that there are some types of "economically valued work" that are morally, objectively bad, and thus undermine the goodness of work as such, even if valued economically.

FM3-Market Spontaneity is a description of the nature of free markets. This seems consistent with both E1-Rationality, E2-Freedom, and E3-Relationality. Such a system allows for a context for human beings to actualize freely their rational and relational capacities in a variety of economic arrangements that are valued by those participating. FM3-Market

Spontaneity allows for the possibility (but not the necessity) of MV_{1-4} (Human Dignity, Solidarity, Goodness of Work, and Education). In such a system, MV_2-Solidarity especially would simply be one such arrangement that those participating in a cooperative would find economically valuable. Perhaps it would be fair to say that FM_3-Market Spontaneity combined with FM_2-Relative Economic Value is what allows a worker-owned cooperative such as the Mondragon Cooperatives to flourish. Those who value cooperatives have the freedom of market permissive spontaneity to organize themselves in a robust way in order to express the value of solidarity.[25] Finally, FM_3-Market Spontaneity (especially 3.1-Specialization) very much allows for E_{1-3} (Rationality, Freedom, and Relationality) and MV_{1-3} (Dignity, Solidarity, and Goodness of Work) to be manifest. Specialization allows for particular individuals to fully express their inherent capacities for what they do best, which brings dignity for the individual, solidarity and inter-dependence with others, and allows one to see the goodness of their own individual work in light of this inter-dependence and solidarity.

FM_4-Political Liberty regards the antecedent structural requirements for free markets. (Property rights are especially salient here.) The cooperative value MV_2-Solidarity works out practically in the fact that Mondragon cooperative members each "buy into" the cooperative. The workers are the owners. For those who value the wide distribution of property, the right to do so (I take this to be a natural negative right) is absolutely necessary for the exemplification of MV_2-Solidarity.

FM_5-Private Property is a general restatement of E_4-Falleness as discussed earlier in this chapter, and it is a good recognition of this reality. If FM_5-Private Property is true, then it seems clear to me that the cooperative value of MV_2-Solidarity, again exemplified in the wide dispersion of power to cooperative members, may allow for greater democracy and less possibility of managerial dictatorial power in business in an analogous way that dictatorial power is consolidated in politics. That MV_2-Solidarity is a way of exemplifying FM_5-Private Property.

This completes this brief (and rather cursory) overview of the compatibility of the values of Mondragon (which I argued are grounded in facts both theological and rational) and their compatibility with free-market

25. I do believe that MV_1–MV_5 are real moral values, part and parcel of the facts of E_1–E_5. However, they may be treated as economic values as well. When considered as economic values (which are relative to those who hold them), they become possibly expressible (i.e., exemplified) best when they occur in a system which allows for their free expression. It seems to me that Nash's description of a free-market system is one that contains the greatest possibility for such arrangements.

concepts.[26] It seems to me that free-market concepts are compatible with such cooperatives' values.[27] They provide a possible way to exemplify E5-Redeemability of human life.[28] This is one possible, and historically workable model of how Christian ontological realism can be worked out in a practical way.

13.7 CONCLUSION: EVERY DAY IS "TAKE ONTOLOGY TO WORK DAY"

Connecting deep issues in ontology (i.e., metaphysics—a study of reality) with economic theory and applying these ideas to a particular case to test for compatibility has been the purpose of this chapter. I have argued that from common-sense experience we can know what existence is (essential exemplification). From this knowledge, we can see what essences are (including human essence). I have considered how human essence and knowledge about it (from both general rational reflection and from theological revelation) can inform economic thinking. I then turned to a comparison of an understanding of free markets with this knowledge and have shown how both free markets together with Christian metaphysical realism are compatible with the particular case of Mondragon Cooperative values.

Let me conclude with a quotation from Jacques Maritain, the bridge between Christian ontological realism and Mondragon. Maritain states, "In the last analysis it is because God is the Act of Existing Itself, in His ocean of all perfection, that the love of that which is better than all goodness is that in which man attains the perfection of being."[29] Part of human life involves our economic activity. A thoroughgoing Christian realism ought to see our economic activities as a means to attaining the perfection of our being, the exemplification of our essences as God's children destined for good work prepared for us.

---

26. For an additional discussion of the relationship between Mondragon and capitalism, see Hindmoor, "Free Riding off Capitalism." Hindmoor writes, "Mondragon depends upon the achievements of the capitalist economy within which it is embedded" (218).

27. For a popular discussion from a free-market perspective of Mondragon within the context of the economic philosophy of distributism, see Deavel, "What's Right with Distributism," and Deavel, "What's Right with Distributism." For a popular level "distributist" response to Deavel, see Storck, "What's Wrong with Distributism."

28. FM1–5 certainly don't guarantee either E5-Redeemability or MV5-Education, but do allow for their possibility.

29. Maritain, *Exitence and the Existent*, 49.

PART 5

Reality Restored
We Have Fought the Long Defeat

CHAPTER 14

The Long Defeat
and Our Final Gladness

14.1 The Long Defeat

14.2 From Part to Whole

14.3 From Common Sense through Scripture to Our Final Gladness

14.1 THE LONG DEFEAT

I arrive at the beach. I feel the cool, wet sand at my feet. I taste the saltiness of the ocean water on my lips. I hear the sound of the crashing surf. I smell the freshness of the sea air. I see waves breaking offshore. These things are real. Every person knows what is real from ordinary common-sense experiences like these. They also tell us more. They tell us about the nature of reality itself, about existence itself. But, everyone leaves the beach eventually. There is always a final wave, the paddle back to shore and the journey home. The ordinary common-sense things of this world which teach us so much about the nature of what is, eventually fade. If the things of this world *everlastingly* wind down that would be nauseating indeed.

Some years ago, I was listening to an audio recording of J. R. R. Tolkien's *Lord of the Rings*, and I noticed a phrase that I had unthinkingly passed over in my previous readings. The line is from Galadriel's conversation with Frodo. She says that she has "fought the long defeat."[1] This struck me when

1. Tolkien, *The Lord of the Rings*, 357.

I really heard it. Tolkien said that as a Christian he didn't expect "'history' to be anything but a 'long defeat,'" but he adds that history does contain "some samples or glimpses of final victory."[2]

There is something right about this idea. Common-sense realism has had a rough go of things over the last half of a millennium, and especially over the last century, both philosophically and culturally. Orwell saw that common sense would be the greatest of heresies under totalitarianism, whether that totalitarianism is political or intellectual. Regarding culture post-World War II, Tolkien wrote to his son Christopher, "You and I belong to the ever-defeated never altogether subdued side."[3] Perhaps common-sense realism is like that: ever-defeated but never subdued. The long defeat is real, but so is the life to come.

Common-sense realism is heretical today according to the secular orthodoxy of our times. This should cause no alarm among common-sense realists. Defending the obvious from philosophies that deny the obvious is a noble calling; we must fight that good fight. Yet, the defense of common sense is the fight of a long defeat. It is *long* because the human intellect and human will continually strive toward themselves rather than *what is*. It is a defeat, because in the end, the world of common sense is not a dream, but it will someday seem like one.[4] The common-sense world that we know, love, and defend is passing away, but it will be renewed. And when we see the One in whom all things have there being no defense will be needed for such love.

14.2 FROM PART TO WHOLE

In chapter 1, I mentioned a question raised by a student in a recent philosophy course. The question was: "Is there just one reality or does each person have their own reality?" Well, if we each have our own reality, then reality is no longer real, eggs are no longer eggs, and the broad daylight of the brotherhood of man, has darkened to the twilight of "every man for himself." And if reality is no longer real, then it is impossible for students to get at the nature of reality even in a *fragmented* or *partial* way let alone from the fragment/part to the whole, through common-sense experience to the fullness and whole of *what is*.

---

2. Tolkien, *The Letters of J. R. R. Tolkien*, 255.

3. Tolkien, *The Letters of J. R. R. Tolkien*, 89.

4. I owe this idea to George MacDonald, who I believe borrowed it from the poet Novalis.

I argued in chapter 2 that from our ordinary sense experiences, we are reasonable in believing that existence is essential actualization. Things exist because they exemplify their essences. Human beings are therefore capable of knowing existence through the fragmentary nature of experience. We have a glimpse of the whole nature of existence (of being, of reality, of *what is*) through our experience of the fragments of being in our ordinary sense experiences.

Hans Urs von Balthasar in *Das Ganze im Fragment* (*Man in History: A Theological Study*) also recognizes this ability when he states,

> Man exists in a transcending extension beyond himself, not only toward something and his environment, but toward the world, toward being in general. Wherever being is illuminated, however obscurely, there is his humanity, and he becomes illuminated to himself as spirit. There he exists in the freedom which has not only arrived at the real, but also been able to distance itself from every individual piece of reality.[5]

Hans Urs von Balthasar also shows that common-sense realism is part and parcel of the Christian faith. As Christians, we are to model our lives after Jesus, and Balthasar shows how Jesus himself in his humanity experienced the delight and wonder of *what is*, which is arrived at through our common-sense experiences. According to Balthasar, Jesus, when he was a youth, measures the extent of being and discovers the delightful "depth . . . of *being*: of one's own, of other people's, of that of the nature around one. Existence itself unintelligible, is woven from the stuff of wonders. . . . Reality itself is what is wonderful: frightening and seductive, burdensome to the point of melancholy, yet inviting one to a secret, continual feast."[6]

Balthasar also makes a similar point to our knowledge of existence that Edith Stein made in chapter 3 when she argued that from our own common-sense experience of ourselves, we can come to know that there is Eternal Being. In his discussion of time, Balthasar writes:

> Time results from the radical not-being God of the creature and, for Augustine, that means that it is rooted in its (bodily or spiritual) materiality. Time is the principle of total differentiation from God and all similarity to God originates in what calls the creature back to God, the power of the Logos drawing form out of material substance. Precisely because matter is not in opposition to God, . . . and indeed is the definite basis of all the good created works of God, creaturely time is good in itself and does

5. Balthasar, *Man in History*, 219.
6. Balthasar, *Man in History*, 260.

not express a fall. The creature called from the realm of nothingness into being by God has this longing for the source of being,
the transcendent (and, therefore, extratemporal) being of God.[7]

Thus, from our awareness of the existence of ourselves, we become aware of
eternal being. The next question is, how do we respond to our knowledge?

Balthasar shows this step of faith when he discusses the youthfulness
of Jesus and his saints. Following Georges Bernanos, Balthasar exclaims, the
"Saints are, above all, young. They are fifteen years old, even if . . . they are
crushed by the weight of physical and moral death. All their thinking flows
from youthful spirit."[8] Recently I took my fifteen-year-old son and some of
his buddies surfing after school. The waves were much larger than normal
that day, but the boys insisted that I take them to a spot that I wasn't sure
they could even make the paddle out. We parked in the parking lot and
walked to the beach. One look at the giant surf, and I said, "Forget it, let's go
to a smaller spot." The waves where huge, pounding walls of cold saltwater.
But the three fifteen-year-olds charged out there like David against Goliath;
ready to slay their giants, "In the name of the LORD Almighty, the God of
the armies of Israel!" Nothing was stopping them. As I watched my son
get sucked out into the ocean in a rather powerful rip current, I thought,
well this may be my last look at him, drifting out into the Pacific never to
be seen again. (I wonder if David's brothers thought that when he charged
Goliath?!)

While watching in terror, I pulled up the emergency number to the
local lifeguard station on my phone while I witnessed all three boys get just
absolutely pounded, over and over, by waves that were bordering on ten
feet high. Only one of the three boys caught a wave that afternoon, but after
about forty-five minutes of getting hammered by the surf, they were swept
to shore and with the biggest smiles on their faces said to me, "That was
awesome!"

People of faith are fifteen-year-old surfers charging into the sheer
overwhelming power of *what is*, "even if they are crushed by the weight
of death." Paddling out is always a risk. As Tolkien wrote, "It's a dangerous
business, Frodo, going out your door. You step onto the road, and if you
don't keep your feet, there's no knowing where you might be swept off."[9]
Surfing and our response to the gift of existence is a lot like that. By grace,
through faith, stepping off the shore of our fragments of sense experience
and self-knowledge into reality is a gift that leads us to the Giver.

7. Balthasar, *Man in History*, 23.
8. Balthasar, *Man in History*, 265.
9. Tolkien, *Lord of the Rings*, 74.

14.3 FROM COMMON SENSE THROUGH SCRIPTURE TO OUR FINAL GLADNESS

The logic of both the teleological and sacramental nature of our experience of existence leads us from the fragment of existence in common-sense experience to the whole of God's love in our relationship with the Holy Trinity. This is primarily done through revelation in Scripture and especially in the incarnation. Knowledge of reality at this point is received also as a gift, similarly to the reception of reality through sense experience and experience of ourselves. That reality is personal was argued in chapter 3.

Balthasar makes it clear that it is in Christian revelation that the fragment of reality—even in revelation, which we experience teleologically—lead us to the whole. Remember St. Paul's words in 1 Corinthians 13:12, "For now we see only a reflection as in a mirror; then we shall see face to face. Now I know in part; then I shall know fully, even as I am fully known." Balthasar writes, "Faith alone contains a fulfilling hope . . . because, beyond all intermediate stages in time it grasps fulfillment, nay is grasped by it. It reaches for the goal that has already reached it (Phil. 3.12–13). Faith grasps the whole in every fragment because it is already grasped by the whole and incorporated into its body."[10]

But Christian faith is not blind faith. Rather, "faith is our step of trust to rely on what we have good reason to believe is so."[11] What we have good reason to believe comes to us through common-sense real experiences regarding the nature of existence. Through these experiences we can know that existence is real and it is independent from us. We can fill in this knowledge with the eternality of being from Stein's interior phenomenology. Finally, we are given Christian revelation claims. Scripture shows us reality is personal. Scripture completes our concept of existence and shows that what we know about existence from general revelation is not only compatible with Scripture, but that Scripture is what one might expect to find next along the path of discovery of the real nature of existence.

Finally, it is important to remember that although Christian revelation culminates in Jesus and completes what we begin to see from common sense, it is also works with it, especially in our knowledge of the incarnation. Let me conclude with a passage from St. John's First Epistle to summarize how our knowledge of the incarnation presupposes common-sense realism, and how the incarnation fulfills what we know from natural reason. John writes:

10. Balthasar, *Man in History*, 334.
11. Koukl, *The Story of Reality*, 137.

> What was from the beginning, what we have heard, what we
> have seen with our eyes, what we have looked at and touched
> with our hands, concerning the Word of Life and the life was
> manifested, and we have seen and testify and proclaim to you
> the eternal life, which was with the Father and was manifested to
> us what we have seen and heard we proclaim to you also, so that
> you too may have fellowship with us; and indeed our fellowship
> is with the Father, and with his Son Jesus Christ. These things
> we write, so that our joy may be made complete. (1 John 1:1–4)

Those who knew Jesus really heard, saw, and touched the Great I Am. They really knew that Jesus had a human body, lived a fully human life, really died on the cross, and really rose again. Those eyewitnesses had a common-sense awareness *of what is*, of Jesus, the I Am. It is Jesus' gift of existence that leads us teleologically and sacramentally into the very loving fellowship of the Trinity.

God gives us fragments in general revelation and gives us direct knowledge of himself in special revelation and gives himself entirely in the incarnation, bringing us into fellowship with himself. As Balthasar concludes, so shall we. The "tread of the believer through time toward the risen Christ is the true progress of the world. It alone sets creation as a whole in true movement toward God. It implants into all the vanity of earthly activity an eternal soul. As faith, it does not seek to replace sight (2 Cor. 5:7). . . . In this there is certainty, 'If God is for us, who is against us? He who did not spare his own Son but gave him up for us all, will he not also give us all things with him?' (Rom. 8:31–32)."[12] From the fragmented long defeat, to the whole of glory, from common sense to eternal happiness, this is our "final gladness."[13]

---

12. Balthasar, *Man in History*, 335.
13. Belloc, *The Four Men*, 250.

Works Cited

Aertsen, Jan. *Medieval Philosophy and the Transcendentals*. Leiden: Brill, 1996.

Altuna, Larraitz. *La Experiencia Cooperative de Mondragon: Una Síntesis General*. Eskoriatza, Spain: Lanki-Huhezi, 2008.

Anderson, James F., and Norris W. Clarke. *An Introduction to the Metaphysics of St. Thomas Aquinas*. Chicago: Regnery, 2008.

Aquinas, Thomas. *The Divisions and Methods of the Sciences*. 3rd ed. Translated by Armand Maurer. Toronto: Pontifical Institute of Mediaeval Studies, 1963.

———. *An Introduction to the Metaphysics of St. Thomas Aquinas*. Translated by James F. Anderson. Chicago: Regnery, 1953.

———. "On Being and Essence." In *Selected Writings of St. Thomas Aquinas*, translated by Robert P. Goodwin, 33–67. Indianapolis: Bobbs-Merrill, 1965.

———. *On the Power of God, First Book*. Translated by the English Dominican Fathers. Reprint, Eugene, OR: Wipf and Stock, 2004.

———. *Summa Theologica*. Vol. 1. Translated by Fathers of the English Dominican Province. Chicago: William Benton and Encyclopedia Brittanica, 1923.

———. *Truth*. Vol. 1. Translated by Robert W. Mulligan, SJ. Reprint, Eugene, OR: Wipf and Stock, 2008.

Aristotle. *Metaphysics*. In *The Basic Works of Aristotle*, edited by Richard McKeon. New York: Random House, 1941.

Audi, Robert. *Epistemology: A Contemporary Introduction to the Theory of Knowledge*. 3rd ed. London: Routledge, 2010.

Azurmendi, Joxe. *El Hombre Cooperativo*. Mondragon, Spain: Caja Laboral-Euskadiko Kutxa, 1984.

Balthasar, Hans Urs von. *Man in History: A Theological Study*. London: Sheed and Ward, 1968.

Barbour, Hugh. "Bonum Communius Ente: On the Priority of the Good." *Proceedings of the International Congress on Christian Humanism in the Third Millenium: The Perspective of Thomas Aquinas*, September 21–25, 2003, 169–81. http://www.past.va/content/dam/past/pdf/international_congress_2003/international_congress_2.pdf.

Belloc, Hilaire. *The Four Men*. London: Nelson, 1911.

———. "The Roman Road." In *Hills and the Sea*, 217–23. New York: Scribner, 1906.

———. "The Sign of the Lion." In *Hills and the Sea*, 285–96. New York: Scribner, 1906.

Biletzki, Anat, and Anat Matar. "Ludwig Wittgenstein." In *The Stanford Encyclopedia of Philosophy* (Spring 2020 ed.), edited by Edward N. Zalta. https://plato.stanford.edu/archives/spr2020/entries/wittgenstein/.

Bloom, Alan. *The Closing of the American Mind.* New York: Simon and Schuster, 1988.

Boulter, Stephen. *The Rediscovery of Common Sense Philosophy.* New York: Palgrave Macmillan, 2007.

Chesterton, G. K. "The Life of Stevenson Mr. Graham Balfour's Biography." *London Daily News,* October 18, 1901.

———. *Orthodoxy.* New York: Lane, 1908.

———. *St. Thomas Aquinas.* 1933. Reprint, New York: Sheed and Ward, 2009.

Copleston, Frederick. *A History of Philosophy.* Vol. 3. Westminster, MD: Newman, 1953.

———. *A History of Philosophy.* Vol. 9. New York: Doubleday, 1994.

Craig, William Lane. *The Kalām Cosmological Argument.* London: Macmillan, 1979.

Deavel, David. "What's Right with Distributism." *Intercollegiate Review,* July 29, 2013. https://isi.org/intercollegiate-review/whats-right-with-distributism/.

———. "What's Wrong with Distributism." *Intercollegiate Review,* August 5, 2013. https://isi.org/intercollegiate-review/whats-wrong-with-distributism/.

Dewey, John. *Experience and Nature.* London: Allen & Unwin, 1929.

Frame, John. *The Doctrine of God.* Phillipsburg, NJ: P & R, 2002.

Galilei, Galileo. "From The Assayer (1623)." In *The Essential Galileo,* edited and translated by Maurice A Finocchiaro, 185–89. Indianapolis: Hackett, 2008.

Gilson, Etienne. *Being and Some Philosophers.* 2nd ed. Toronto: Pontifical Institute of Medieval Studies, 1952.

———. *Methodological Realism.* San Francisco: Ignatius, 2011.

Groothuis, Douglas. *On Jesus.* Belmont, CA: Wadsworth, 2003.

Grossmann, Reinhardt. *The Categorial Structure of the World.* Bloomington, IN: Indiana University Press, 1983.

Heidegger, Martin. "What Is Metaphysics?" In *Existence and Being,* 359–92. London: Vision, 1949.

Heraclitus. *Heraclitus.* Translated by Philip Wheelwright. Princeton, NJ: Princeton University Press, 1959.

Hindmoor, Andrew. "Free Riding off Capitalism: Entrepreneurship and the Mondragon Experiment." *British Journal of Political Science* 29 (1999) 217–24.

Homer. *The Illiad.* Translated by A. T. Murray. London: Heinemann, 1928.

———. *The Odyssey.* Translated by Robert Fagles. New York: Penguin, 1996.

Hook, Sydney. *The Metaphysics of Pragmatism.* 1927. Reprint, Amherst, NY: Promethius, 1996.

———. *The Quest for Being.* London: Macmillan, 1961.

Horgan, Terry, and Matjaž Potrĉ. *Austere Realism.* Cambridge: MIT Press, 2008.

———. "Blobjectivism and Indirect Correspondence." *Facta Philosophica* 2 (2000) 249–70.

James, William. *The Principles of Psychology.* Vol. 2. London: Dover, 1890.

Kant, Immanuel. *Groundwork of the Metaphysics of Morals.* Translated by Mary Gregor. Cambridge: Cambridge University Press, 1998.

———. *Immanuel Kant's Critique of Pure Reason.* Translated by Norman Kemp Smith. 1923. Reprint, London: Macmillan, 1956.

———. *Kant's Prolegomena to Any Future Metaphysics*. Edited by Paul Carus. Chicago: Open Court, 1902.

Klubertanz, George. *Introduction to the Philosophy of Being*. Eugene, OR: Wipf and Stock, 2005.

Koukl, Gregory. *The Story of Reality*. Grand Rapids: Zondervan, 2017.

Kreeft, Peter. *Philosophy 101 by Socrates*. San Francisco: Ignatius, 2002.

Lacey, A. R. "Relativism." In *A Dictionary of Philosophy*, 296–98. 3rd ed. London: Routledge, 1996.

Lewis, C. S. *The Abolition of Man*. New York: MacMillan, 1947.

———. "Christian Apologetics." In *God in the Dock*, edited by Walter Hooper, 89–103. Grand Rapids: Eerdmans, 1970.

———. "Funeral for a Great Myth." In *Christian Reflections*, edited by Walter Hooper, 102–16. 1967. Reprint, Grand Rapids: Eerdmans, 2014.

———. *The Screwtape Letters*. New York: MacMillan, 1996.

Lockridge, S. M. "My King." 1976. https://www.thegospelcoalition.org/blogs/justin-taylor/well-i-wonder-if-you-know-him/.

Maritain, Jacques. *Existence and the Existent*. New York: Pantheon, 1948.

MacIntyre, Alasdair. "Relativism, Power and Philosophy." *Proceedings and Addresses of the American Philosophical Association* 59 (1985) 5–22.

McDaniel, Charles. *God & Money: The Moral Challenge of Capitalism*. Lanham, MD: Rowman & Littlefield, 2006.

Molina, Fernando. *José María Arizmendiarrieta, 1915–1976 Biografía*. Mondragon, Spain: Caja Laboral-Euskadiko Kutxa, 2014.

Molina, Fernando, and Antonio Miguez. "The Origins of Mondragon: Catholic Co-operativism and Social Movement in a Basque Valley (1941–59)." *Social History* 33 (2008) 284–98.

Mondragon. *Annual Report 2014*. http://www.mondragon-corporation.com/wp-content/themes/mondragon/docs/eng/annual-report-2014.pdf.

Moregan, Christopher. *Christian Theology: The Biblical Story of Our Faith*. Nashville: B & H, 2020.

Moreland, J. P. "Grossman on Property-Instances and Existence: Suárez's Way Out." *Studies in the Ontology of Reinhardt Grossman*, edited by Javier Cumpa, 77–190. Frankfurt: Ontos, 2010.

———. *Scaling the Secular City*. Grand Rapids: Baker, 1987.

———. *Universals*. Chesham, UK: Acumen, 2001.

Moreland, J. P., and William Lane Craig. *Philosophical Foundations for a Christian Worldview*. Downers Grove: InterVarsity, 2003.

Mosteller, Timothy. *Contemporary Perspectives on C. S. Lewis' Abolition of Man*. London: Bloomsbury, 2017.

———. "The Incompatibility of a Thomistic View of Existence and Natural Existence Monism." *Forum: Supplement to Acta Philosophica* 3 (2017). http://forum-phil.pusc.it/articoli/vo3-a19.

———. *Relativism: A Guide for the Perplexed*. London: Continuum, 2008.

———. *Theories of Truth: An Introduction*. London: Bloomsbury. 2013.

Moyce, David. "Man Goes under Knife to Turn Himself into Real-Life 'Parrotman.'" *Huffpost*, April 4, 2019. https://www.huffpost.com/entry/ted-richards-parrotman-ripleys-travel-channel_n_5d1cf037e4b01b834730b2e9, last accessed 2/12/20.

Nash, Ronald. "The Economic Way of Thinking Part 1." October 1, 1993. Foundation for Economic Education. https://fee.org/articles/the-economic-way-of-thinking-part-1/.

———. "The Economic Way of Thinking Part 2." November 1, 1993. Foundation for Economic Education. https://fee.org/articles/the-economic-way-of-thinking-part-2/

———. "The Economic Way of Thinking Part 3." December 1, 1993. Foundation for Economic Education. Accessed at: https://fee.org/articles/the-economic-way-of-thinking-part-3-the-free-market-system/.

———. "The Economic Way of Thinking Part 4." January 1, 1994. Foundation for Economic Education. https://fee.org/articles/the-economic-way-of-thinking-part-4/.

Nelson, Michael. "Existence." In *The Stanford Encyclopedia of Philosophy* (Winter 2012), edited by Edward N. Zalta. http://plato.stanford.edu/archives/win2012/entries/existence/.

Origen. "A Letter from Origen to Gregory." In *The Ante-Nicene Fathers*, vol. 4, edited by Rev. Alexander Roberts and James Donaldson, 393–94. New York: Scribner, 1926.

Orwell, George. *1984*. New York: Signet Classics, 1949.

Parmenides. "Fragments of Parmenides, Concerning Truth." In *The First Philosophers of Greece*, translated by Arthur Fairbainks, 89–97. London: Kegan Paul, 1898.

Peirce, C. S. "The Fixation of Belief." *Popular Science Monthly* 12 (1877) 1–15. Conducted by E. L. Youmans and W. J. Youmans. New York: Appleton, 1878.

———. "How to Make Our Ideas Clear." *Popular Science Monthly* 12 (1878) 286–302. Conducted by E. L. Youmans and W. J. Youmans. New York: Appleton, 1878.

———. "Immortality in Light of Synechism (1893)." In *The Essential Peirce Selected Philosophical Writings*, vol. 2, *1893–1913*, edited by the Peirce Edition Project, 1–3. Bloomington: Indiana University Press, 1998.

Plato. *Republic*. Translated by G. M. A. Grube. Revised by C. D. C. Reeve. In *Plato: Complete Works*, edited by John M. Cooper, 971–1222. Indianapolis: Hackett, 1997.

———. *Theatetus*. Translated by M. J. Levett. Revised by Myles Burneat. In *Plato: Complete Works*, edited by John M. Cooper. Indianapolis, IN: Hackett, 1997.

Pojman, Louis. "Relativism." In *The Cambridge Dictionary of Philosophy*, edited by Robert Audi, 690–91. Cambridge: Cambridge University Press, 1995.

Poplin, Mary. *Is Reality Secular?* Downers Grove: InterVarsity, 2014.

Redmond, Walter. "A Nothing That Is: Edith Stein on Being without Essence." *American Catholic Philosophical Quarterly* 82 (2008) 71–86.

Rorty, Richard. *Philosophy and the Mirror of Nature*. Princeton: Princeton University Press, 1979.

Rummel, R. J. *Death by Government*. Brunswick, NJ: Transaction, 1994.

Russell, Bertrand. "A Free Man's Worship." In *Mysticism and Logic*, 46–57. London: Longmans, Green, 1919.

Sartre, Jean Paul. *Exisentialism and Humanism*. Translated by Philip Mairet. London: Methuen, 1960.

Sayers, Dorothy. "Why Work?" In *Letters to a Diminished Church*, 118–39. Nashville: Nelson, 2004.

Schaffer, Jonathan. "Monism." In *The Stanford Encyclopedia of Philosophy* (Summer 2015), edited by Edward N. Zalta. http://plato.stanford.edu/archives/sum2015/entries/monism/.

Schall, James V. "On Disliking Champagne but Delighting in Existence" *Generally Speaking*, February 1997. http://thehilairebellocblog.blogspot.com/2012/05/on-disliking-champagne-but-delighting.html.

————. "To Go and Look at the Roman Road." *University Bookman* 41 (2001) 46–48.

————. "Why Do Things Exist? On the Meaning of Being." *Ignatius Insight*, September 24, 2007. http://www.ignatiusinsight.com/features2007/schall_existence_sep07.asp.

Sharkey, Sarah Borden. "Edith Stein and Thomas Aquinas on Being and Essence." *American Catholic Philosophical Quarterly* 82 (2008) 87–103.

Siegel, Harvey. *Relativism Refuted: A Critique of Contemporary Epistemological Relativism*. Dordrecht: Reidel, 1987.

Smith, James K. A. *Who's Afraid of Relativism?* Grand Rapids: Baker, 2014.

Southern Baptist Convention. *Baptist Faith and Message 2000*. http://www.sbc.net/bfm2000/bfm2000.asp.

Stark, Rodney. *How the West Won*. Wilmington, DE: Intercollegiate Studies Institute, 2014.

————. *The Victory of Reason*. New York: Random House, 2005.

Stein, Edith. *Finite and Eternal Being*. Washington, DC: ICS, 2002.

————. *Finite and Eternal Being*. Unpublished translation by Walter Benjamin, forthcoming.

Storck, Thomas. "What's Wrong with Distributism: A Response." *Distributist Review*, August 23, 2014. http://distributistreview.com/whats-wrong-with-distributism/.

Tolkien, J. R. R. *The Letters of J. R. R. Tolkien*. Edited by Humphrey Carpenter. Boston: Houghton Mifflin Harcourt, 2000.

————. *The Lord of the Rings*. Reprint, Boston: Houghton Mifflin, 2004.

Uzquiano, Gabriel. "Quantifiers and Quantification." In *The Stanford Encyclopedia of Philosophy* (Fall 2014), edited by Edward N. Zalta. http://plato.stanford.edu/archives/fall2014/entries/quantification/.

Vallicella, William. "The Moreland-Willard-Lotze Thesis of Being." *Philosophia Christi* 6 (2004) 27–58.

————. *A Paradigm Theory of Existence*. Dordrecht: Kluwer, 2002.

Whyte, William, and Kathleen Whyte. *The Making of Mondragon*. 2nd ed. Ithaca, NY: ILR, 1991.

Wilhelmsen, Frederick. *Man's Knowledge of Reality*. Englewood Cliffs, NJ: Prentice Hall, 1956.

————. *The Paradoxical Structure of Existence*. London: Routledge, 2017.

Willard, Dallas. "The Absurdity of Thinking in Language." *Southwestern Journal of Philosophy* 4 (1973) 125–32.

————. "Attaining Objectivity: Phenomenological Reduction and the Private Language Argument." In *Topics in Philosophy and Artificial Intelligence*, edited by Liliana Albertazzi and Roberto Poli, 15–21. Bolzano, Italy: Istituto Mitteleuropeo di Cultura, Bozen, 1991.

————. "The Bible, the University and the God Who Hides." In *The Bible and The University*, edited by David Lyle Jeffery and C. Stephen Evans, 17–39. Scripture and Hermeneutics series. Milton Keynes, UK: Paternoster, 2007.

————. *The Great Omission*. New York: Harper Collins, 1996.

————. "How Concepts Relate the Mind to Its Objects." *Philosophia Christi* 2 (1999) 5–20.

————. "Integrity of the Mental Act: Husserlian Reflections on a Fregian Problem." In *Mind, Meaning and Mathematics*, edited by Leila Haaparanta, 235–62. Dordrecht: Kluwer, 1994.

————. "Knowledge and Naturalism." In *Naturalism: A Critical Analysis*, edited by William Lane Craig and J. P. Moreland, 24–48. London: Routledge, 2000.

————. "Language, Being, God, and the Three Stages of Theistic Evidence." *Does God Exist?*, edited by J. P. Moreland and Kai Nielsen, 197–220. Amherst, NY: Prometheus, 1993.

————. "Phenomenology and Metaphysics." Unpublished manuscript. http://www.dwillard.org/articles/individual/phenomenology-and-metaphysics. The paper was read at the APA Symposium "Husserl's Ontology," with Barry Smith and David Smith, San Francisco, March 30, 1995.

————. "Predication as Originary Violence: A Phenomenological Critique of Derrida's View of Intentionality." In *Working through Derrida*, edited by G. B. Madison, 120–36. Evanston, IL: Northwestern University Press, 1993.

————. "The Redemption of Reason." Transcription from an address given at The Academic Symposium on "The Christian University in the Next Millennium" at Biola University, La Mirada, CA, February 28, 1998. http://dwillard.org/articles/redemption-of-reason-the.

————. "Theory of Wholes and Parts and Husserl's Explication of the Possibility of Knowledge in the *Logical Investigations*." In *Husserl's Logical Investigations Reconsidered*, edited by Denis Fisette, 163–82. Dordrecht: Kluwer, 2003.

————. "Toward a Phenomenology of the Correspondence Theory of Truth." http://www.dwillard.org/articles/individual/toward-a-phenomenology-for-the-correspondence-theory-of-truth. Published in Italian as "Verso Una Teoria Fenomenologica Della Verita Come Corrispondenza," *Discipline Filosofiche* (Bologna) 1 (1991) 125–47.

————. "Truth: Can We Do Without It?" *Christian Ethics Today* 5 (1991). http://pastarticles.christianethicstoday.com/cetart/index.cfm?fuseaction=Articles.main&ArtID=472.

————. "Truth in the Fire: C. S. Lewis and the Pursuit of Truth Today." The Independent Institute, July 21, 1998. https://www.independent.org/publications/article.asp?id=1669.

————. "What Significance Has 'Postmodernism' for Christian Faith?" 2020. https://preachitteachit.org/articles/detail/what-significance-has-post-modernism-for-christian-faith/.

William of Ockham. *Philosophical Writings: A Selection*. Translated by Philotheus Boehner, O.F.M. Indianapolis: Bobbs-Merrill, 1964.

Wippel, John. *The Metaphysical Thought of Thomas Aquinas*. Baltimore: Catholic University of America Press, 2000.

Index